BARGAIN BOATS
and
BUDGET CRUISING

BARGAIN BOATS
and
BUDGET CRUISING

The fine art of selecting a great boat, outfitting it, living aboard, and cruising on a minimal budget

by
Todd Duff

Seaworthy Publications, Inc. • Melbourne, Florida

Bargain Boats and Budget Cruising

The fine art of selecting a great boat, outfitting it, living aboard, and cruising on a minimal budget

Copyright © 2021 by Todd Duff
Published in the USA by:
Seaworthy Publications, Inc.
6300 N. Wickham Rd
Unit 130-416
Melbourne, FL 32940
Phone 310-610-3634
email orders@seaworthy.com
www.seaworthy.com - Your Bahamas and Caribbean Cruising Advisory

Illustrated by **Adriana Reynal, Graphic Designer**. You can contact her at: **adriana.exploremyworld@gmail.com**

The aerial photo of the boat on the front cover and the boat tied to a tree on the back cover are courtesy of **Gary Felton Photography (https://garyfelton.com).**

Library of Congress Cataloging-in-Publication Data

Names: Duff, Todd, 1955- author.
Title: Bargain boats and budget cruising : the fine art of selecting a
   great boat, outfitting it, living aboard, and cruising it on a minimal
   budget / by Todd Duff.
Description: Melbourne, Florida : Seaworthy Publications, Inc., [2021] | Summary: ""Bargain Boats and Budget Cruising" is about how the ordinary person, one who does not have a trust fund or hundreds of thousands of dollars saved up, can still embark and see the world, or live-aboard a sailing vessel for extended periods in beautiful places without waiting for years and years to save up enough money before they can start, or without the need to work for decades to "retire" afloat. This book is for those who wish to go now; who want to live this exciting lifestyle immediately, rather than waiting any longer; dreaming of waving palm trees while standing on a distant shore. Or worse, trapped in a city in the middle of a continent working a job they hate, to pay for the house or apartment they need to work that job and pay for the vehicle they need to get to that job, plus insurance, utilities, and the myriad other annoyances that can hinder experiencing an incredibly simple, healthy, exciting, and fulfilling life. In "Bargain Boats and Budget Cruising," accredited Marine Surveyor and long-time cruiser, Todd Duff, provides lessons learned from 40+ years of experience buying, selling, surveying, outfitting older sailboats, and taking them cruising the world. This book is not only a guide for making the long-term cruising lifestyle a reality but also a resource on what to look for when searching for that perfect bargain boat to take you away. These pages are packed with valuable information on how to avoid common mistakes and provide the reader with the tools needed to help make wise decisions in the boat-buying process. You'll find lots of details on the best places to find super buys on cruising boats, ways to zero in on that ideal vessel, negotiate for the best value, and how to outfit it for world cruising without going broke in the process. It is a primer on how the average man or woman can achieve the freedom of sailing the world's oceans on a minimal budget. "Bargain Boats and Budget Cruising" is a one-stop guide to making the increasingly popular lifestyle of world cruising available and possible RIGHT NOW, without the need to save for decades to make that happen. In this book you will find: Reviews of over 40 outstanding cruising designs. Why go world cruising and who is really doing it? What's it like out there? Where are the real bargains to be found? Keys to negotiating for the best value on a boat. What dangers and pitfalls to be aware of and how to avoid them"-- Provided by publisher.
Identifiers: LCCN 2021025960 (print) | LCCN 2021025961 (ebook) | ISBN
   9781948494533 (paperback) | ISBN 9781948494540 (epub)
Subjects: LCSH: Offshore sailing. | Boats and boating. | Boats and
   boating--Equipment and supplies. | Sailboat living.
Classification: LCC GV811 .D84 2021 (print) | LCC GV811 (ebook) | DDC
   797.1--dc23
LC record available at https://lccn.loc.gov/2021025960
LC ebook record available at https://lccn.loc.gov/2021025961

Table of Contents

Preface

There are many online blogs and forums about offshore and long-distance sailboat cruising offering a wide range of opinions from both 'newbie' sailors and experienced cruisers alike who are hoping to gain or provide additional insights into achieving and maintaining this fantastic lifestyle. These web pages and forums run the gamut from super helpful to downright trolling sites! Over the years there have been many books published which have within their pages suggested how best to buy and outfit a sailboat for long-distance cruising, and many more which discuss systems, energy management, seamanship, navigation, and boat-keeping. Others deal with cruising from port to port and country to country safely, and some books explain storm tactics, anchoring methods, and a myriad of other specific aspects of what is becoming a more and more popular alternative lifestyle for thousands of people every year.

This book is to some extent about some of these issues, concerns, and skills, but more importantly, it is about how the ordinary person, one who does not have a trust fund or hundreds of thousands of dollars saved up, can still embark and see the world or live aboard for extended periods in beautiful places without waiting years and years to save up enough money before they can start, or without the need to work for decades to 'retire' afloat. This book is for those who wish to go now; who want to live this exciting lifestyle immediately, rather than waiting any longer; dreaming of waving palm trees while standing on a distant shore or worse, trapped in a city in the middle of a continent working at a job they hate doing in order to pay for the house or apartment they need to work that job and pay for the vehicle they need to get to that job, and insurance, and utilities, and the myriad of other annoyances that can hinder experiencing a truly simple, healthy, exciting, and fulfilling life.

So how then do I believe I can add additional valuable insights to this discussion? Let's start a few decades back.

One blustery spring morning in the upper Midwest in 1981, with the last vestiges of snow still melting, I woke up with an undeniable urge to see if I could find a sailboat to buy. This desire had been festering for quite some time. When I was 19 years old and living in the hinterland of Wisconsin, I bought a 1956 48-passenger Dodge school bus that someone had converted into a hunting cabin slash primitive RV complete with four bunks, a settee-style couch, a small dinette, and a linear galley with a propane fridge, plus a small loo in the back. It was pretty well-done actually if you didn't think about the worn-out engine or the ugly paint job. But it cost me my faded green 1969 Impala with no rear window and $500 of hard-earned cash to buy, and I immediately set about putting it right. I will always consider this my first cruising experience.

I drove that bus all over the Midwest the next year with my rock band as 'crew' and managed to save up enough money so that by my 20th birthday I found myself out in Colorado with my best friend and an ever-changing crew of young people and animals accompanying us on our travels.

Somewhere in these journeys, I began to draw boats and dream about living aboard and cruising on the oceans rather than just the land. So I started to check out every book I could find and read about yacht design, cruising, and sailing. I think I read every book there was from local libraries on sailing and cruising and so by the time I got back from my epic trip out west I had decided that one day, I too would sail the world's oceans on my own sailboat. There was just one problem: Virtually every book I read seemed to have people sailing in these zillion dollar boats who were retired, people with trust funds, or some other source of income that I just couldn't fathom. And when I bought the occasional sailing magazine, the boats advertised in the back of these glossy publications were all so far out of my financial resources that they seemed virtually unattainable on my meager musician's income.

So over the next few years, I read more and dreamed a lot and began to try to figure out if there might somehow be a boat out there that I could afford that could take me across oceans and allow me to realize some of the dreams I had of beautiful tropical anchorages and exotic far-off lands.

Lucky for me, when I was a child my father had gone into a partnership on a couple of sailboats with a friend, and although he was never really totally infected with the sailing bug, it sure made a huge impression on me! While I have memories of sailing from as early as six years old, by the time I was twelve we had moved away from the water and our family bought a powerboat. I learned how to be a good ski boat operator, leaving my minimal sailing skills dormant.

So on that early spring morning with the last of winter's snow still melting, I knocked on my next-door neighbor's door and asked my buddy Ron if he wanted to go help me look for a boat. I knew that boat shopping with only $500 in my pocket wasn't exactly the easiest or most promising undertaking, but I was sure there'd be something out there I could afford. Heck, I didn't even care if it had a hole in the side... I could fix it and take it sailing!

At the very first place we stopped, I asked if they had any used sailboats. The salesman looked at my long hair and well-worn clothing and correctly surmised that I was probably a

bottom feeder, so he said, "There's an old wooden boat out back, go take a look."

There, under a blue tarp with a bit of melting snow and pools of cold water trapped in the folds, nestled the most beautiful 16' wooden sailboat I had ever seen. She was a 1950s wooden Comet class daysailer/racer that was clearly past her racing days and needed to have her brightwork refinished. But poking around I didn't find any soft spots (I found those later) and so I trudged back across the muddy boatyard to ask the salesman how much it was. He pointed me in the direction of one of the workers who he told me was the boat's owner.

"She's mine and I've got no use for her, I've bought a new boat," he told me. "I'll take $500."

To which I responded, "I'll take her!"

Over the next summer, when I wasn't out on tour with my band, following some needed TLC, I sailed her every spare minute I had.

The following spring, I refurbished her even more and put an ad in the local newspaper. She sold for a tidy profit to the first person who looked at her and with that money and a fistful of money from selling one of my big spare amplifiers, I set out to look for a *real* cruising boat—one you could sleep aboard!

I drove to the closest big city (Chicago) and found a sleek and narrow 26' wooden boat with an elaborate trailer that alone was worth what the owner was asking for the whole boat. But this boat *did* have a hole in its side! The owner had been sanding her hull in preparation for repainting the topsides when his sander went through the hull! But it was only a little hole, so I was sure I could fix her. Luckily I am fairly handy, and I had just enough money to buy the boat and still had a couple of hundred dollars left over to buy some epoxy and some wood.

I trailered the boat back up to Wisconsin using a borrowed truck and found a local boatyard with a shed big enough to fit her inside. It was late spring and many of the boats had already been launched for the season, so they had an inside storage space that they rented to me at a price I could afford, and I set about figuring out how to repair the hull.

Thank goodness I had read virtually every book on boat repair I could find in the preceding years because I ultimately needed all the help I could muster as the repair grew into a complete rebuild of the entire port stern quarter from the keelson to the deck, and part of the afterdeck too! But what a great learning experience! I think some of that even rubbed off on my first son because he spent parts of some workdays in the shade in his playpen watching me repair the complex compound curves of the structure I was rebuilding.

Wow! Did that boat sail great! I found a mooring for her off the University of Wisconsin on Lake Mendota, the small inland lake nearby, and spent many a night aboard her that summer and the following summer as well. I honed my sailing skills for the day that I would eventually reach the ocean. I got very used to sailing the engineless 26' sloop and often while under sail I would dock her solo to pick up friends or to take on water. But soon I realized that if I really wanted to cruise, I needed a boat with more volume and more berths for my growing family and that while a svelte ex-racing boat might be a lot of fun to sail, it was not necessarily what one should take out on the open ocean.

During this period, I quit my band to be home for my growing family and took a job at what was then the world's largest Laser sailboat dealer that also sold AMF sailboats, canoes, kayaks, and all manner of small watercraft. They also took on consignment small trailerable cruising sailboats up to about 26' and this is where I accidentally found my next profession.

Interestingly enough, because there were so many boats to take care of and all manner of repairs and modifications that needed doing, with my woodworking and mechanical skills, I became the chief 'fix it' guy and also helped to sell the trailerable sailboats as needed. This, and my increasingly busy schedule with fixing other people's boats, led to me being called upon occasionally to make bank valuations or insurance surveys on people's boats. So with no prior knowledge as to how those should be written other than what I learned from a few books on the subject, I began doing marine surveys. I also worked at the same time learning how to sell sailboats and enjoyed success with that too.

Over the next few years I ended up buying and selling a few more boats, each one a little newer and more complex in my quest toward getting something large enough and able enough to take my family sailing to the tropics, which had been my dream all along. Somewhere along the way in this time-frame, my wife, who when we met probably thought she was marrying a soon-to-be-famous rock star, came to the sad realization that she had married a certified boat bum. One whose main desire in life seemed to be to live in shorts and T-shirts and sail around with the only apparent goal of going barefoot on sandy beaches and swimming amongst tropical reefs. So she left and we went our separate ways.

Several more years passed while I owned a series of other boats and during that time I remarried and eventually went sailing to 13 countries on a boat I had rebuilt nearly from scratch. After returning to the US from a two-year cruise sailing the Eastern Caribbean, I ended up on the mid-Atlantic Coast of the US where I set about earning some money for further adventures. Because I had rebuilt a couple of boats down in Florida and had met some interesting people in the yachting industry while doing that, my reputation preceded me up the coast and so by the time we arrived in the Chesapeake Bay, I had a job waiting for me at the largest yacht brokerage in the region, and one of the biggest in the world. I fell into a super-high-volume used sailboat sales job in what was at that time one of the busiest marketplaces for cruising boats in the entire world: Annapolis, Maryland. So over the next seventeen years, in between 'sabbatical' cruises with my family, I worked as a yacht broker.

For a brief period in the mid-nineties I tried to settle back into marine surveying, but people kept wanting me to help them find boats, and with the lower-paying job of looking people's boats over, I just couldn't make ends meet with my family of four kids and a wife in an expensive Maryland economy. To still be able to save for long sailing trips, I kept at the brokering, but I also kept my love of working on boats and finding and fixing problems satisfied by buying and selling a succession of boats; a habit I have maintained throughout my entire life and as I write this book, I am now on the 56th sailboat that I have bought, sailed, repaired or rebuilt and cruised. Some of these were sailing and racing dinghies, some were sloops and cutters, a few were ketches, two were schooners, and one was a brigantine. As I have grown older, I have more and more often just project-managed major refits on my various boats, and as a broker or surveyor, I have overseen or assisted in the logistical aspects of hundreds of partial or complete refits for clients and friends. And while all this was going on, about every second or third year, I would take off with my partner and kids aboard and go cruising for a year or two, each time going to a different part of the world. When I started to run out of money, we would sail back to the Chesapeake, the brokerage would clear a desk for me and I'd set back to work in yacht sales. During this time I helped people buy and sell boats or surveyed hundreds of boats. Because I was always willing to work with entry-level buyers in the lower end of the budget spectrum and was not afraid to submit what I considered to be realistic bids on overpriced boats, I was sometimes referred to behind my back by other brokers as 'Lowball Todd'. But this bothered me not one little bit because I sold more boats than anyone in the company, and in some years sold more boats than anyone in the entire region. And in the process, I made a lot of really great lifelong friends with people who had started as my clients!

In 2004, I moved to the Caribbean full-time because I had been selling more and more boats down there and quite frankly, the sailing is just a heck of a lot nicer in that area than it is up north—to me anyway! Then in 2010, I took off on a 27-country cruise that lasted six years, ending up in Fiji. Returning to the workforce in the Caribbean I was impressed with how many new people were coming into the liveaboard cruising lifestyle. I began to see the need for a more detailed and accurate assessment of what the best and worst boats were, how to properly prepare for long-term sailing adventures, and how to do so on the lowest budget possible. Having now lived aboard full-time for over thirty-five years, and having spent fifteen of those years cruising full-time, I think I understand the liveaboard part pretty well. And having now personally been involved in the sale of close to a thousand sailboats, and having been through as many marine surveys and sea trials on all variety of boats of all types and in all kinds of condition, I can honestly say that I am uniquely qualified to give a well-rounded assessment of what to watch out for, good and bad, when buying or outfitting and living aboard a sailboat while cruising, at anchor or in port; and in doing so on a tight budget.

So please allow me to lay out what I have learned in my four-plus decades of this life experience and hopefully some of what I have picked up will be of use to those who wish to sail and cruise on a small budget, who want to see the world from the deck of their own boat, but don't want to wait until they are too old to deal with the physical rigors that ocean sailing sometimes requires, and who want to make the whole process as much fun as possible. Welcome to my world. Let's have some fun, and let's go sailing!

Chapter One

Who Are We and Why Do We Go Cruising?

As a marine surveyor, former yacht broker, and longtime cruiser, something interesting has come to my attention of late: world events and in particular recent geopolitical developments, and the recent pandemic health crisis has brought about a fairly urgent response from many people who feel the need to be able to 'get away'. I've seen all sorts of Internet posts about US citizens threatening to move to remote areas of Canada, Chile, or wherever, if 'So and So' gets elected in the next election, or to protect themselves from the next global pandemic. I have met many Americans and Europeans who have left their homes in major population areas in search of saner, more peaceful, and warmer places to live. In general, from where I sit (safe and happy aboard my sailboat in the British Virgin Islands) it seems to me that there are probably still a lot of discontented, possibly unhappy, maybe even scared people out there who want to get away from the madness of twenty-first-century urban life, but just don't know where to go or how to go about it.

Recent events with the ever-increasing threat of emerging pandemics and increasing authoritarian controls within world governments have made many people feel the need to have a way to get away if and when things begin to feel unsafe. But most don't have a good idea of how to accomplish this. Although RV sales have skyrocketed in recent years, with an RV you are still stuck on land and how on earth would that help you if you truly wanted to extricate yourselves to seek a saner and safer way of life?

And then there are the sailors. These people *do* know how to get away, and most have a pretty good idea of where to go and how to go about doing it. They are the lucky few who already own an oceangoing sailboat they could escape on if and when the local environment gets just a little too unfriendly. I would not be surprised over the coming years to see a much higher number of people heading out to go cruising if for no better reason than to distance themselves from the heated and sometimes deliberately misleading rhetoric of politics, increased health concerns, pressing human congestion, collapsing ecosystems, or simply as a means of avoiding the pressures of an increasingly fast-paced modern society, to reassess their lives out on the open ocean, visiting isolated tropical islands, remote northern anchorages, and small countries where one can still find solitude and peace in place of incessant media bombardments, misleading political yammering, traffic jams, and overcrowded, germ-infested cities.

These lucky people own sailboats that could best be described as 'Escape Pods'. I wrote about this a few years back in one of the big sailing magazines and the term seems to have caught on—like the science fiction books and movies, where large spaceships had escape pods to allow people to get away when danger was threatening the integrity of their mother ship, world cruising sailboats can offer the same safety net for sailors who realize that until things settle down again at home, or if things get just a little too uncomfortable, that their escape pods can carry them far away to the safety of distant shores, unaffected by the politics, diseases, or the aftermath of bad government decisions. These same escape pods can become safe homes and perfect havens in which to make the transition from refugees to becoming emissaries of goodwill and a positive influence on the people they meet during their travels.

Despite all the scary news and xenophobic fearmongering that goes on as part of modern societies' belief that only when you are home in your own country (paying taxes and feeding the market economy) are you safe and secure. There is a terrific, wonderful, clean, and enticing world out there. If you avoid the major sailing centers and big, well-known ports and instead go to the smaller places like the northern Cook Islands, Kiribati, or the more remote islands of Tonga or Fiji, you'll find people living in the most basic of political environments. The same holds true for almost any small country or remote outpost of civilization. More often than not you'll find rational ideals, goodwill, and caring for one another as the cornerstones of their societies. Greed is often less of a problem in many small populations because almost everyone has about the same earning potential, and everyone can achieve almost anything within the structure of the society that they are willing to work hard enough to capture.

What better time in the history of the world to go ocean cruising than right now? With the current and continuing state of world affairs, I expect that we will see a huge surge of 'sailing refugees' in their own escape pod sailboats setting out upon the world's oceans and fanning out on the four winds to find a new beginning in places not yet stricken by twenty-first-century greed and corruption. Living in the major population centers it is easy to believe that the world is getting too crowded and yet human beings are for the most part extremely social and choose to group themselves in centers of high concentration. We as world-cruising sailors can shed to a large extent the need for the infrastructures of modern society and we can go virtually wherever we wish and thereby avoid most of the pitfalls of modern urban life; crime, overcrowding, exploitation, lack of freedoms, and the effects of the incessant media urging people to *buy-buy-buy*.

In most cases, sailors can decide for themselves when it is time to leave or arrive in a country or even to avoid countries altogether. True enough, the entire world is more or less claimed by one country or another, but in many of the less populated areas it is still possible to find a spot, anchor your boat and live for extended periods, and as long as you don't become a burden to the local populace, you will generally be tolerated, and if you're a positive person, are compassionate and caring, you will almost always be accepted. If you are lucky enough to find an uninhabited island you like (and there are many possible candidates), in some areas of the world, simply being there may be enough of a claim to allow you to stay on for a while. Should your enclave of sanity be found out, as long as you are working within the confines of the national government's regulations and restrictions, you will likely be allowed to enjoy your sanctuary free of official intervention.

Many of our good friends, however, live their lives on the sea by staying more or less in constant motion. They arrive at one island group and spend several months, then sail on to the next, and then on again, and eventually a year or more later, they return to the first. This is not uncommon both with Atlantic sailors making yearly voyages to and from the Caribbean islands and with Pacific sailors doing the Tonga, Fiji, New Zealand triangle. I know people who have been doing this for years who are quite happy with friends in many different countries that they see on a yearly or semiannual basis. Others keep sailing in one direction and end up sailing around the world and then take a new route on the second or third time around.

If you are fed up with the way the society you have been living in is headed and are lucky enough, or smart enough, to have the ability to sail, or are at least willing to learn, then maybe you should consider taking on the vagabond lifestyle of the cruising sailor. We are not total dropouts. We pay our taxes on income earned, we keep in contact with family and friends via email, social media, and phone calls, and we even occasionally fly home to visit loved ones. But what we *don't* do is sit in our urban or suburban homes in debt, taxed, and charged for everything from water to electricity (which we get free from the sky, the sun, and the wind) and with our every move regulated and constricted. While many travel restrictions are currently in place at the time of the final editing of this book, the fact is this pandemic will pass, and once again, cruising sailors will be free to go whenever and virtually wherever we wish, and in many areas of the world, we are free to stay for extended periods. We are not prisoners of society but are the free spirits of the world who have the guts to leave the familiar, the allegedly safe and secure behind, and to head out into the unknown to make the best of what we find.

I can think of no loftier goal in this world than to become emissaries of goodwill and positive influences on the people we meet on our world travels. Fed up with your life at home and want a change? Go find yourself an escape pod and jettison the trappings of modern society that are keeping you held as a prisoner of a society that has lost its sense of reason. Escape to the freedom of the open ocean and see where the four winds will take you.

There is still a great big world out there and it's yours to discover. Hop aboard your escape pod and head out. You are a prisoner no longer; freedom hovers just over the horizon!

***

During my many years of cruising, I have noticed there seem to be three distinct groups of people who are 'out there' traveling the world's oceans. The first and probably most populous group are and probably always will be what we call 'retirement cruisers'. For these people, life is pretty simple. Theoretically, they have saved up a nest egg for many years and managed to acquire a nice boat, get it equipped the way they want it and then they simply cruise from country to country living on retirement pensions or interest from investments. While this is the largest group of people you will likely meet while coastal cruising or in areas like the Caribbean or the Med, the farther off the beaten path you get, the fewer of these people you will meet. It seems that for the most part 'retirement cruisers' spend most of their time traveling in groups and spend the majority of their time at anchor in the most popular ports of the world where they hang out with others just like them. Although the needs and challenges many of these retirees face are similar to the challenges the other two groups face. Their advancing age and years of conditioned lives of comfort and ease has them often sailing on expensive yachts with all the amenities and this alone puts most of this group outside the scope of this book.

However, we know of many people who are at or near traditional retirement age who are *not* wealthy, and even if they are collecting a pension, it may be a small amount from social security or savings that only gives them a limited amount of money each month with which to not just survive but to maintain their vessel too. Many of these people sail on older boats because that is what they can afford. For these people, paying close attention to the following chapters may prevent them from falling into the trap of buying a boat that is more expensive to maintain in the long term than their fixed income will allow and will hopefully help them to understand that while comfort at anchor is important, in reality, as long as the boat they own can be sailed easily, can be maintained in top condition within their long-term budget and provides them with a safe and comfortable home that this will serve them far better than a super complicated and expensive to maintain boat that will bleed them dry when things begin to wear out and fail.

While it is easy to fall into the trap of thinking that life afloat cannot be comfortable without all kinds of luxuries like air conditioning, washer/dryers, generators, and dishwashers, remember that the people who own boats with all these amenities are paying a high price to keep everything in working order and while these yachts may look and feel elegant at anchor in some beautiful bay, the reality is that the beautiful palm-fringed beach and the mountains behind it and warm clear waters surrounding it will look and feel exactly the same no matter what boat you are floating on! So to this group of sailors—those of advancing age who wish to take on this cruising liveaboard lifestyle—please consider carefully the content of the following chapters while you are choosing your retirement cruising home.

The second most populous group we find out cruising the world's oceans are what I call 'the adventurers'. These are people who may be in their early twenties or even up into their forties or fifties and are 'out there' sometimes single-handing, sometimes with a revolving door of friends and family, or sometimes as a couple who are sailing from country to country, working odd jobs, or leaving their boat from time to time to fly home to work and then returning to carry on. To this group of people, I hope to introduce some insights on how to choose a vessel that is safe, seaworthy, and strong because these sailors are the types that seek out the unexplored areas, the distant reef-strewn bays to dive, the remote shorelines to surf, or the navigationally challenging fjords and inlets to access pristine hiking or mountain climbing. Choosing a yacht with which to undertake adventurous off the beaten path sailing is vitally important and making those choices with 'eyes wide open' to the realities of repairing and maintaining said vessel is important beyond measure.

The third-largest group of sailors that we meet out there these days is the families.

Raising my kids on the sea gave them what I think of as a huge advantage over most of the kids growing up today in a modern land-based society. Cruising kids often become more self-reliant and more confident of their skills simply because they soon realize that what they say and do matters, a lot. For example; give a 13-year-old child a night watch with everyone sleeping below while they alone are in charge of the boat as it plows along at seven knots on a moonless night hundreds of miles offshore and it teaches them a sense of responsibility that many adults rarely even experience. All too often in modern society, teenagers are left feeling unimportant and ineffectual—like what they do and say doesn't matter. On a cruising sailboat, the actions of every single person matter and the responsibilities and challenges they share, no matter what age they are, have a huge impact on shaping their feelings of self-worth that may be lacking in many of the aspects of modern shore-based society. From my observations over the last forty years, cruising kids are often far more able to communicate easily with adults or kids that are outside of their age and language group and almost assuredly have a more worldly outlook on life than children who grow up within the confines of a land-based society that is often overshadowed by the incessant bombardment of tainted media and peer pressure.

Cruising families do however face special challenges while sailing the world's oceans that shape how they sail and where they congregate. First and foremost, of course, is the necessity of providing an exceptional education for their children and so homeschooling becomes a major aspect of onboard life. Finding other 'kid boats' is also important so that the parents can provide their children with others to interact with, and of course, most younger families have parents who must do something to bring in an income, so stopping in different ports around the world to work or operating a business remotely from the boat becomes another important aspect of life afloat. Because of this, choosing a boat that has space for every child, that allows for a possible workspace and a comfortable spot for doing schoolwork, and is safe and easy to sail shorthanded (because many times one parent will have to tend to the children while the other operates the boat) becomes of primary importance.

While many of the newer 'charter style' monohull sailboats and catamarans seem to lend themselves to being ideal for a family, other considerations that I will bring to light in the following pages should be carefully weighed when choosing your floating home.

Having now lived for many years as a participant in each of these three groups of sailors, I find it exciting and promising that thanks to the longevity of fiberglass as a building material and the advances that have been made in coating materials for metal yachts, and because of the proliferation of quality production yachts that have been built over the past five decades, that purchasing a great world-cruising sailboat—no matter what age group you are in—has never been easier, or less expensive in real dollars than it is today.

Chapter Two

What Attributes Define a Good Cruising Boat?

Having owned quite a few boats over the years and sailed on many hundreds of others, I realize that as I grow older, I have become 'boat sick' and somewhat jaded on what I find exciting, interesting, or special. And to me, if you can't be excited about your boat, then why own it? Boats cost a lot of money to buy and to maintain and take a lot of time to keep in good condition, so you've got to love your boat or the whole experience becomes an ordeal.

Deciding on what boat is worthy of your love also requires a bit of logic. As a long-time yacht broker and marine surveyor, I have seen many people attempt to approach the entire buying process with a great deal of research and logical thought, only to throw all the logic out the window when a particular boat strikes them as beautiful, exciting, or romantic. Once that happens, the logic process may change to become a way of justifying what may be an illogical emotional response! But of course, being 'in love' with your boat will ultimately be quite important in that it will lead you to take good care of the boat so that it can take good care of you.

The logic part is the most important part of the search for the perfect cruiser. Try to keep that part alive up until the very last moment during the choosing process and if you are lucky, you may be able to quell the 'love' part until after you have made a successful, logical decision.

So what's logical to look for in a cruising yacht? Let's assume for the moment that the type of cruising we are talking about is long-distance sailing and a long-term liveaboard lifestyle. This is the type of cruising where having

the right boat makes the biggest difference. Okay, many successful long-term cruises have been made on boats that are far from ideal, and this is largely because the adage of 'the best boat to go cruising on is the one you own' is not far off from a logical perspective. However, if you are lucky enough to be boatless, or to realize that you have the time and flexibility to take a look at the entire marketplace to search for the very best boat for your type of cruising, then there are three key points to keep in mind:

1. A good cruising boat should be easy to maintain—be sure that whatever boat you choose can be maintained easily within the skill sets you possess. Otherwise, you may end up being sabotaged into hiring others to work on your boat. This can become unsustainably expensive or even impossible—particularly when in remote places.

2. Make sure the boat can be maintained within the budget you have created. This is a close cousin to #1, but maintaining a boat is also considering things like periodic replacement of key items like

engines, sails, rigging, and systems. Be sure that the choices you make in these departments are replaceable within the long-term budget you have in mind.

3. Comfort and living space—too many people fall into the trap of trying to buy the biggest boat they can afford and end up with more boat than they need. Large spaces are wasted when they are not filled with lockers. A safe and comfortable main saloon is one that is adequate for two to four or slightly more for a big family and yet allows easy access fore and aft without the potential for being thrown a long way to the opposite side in a sudden lurch. It can be argued that as long as there are secure places to sit and eat and socialize, any extra space is meaningless. Comfortable places to read, or sleep, and navigate should take precedence over the 'light and airy', wide-open spaces.

When is Big Too Big and When is Small Too Small?

The case for the right size boat for cruising

We've probably all heard the old saying that "Everyone owns a boat that is two feet too small," and that it is the natural progression of boat ownership to keep buying bigger and bigger boats your whole life. If this is accurate, then surely the day must come when your boat becomes so large that you can no longer take it out without a crew aboard. Even though it's true that the larger the boat, generally speaking, the more comfortable it is at sea, many other factors must be considered when choosing the right size boat and deciding on what is too big or too small for comfortable long-term cruising.

Long-term cruising does not have to mean crossing oceans, or even doing lengthy coastal hops. Long-term cruising could mean living aboard in different anchorages around any area where you spend the majority of your time aboard and move the boat often enough so that you are not simply 'living aboard.' For the sake of argument, we will dismiss the majority of the larger-crewed superyacht-type vessels because these are not the homes of the owners. In most cases these yachts are staffed by crews of professionals who, although spending the majority of their time on the boat and moving from time-to-time, are still not experiencing life in the same way that a couple or family who are off on a two- to five- or more year cruise are. I have met many of these superyacht and maxi boat crew who owned their own modest-sized boats that they would return to whenever they are not working, and in most cases, these are vessels that can be easily handled by just one or two people. I mean, who wants to always need to have a crew aboard your home and put up with all of the idiosyncrasies of living with people who aren't family. Unless you are getting paid to do it, forget it!

On one of my most recent trips through the Panama Canal, I noticed that the majority of the husband/wife or couple crews were sailing on boats that were between 38-52 ft. Many of the larger boats were much more 'gadget intensive' than the smaller boats and certainly more complicated and sophisticated than what was typically seen out cruising twenty years ago. Nowadays, it is not uncommon to see the larger cruising boats with electric winches, bow thrusters, electric furling, and complicated electrical and mechanical systems to support things like multi-zone air conditioning, washer dryers, big watermakers, and computerized navigation systems all of which must be maintained in top condition or the owners will suffer the consequences of either being stuck in port awaiting repairs or worse: finding themselves in a situation that they cannot handle without the electric or hydraulic assistance of these systems. Granted, if one is an engineer type and is willing to spend a small fortune maintaining the systems aboard a big, complicated boat to the same standards that airplanes are maintained, then this is not such a concern. But too many times I have seen couples on large, complicated yachts who are often older and less fit than younger crews aboard some of the smaller boats who, because of lack of substantial investments in systems maintenance, are broken down in some marina or anchorage and living like prisoners to a boat that cannot be safely sailed without the equipment necessary to handle the heavy loads and huge sails and anchors onboard. That is an example of where big is too big!

In many cases, I have seen the crews of smaller vessels coming and going more often through an anchorage and one has to wonder if this isn't because their boats are so much easier to sail and get underway that the temptation to put the hook down and just stay is not nearly as strong as the lure of another bay, a beautiful island, or a special beach. And getting there with the smaller, less complicated boat is often easier too.

I remember back in the early nineties being anchored in Prince Rupert Bay in Dominica. Onboard with me on our comfortable and easily handled 32' cutter were my wife and two children. We had been on the move more or less constantly, for almost two years. One afternoon a large ketch came into the bay with an older couple aboard. They anchored right next to us. The next morning we upped anchor under sail and went to the other end of the bay for a couple of days, then sailed back to our old spot for another day and then went on down the chain, island hopping all the way to Grenada. On our way back up the island chain six weeks later, the big ketch was still at anchor in the same spot. I wondered if this was because it was a major undertaking to bring up the anchor and set all the sails and make her way on to another place, weaving through another crowded anchorage and that they just stayed put because it was too difficult to do otherwise? If they had owned a more manageable size boat that could have been sailed single-handed by either one of them, then wouldn't they have been more comfortable moving on to new places?

Sure, a big boat is more comfortable at anchor, and usually has an easier motion in a seaway, but how big must a boat be to be safe, secure, and keep her crew happy? Of the 56 sailboats I have owned, I have lived aboard or cruised on 24 of them, from 20-64 feet in length. I believe I can say with certainty that the amount of fun one can have aboard a sailboat has virtually no correlation to its size or amenities. Take a look at people like Lin and Larry Pardey who completed many major world voyages aboard their 24' and 29' engineless cutters and look at the countless other small boat voyagers who have written about their exploits sailing vessels that would be considered 'too small' for most people's taste in this day and age.

I believe it can be safely said that size in and of itself has little to do with seaworthiness. Many epic voyages and even circumnavigations have been safely completed in vessels under thirty feet. But is it also inarguable that a smaller boat has a quicker motion? There is a point where, especially for older people, that the way a very small boat moves through the water may be too quick and unsteady to be truly comfortable. But in an argument for a larger boat, I have also seen cases with couples who started out cruising on a small boat and then had three children along the way, picked up a couple of pets, and were stressed for space for everyone. This is a case where small is too small!

In my career, I have been lucky enough to have sailed on hundreds of different types of sailboats. Over the years, I have concluded that for an average fit couple the upper size limit for a cruising yacht should be between 20-35 thousand pounds of displacement, and that if additional adult crew are added, then adding another 10,000 or so pounds with each person will still generally allow for relatively easy boat handling. If a boat weighs much less than 20,000 pounds then the motion will be quicker and harder on the body, and above 35,000 pounds, the size of the sailing gear and the effort involved in sailing may make it too difficult to handle when the wind and seas are up.

The length of the waterline also has a huge impact on how a boat will feel in large seas. If the waterline is too short and the corresponding rocker in the hull (shape fore and aft) is too great, then a lot of forward effort is spent hobby horsing up and over waves, but if it is too long, then it is easy to get tripped and boarded by solid water if the yacht is straddling two very close waves while running downwind. This is why I find myself gravitating to boats with waterline lengths of between 27 and 42 feet. Modern yacht designs are often built with flatter runs fore and aft to try to negate the hobby horsing tendency, but this often results in a vessel that will pound heavily when going to windward.

The next biggest issue for choosing the right size boat for cruising after the comfort aspect has been taken into account is its carrying capacity, or *storage space* if you prefer. Deciding on where you will be cruising can have a strong influence on this consideration. If you are planning a voyage through the Northwest Passage or to other remote areas, then enormous fuel capacity is a must, and the ability to carry months of food and a ton or two of spare parts might be nice, but if you have plans to only cruise the Bahamas or Caribbean Islands, then much smaller capacities may be acceptable. Owning a boat with hundreds of gallons of fuel capacity and then only using the engine a little each year means you are not only wasting space but carrying around extra diesel is inefficient and not good for the fuel. And of course, sailing around with mostly empty tanks isn't good either.

Desalinators have allowed for much smaller water tankage and many modern cruisers are sailing offshore with water capacities that would have been considered inadequate a couple of decades ago. Of course, having tanks large enough to easily make port on a long passage without the watermaker is only prudent and we have had watermakers fail on passages in the past. It is arguable though that for a couple, having much more than 100 gallons in water capacity may be unnecessary.

Refrigeration is nice and many consider it a necessity. We have however cruised many years with no refrigeration on previous boats and learned to live without it. Deep freezers are becoming more and more common with the proliferation of larger cruising boats, but of course, these require much more power to maintain which means having very large solar arrays and wind generators or relying on a diesel engine or generator to provide the power. More expense and complication are the by-products of these systems.

I have met very few long-term cruisers who felt that air conditioning was a necessity. But living aboard and cruising some areas of the world might be made a lot more pleasant with this option onboard. Again, weighing the added expense to buy and maintain these systems and run them on a long-term basis should be carefully considered. Perhaps adding a few hatches and some additional opening ports would be a lower cost and easier to maintain solution?

In the end, a person, couple or family should, if at all possible, spend some time aboard a boat of the approximate size and layout of what they intend to cruise on before moving up (or down) in size. Chartering a 50' sloop for a couple of weeks with all the systems and gadgets might lead you to realize that you just don't need all that space and that the sails are just too much to handle in adverse conditions. However, spending a week or two aboard a 24-footer might lead you to decide that sometimes, bigger *is* better!

Back in the late 80s after finishing my first long cruise, I had gotten my first case of the dreaded boaters' disease "bigger boat-itis," which led me to sell my trim and easy-to-sail 33' sloop to buy a heavy, complicated 45' ketch with all the offshore 'goodies'. I now had two autopilots, a windvane self-steering gear, six solar panels, two refrigeration systems, a wind generator, eight batteries, seven sails, a super complicated engine room full of switches, dials, and gauges of all kinds. She had been a crewed charter vessel in her early life and by the time I got her, she had a plethora of not immediately obvious problems.

After months of hard work, I had only taken her sailing a few times. After two years, I realized that we weren't much closer to having her completely ready to go cruising than when I had bought her, although my bank account was being worked hard as I bought more giant gear and expensive spare parts and replacements for systems that were proving unreliable. Worst of all, I discovered that we tended to not go sailing if it was only for a fun evening sail or a short distance. The amount of effort involved in getting the boat ready and off the dock, or the anchor up and all the sails uncovered and set was not worth the rewards that a short sail would give—so I bought an 18' daysailer to go sailing on! Meanwhile, a couple across the dock from us lived aboard a Westsail 32. They went sailing several times a week—sometimes only for an hour or two. I grew to envy them and would often meet them out on the water on my small daysailer. One day a friend asked me, "You want to go back out cruising again, right? Why do you need such a big, complicated boat? Maybe you should just buy a smaller boat and take off; forget all the gadgets and just go have fun." Nine months later I had done just that: sold the big ketch and sailed off on a super nice Westsail 32—visited thirteen countries in two and a half years and never once regretting having gotten rid of the larger boat.

I don't want to sound like I am suggesting that everyone should be cruising on small boats and nowadays, with so many terrific older mid-size cruising boats out there on the used market, choices abound for what might be the right size for cruising. For me, at that time, a smaller boat was perfect. I later went up in size several times and even cruised a fair amount on my 64' brigantine with a full crew of paying guests, family, and friends. But in the end, what might have seemed too small, or too large, was all in my mind.

Take a good hard look at the kind of people you are. If you enjoy repairing things and maintaining systems to perfection and can afford to do so, then by all means go for a complicated, larger boat. But if you hate fixing things, or don't feel comfortable reefing a 500 sq ft mainsail during a 2:00 a.m. squall, disassembling a generator, or surgically repairing a watermaker, then maybe a smaller boat with fewer systems might be a better choice. If you want to have the freedom to up anchor and sail away at the drop of a hat, keep that in mind while choosing your future cruising home.

In the end, what is too big or too small has little or nothing to do with seaworthiness or safety, it's all about how you want to spend your time and how willing (or able) you are to maintain your cruising home to seaworthy standards. Choose a boat that is big enough to support the basic systems you feel you need to have, and small enough so that you will want to sail her often... and far.

The right rig for cruising

One of the greatest aspects of offshore and coastal cruising is meeting other like-minded souls out there, sailing the world's oceans as you are doing, dealing with the same logistics and difficulties, and reaping many of the same rewards. Of course, mixing with the local people, blending in with the cultures of the various countries we visit, learning what we can, and sharing what we have with others is largely what cruising is about, but it is also about meeting and befriending other cruisers.

Often, after a passage or when in a friendly port, I will find myself socializing with other cruisers who have come from so many different backgrounds, countries, and ways of life, and yet, we all find ourselves in the same places doing the same sort of things, so a bond is often formed. Go to any cruiser bar or beach-side potluck and sooner or later the conversation will drift to boats, rigs, and systems.

During my many years of sailing various cutters, schooners, and ketches, one of the most common questions I have been asked is: "Why do you sail one of [those]?" The question is not easy to answer and requires a careful analysis of many factors. Having sailed most of my life, I have had experience cruising with many different rigs. Today, with modern sail materials and sail handling equipment, more and more often we see bigger and bigger boats being handled by smaller and smaller crews. It is not uncommon to find sixty-some -year-old couples on 50' or 60' yachts relying on all-electric or hydraulic furling and anchoring systems. When I began cruising, I clearly remember thinking, *I'll never have a roller furling jib. They always fail*! In the early days of roller furling, it was often jokingly referred to as "Roller failing." With the improvements in these gears and the proliferation of manufacturers competing to build the best and most reliable systems, things have sure changed for the better. I now believe that roller furling headsails are probably the single most important safety system developed for sailboats during the 20th century. Roller furling gears keep the crew off the bow and when combined with jiffy reefing or in-mast or in-boom furling, it keeps the crew in the cockpit for all sail handling which can be a real safety factor in big sea conditions.

Conventional wisdom maintains that a sloop is the most efficient cruising rig for upwind work and that cutters, so popular in the days before reliable roller furling became commonplace, are becoming extinct and being replaced by roller headsail sloops and also what are often termed 'double headsail sloops' with two or more roller furling sails all near the stem in the form of a 'Solent Rig' that can be used for different conditions.

Ketches, so popular in the seventies and early eighties, are hardly ever being built anymore and when they are, rarely do you see them in the under fifty-foot range. Most people elect to have a single stick to create the most efficient and simple rig for upwind work. That most long-distance cruising is (hopefully) accomplished on a reach or downwind and these modern designs often rely on very sophisticated, expensive, and complicated sail handling gear that is considered by most to be 'normal' these days, and so little thought is given to some of the more traditional rigs that so often graced anchorages, offshore, and coastal waters in years gone by.

Having been the owner of quite a few sloops, several cutters, ketches, two schooners, and a brigantine over the years, at some of the beach-side discussions about the best rig for cruising, I usually have a different view than most.

Sloops, as we all know, are simple. If you can sail at all, you can probably make a sloop perform reasonably well and if your only goal is to have the simplest, least confusing rig with which to sail, then a sloop is a good choice. For some people, sail handling and trimming of sails is a bother and for many of the sloop sailors who race, having two sails for upwind and a spinnaker for downwind is quite enough of a challenge, thank you very much. Just getting the most out of those two or three sails is satisfying and fun for many and that's okay.

It is generally accepted that cutters were originally developed as a way of offering easier sail handling and greater flexibility in balance than a traditional sloop rig could offer. With the cutter, a smaller jib could be bent on and a staysail could create the extra sail area needed to provide good drive, but each sail was smaller and therefore easier to handle. In the days before roller furling became commonplace, this was a good alternative to dealing with large jibs that would need to be dropped in a hurry in squally or rapidly building conditions. The concept of the cutter is brilliant in that as the sails are reefed and dropped, the sail plan comes well inboard and the mast is more adequately stayed than it typically is with the sloop rig. The downside, of course, is that the rig has more windage, an inner forestay that gets in the way of easy tacking, and more complication. Hence, it can be a more expensive rig to maintain.

Ketches, and to a lesser extent yawls, share some of the simplicity of the sloop rig while offering the ability to have much greater control over the center of effort of the boat. A split rig provides a lot more flexibility in terms of how the sails are trimmed, or which sails are set to achieve a good balance between upwind and downwind performance and offer the potential for self-steering even without an autopilot or windvane. There is no doubt that within normal crew limitations that a properly sailed ketch can carry more sail, longer, in a rising wind than a sloop of similar size. Reaching is a ketch's strong point and we all hope certainly that cruising provides a lot of reaching. If built with relatively long jib luffs and narrow sheeting angles, ketches can do quite well upwind and because typically each sail on a ketch may be slightly smaller than you would find on a similar-sized sloop, the stress on the rig and gear are less and the crew has an easier time sailing the boat as well, despite the extra sail to deal with. 'Cutter ketches', or 'staysail ketches' as they are often called, are quite common and offer tremendous flexibility in changing wind conditions. On one very squally passage up the Yucatan coast aboard one of my staysail ketches many years back, we put a double reef in the mainsail and left the full mizzen, staysail, and full jib out. When the heavy squalls would come through, all we would do was drop the mizzen, which was right in the cockpit, and roll in the jib. We were nearly instantly reduced to a heavy staysail and double-reefed main which worked well in the stronger forty-knot winds. When the squalls would move off, we would simply roll the jib back out and raise the mizzen. The double-reefed main was a little underpowered in the lighter winds between squalls, but we hardly noticed it. Many people also report using just the mizzen, jib, and staysail upwind with the mainsail stowed on the boom in heavier air and we have done that on occasion, but of course, if conditions are squally and variable, dropping and raising a main four or five times in a watch to keep the boat moving well is a bit more work!

Schooners offer even more flexibility when balancing the boat on various points of sail, and in most instances, each sail on a schooner is a bit smaller than you might find on a similar-sized ketch. While headsail luff lengths are usually shorter on a schooner which limits their upwind capabilities, off the wind or running few boats can catch a properly sailed schooner. When rigged with a yardarm and a square sail, they will sail downwind better and with less crew effort than any other rig out there. In the days before self-steering and autopilots, the schooner rig offered the best solution to the dilemma of shorthanded sailing. With a schooner, one can under-trim the main a bit and so when the boat falls off, the main fills properly and pulls the boat back on course. When the boat sails too high, the main loses power and so the center of effort moves forward, and the foresail and jib(s) pull her back on course.

As an interesting tidbit of nautical history, the schooner *America* that sailed across the Atlantic in 1851 managed to beat every racing yacht she was matched against in Europe. Largely because of the success of *America*, racing schooners were still being regularly built for ocean racing and campaigned up until right after World War II. General George Patton of World War II fame's boat that he had intended to cruise on after the war was a beautiful schooner named *When and If*, is still sometimes seen sailing Caribbean waters.

There have been many catboat-type rigs introduced over the years for cruising. The attraction or marketing ploy often promulgated was that the rig was simple, easy to handle, and rugged. With the introduction of roller furling headsails, in-mast furling mains, and in-boom furling, many people that might have chosen a catboat or cat ketch/schooner may be electing to go for the simplicity of these modern furling rigs, and for good reason: they are better upwind performers and are typically better balanced off the wind than a catboat-type rig. All that having been said, as long as one does not mind dealing with a large mainsail and a long boom, the catboat, and cat ketches can be a lot of fun to sail and are great reaching rigs.

The gaff rig has been largely forgotten in the last fifty years and there are only a couple of modern 'character' designs sporting this well-proven and successful innovation. For centuries, the gaff rig was employed as the most suitable way to handle a boomed mainsail. The gaff, when used in conjunction with lazy jacks, makes dropping or raising the mainsail on a reach or even downwind possible, and if a squall comes along, just lowering the peak of the gaff can 'scandalize' the sail, dumping much of the sail's power. Reefing with a gaff rig is very easy and once lowered into the cradle of the lazyjacks, a gaff holds the sail down until gaskets (sail ties) can be lashed in place.

Go into any major cruising port and you will see a broad cross-section of what people consider the best rigs and designs for long-distance voyaging. One thing I have learned is that there is no single 'right answer' for the best rig to take cruising, and I always enjoy seeing a boat with an unusual rig, well handled by a shorthanded crew entering a harbor or on a passage.

It can also be argued that emotions can play a large part in the decision process when choosing the right rig for cruising. I know that it would be easier to sail a modern sloop and in many cases, it would be perfectly adequate, but over the years I have gravitated to more unusual designs and rigs as a way of keeping myself and my crew entertained and I certainly admit that when entering a new port, we are seldom compelled to say, "Oh, look at that beautiful white sloop!" when there is a schooner, brigantine, gaff cutter, or ketch sitting gracefully in the harbor, drawing our attention and eclipsing all the other craft with her beauty.

Some of the more complicated and esoteric rigs of yesteryear are not for everybody and yet I hope that as time goes on we continue to see some of these excellent rigs and traditional designs continuing to sail the oceans, happily taking their crews to destinations far and wide.

Chapter Three

What is a Bargain Boat and How Much Does It Cost?

The adage "A boat will cost as much as you have," may be in some ways true, but in fact, I've learned over the decades that if you do your research and take great care in your boat buying search that in many cases a real bargain can be found. You will be able to find a good boat, get it all sorted out and properly outfitted, and get out sailing for a minimal investment of time and perhaps even energy.

For some, a good cruising boat could be an 18' centerboard trailerable sloop with a small cabin that sleeps two that was acquired for $400 on Craigslist, while others may find their bargain is a 50' catamaran purchased from a bankrupt yacht dealer that has room for all twelve grandchildren! So nailing down exactly how much a bargain cruising boat costs is difficult. However, I will say that there are certain things to look for when you are searching for the best deal out there.

Numero uno: never consider the asking price or even the selling price of a boat to be the *cost* of that boat. When you are considering a boat on which to go long-term sailing, whether it be coastal or offshore, certain things will have to be in top condition. We'll talk more about this in later chapters, but suffice to say that when searching for your bargain, things like newer rigging, chainplates, sails, engines, and electronics are all part of the picture and so sometimes finding a boat that is a little scruffy-looking, but which has all of these important elements in good condition, is a way better choice than a shiny, spiffy-looking boat that will need tens of thousands of dollars and months of maintenance and improvements

put into her before she is ready to take you away sailing.

What parts of a boat's overall structure are the most vitally important and costly to address, and how often do things need to be replaced? Some marine surveyors fall into the trap of capitulating to what is dictated by certain insurers who say that after seven or ten years, standing rigging must be replaced, or that at twenty years, chainplates and keel bolts must be changed out, or that sails over five years old are no good. These are tremendously oversimplified ways to address a complex issue: when must things be replaced and how much will they cost?

Standing rigging is not a simple subject to take on. While there used to be many different grades of stainless steel and even good quality galvanized rigging available, nowadays, almost everything you will find being sold is from China or Korea. While high-quality European wire is still available, it is substantially more expensive and so most manufacturers and riggers use the cheaper wires and expect it to only last seven to ten years. If however, you find an older, high-quality boat such as an Amel, Hallberg-Rassy, or even some of the well-made American boats from the 1980s, it may still have rigging wires that are original and in fine condition! This is especially true for boats sailed in brackish or fresh water, or used seasonally with rigs stored inside during the off-season. But regardless of what boat you find, if it truly needs new rigging, when it comes time to change the wires out, plan on only being able to find the Far Eastern wires.

There are some excellent online sources for costing out replacement rigging and when you are looking at your older boat, whether it needs the rig replaced or not, run the numbers of how much it will come to because if you own it for long enough, you will eventually be changing the rigging out!

More and more often these days traditional designs and some of the more modern designs are being re-rigged with synthetics such as Dyneema. You may also find a great boat that has rod rigging and if you decide to replace it with wire, it can be a daunting process, and rod rigging is extremely expensive to renew. But no matter what you decide on for new rigging, be sure to put the potential costs for this into the equation of how much your 'dreamboat' is going to cost you!

Most production sailboats use stainless steel for the chainplates that hold the rig up and although there are a handful of manufacturers that have used bronze chainplates, which by the way are far superior, or titanium, the vast majority of used vessels you'll find will have some sort of chainplate system made of stainless steel; so changing the chainplates at a certain point will be necessary. Once stainless steel chainplates reach twenty or so years, or if there is any evidence of leaks at the chainplates, most surveyors will suggest at the very least pulling them out and inspecting them. And I have found that unless you are lucky and find a boat that has external chainplates or super easy to unbolt internal chainplates that by the time you've gone to all the trouble of pulling them out, you might as well just buy or build new ones and install them. Then you'll be good to go for about twenty more years, maybe longer! When replacing chainplates, consider using bronze or titanium.

Beware though that titanium and bronze do not tolerate reshaping once installed. Stainless steel can however be reshaped but should be at least 316, (or 316L if they are to be welded) and this material is probably still the most cost-effective metal to use in most instances. Beware of the older boat with 'glassed-in' chainplates as replacing these may turn into requiring the removal of much of the interior joinery of the vessel. This can transform what should be a simple job into a truly daunting project.

Keel bolts are a real debate point and of course, not all keel bolts, attachment systems, or ballast materials are the same, so no blanket statements can be made. It is however good to remember that on any older boat with external ballast, a careful look at the ballast attachment system should be undertaken, and the costs of eventually replacing the bolts should be calculated into the long-term ownership costs too.

Replacing mild steel or stainless bolts threaded into an external iron keel is generally a straightforward and easy to accomplish job. Replacing cast-in stainless J-bolts in a lead keel may require sending the keel to a company that builds keels to get a result that is acceptable enough for an offshore yacht. Some older lead keels had cavities cast in with bolts installed, but most production boats use J-bolts and for example, replacing all the keel bolts on a mid-40s size cruising yacht might cost upwards of twenty-five thousand dollars or even more by the time keel shipping and yard crane and storage fees are added in!

For this reason, a lot of people consider internally ballasted keels to be preferable for a cruising yacht. However, even these types of keels can exhibit problems. The biggest issues to look out for are voids in the keel encapsulation and subsequent ingress of water into the keel cavity. If the ballast is lead, repairing this deficiency can be as easy as draining any water, drying the areas, and filling the voids with epoxy or polyester resin, but if the ballast material is iron, a thorough drying out and preparation of the internal ballast must be made to assure a suitable result. So don't fall into the trap of assuming that just because a boat doesn't have keel bolts that there's nothing to be concerned about. I've seen internally ballasted boats that have taken a heavy grounding and had their ballast fall out! I've also surveyed boats where the hull laminate at the top of the ballast encapsulation has flexed and worked the fiberglass to the point where it is fracturing and beginning to fail. So carefully inspecting and maintaining this critical attachment point, even with an internally ballasted boat, is extremely important. Keeping all that in mind though, it can probably be safely said that it is less expensive in the longer term to own an internally ballasted boat than one with keel bolts.

Cored Hulls vs Solid Laminates

When most yachts were made of wood, they tended to be fairly heavy as a result of the scantling schedules that were arrived at over centuries of trial and error. Plank on frame construction started in the Middle Ages and it can be safely said that through many centuries of experimentation with fishing vessels and trading ships, that by the time yachts were being produced in any significant numbers at the beginning of the twentieth century, rarely did you see a lightly built vessel being launched. Cruising yachts of the 1930s through the 1950s were often either purpose-built vessels emulating traditional fishing or rescue boat designs or were converted workboats built of heavy timbers with oversized fittings designed to withstand years of hard usage. With minimal maintenance they would still provide enough strength and integrity to keep their crews safe in the often precarious weather encountered in the days before modern weather forecasting came about.

Because of the technological advances brought about with the advent of high strength glues and laminated woods developed around the time of World War II, new and innovative advances were made that allowed lighter weight hulls to be built. Then in the 1940s when glass cloth reinforced polyester hulls began to be produced, an entirely new set of structural dynamics were encountered that required the introduction of innovative ways to incorporate this new material. Fiberglass, as it became known in the US, or GRP (glass reinforced plastic) as it was known in Europe proved to be an exceptionally versatile material that for any given thickness or weight could produce a hull that was far stronger than an equivalent wooden hull. But fiberglass, when reduced in thickness to reach reasonable weight vs tensile strength ratios, was far more flexible than an equivalent wooden section. When the first fiberglass hulls were being produced this increased flexibility was not such an issue because the early hulls were basically reproductions of known and accepted wooden sistership designs and so the exceptionally heavy laminated structure was thick enough that flexing was minimized simply with the addition of a few bulkheads and perhaps some transverse floors (structural cross members). But as time went on and the oil embargo of the 1970s created a shortage of fiberglass resins and an exponential cost increase, the boatbuilding industry began to demand lighter (and less costly) ways to build hulls and yacht designers answered this need by creating lighter, wider, shallower bilged designs to facilitate the manufacturing of hulls that had fewer materials in them. In the USA, an engineer by the name of Everett Pearson has been widely credited with the concept of using edge grain balsa wood inside two thin panels of fiberglass to create a relatively lightweight sandwich-type structure that offered increased panel stiffness similar to how a corrugated cardboard box achieves its stiffness, while simultaneously, other engineers had already been experimenting with using plywood inside of deck structures or flat sections of hulls to achieve stiffness and save weight while others experimented with using high-density foam and honeycomb composites as a core to stiffen the panels.

In Europe, manufacturers such as Nautor, Wauquiez, Moody, and others tended to stick with solid laminate structures that used half-round or hat-section stringers built longitudinally inside the hulls along with partial and full athwartship frames, similar to how a wooden boat was built, to achieve stiffness. But in many cases, because most of the early yacht designs were developments of already accepted wooden types, the need for cores to create sufficient panel stiffness wasn't as prevalent in the older designs. By the late 70s and from the 1980s onwards, cored hulls became more and more common. Manufacturers like Whitby, C&C, Tillotson Pearson, and many others jumped on the bandwagon of building lighter cored hulls and in the modern world of yacht building, cored hulls are now nearly as common as solid laminated ones. Is this a good thing? Maybe.

What can go wrong: Cored hulls have the benefits of being very stiff and by virtue of their construction are somewhat insulated from heat and cold and are much lighter weight than a typical solid laminate structure of similar dimensions. The biggest defect I typically find as a surveyor results from an incomplete bond to both sides of the fiberglass skin where the core was never properly attached during the building process. The second-biggest defect often encountered is water ingress into the core lamination. Often these two types of defects are interrelated.

Despite the many early engineering papers touted by various manufacturers of cored hulls suggesting that water would not intrude into a balsa cored hull or deck structure, even when holed, experience in the field has proven otherwise. Balsa (and foam) cores are almost always made up of tiny squares of material lightly attached to a thin woven fabric that allows the wood or foam panels to take on complex compound curves. The small spaces in between the squares are called kerfs and when the panels are laid into a curved section, the kerfs can become fairly wide on one side. The idea is that if enough resin and filler are applied to the side opposite the cloth binder that it will 'squeegee' into all the kerfs and create a perfect unitized bond. My real-life observations on many surveys of cored hulls have proved that this is often not the case. So carefully assessing the integrity of a cored hull

is vitally important because once an organic (balsa or plywood) core is allowed to be wet long enough, it will eventually degrade. Rotten deck cores are quite common as a result of water ingress and yet are typically fairly easy to repair, but rotted or delaminated hull cores can be more of a challenge to overcome. That having been said, no repair is impossible on a boat and so if you end up settling on a cored hull and find areas of moisture intrusion or even delaminations, *don't* necessarily walk away, but *do* be aware of the procedures to remedy this defect and more importantly be aware of what caused the water ingress in the first place. Periodic re-bedding of through-hulls is one area that requires special attention. But I am sure that there are hundreds of cruising boats out there sailing the world's oceans right now that have damp cores and still manage to take their crews safely from port to port. Cored hulls are not taboo but do require that the owner be diligent and observant to assure a safe and seaworthy vessel.

Most fiberglass boats have cored decks too. Coring is one of the easiest and best ways to achieve stiffness in relatively flat deck panels, but the problems here can be similar to the issues addressed about cored hulls above. We will go much more in-depth on how to solve deck and hull problems in subsequent pages, but suffice to say that when trying to ascertain the 'total final cost' of the boat you are considering, repairs to the hull, deck, and rigging are all potential big-ticket items that can drive your total cost up a lot.

Systems on boats are another huge expense and I think it is safe to say that the simpler your boat is, the fewer systems it has, the less it will cost to maintain in the long term.

Foot pumps for your water system can use a lot less water than a pressurized on-demand system and the pumps are less expensive to maintain. Water collection systems from a bimini top, cabin top, or deck can provide as much or more water than a ten thousand dollar watermaker but of course, require regular rainfall to be effective, while an inexpensive homemade watermaker may be an effective solution for cruising in desert areas.

An extra set of hatches or opening port lights will be much less expensive to install or maintain than an air conditioning system and will free up space that would otherwise be taken up with machinery and while appliances like dishwashers and washer/driers may seem essential to people accustomed to living on land, the reality of maintaining these systems and providing the water and energy to operate them should make one seriously question their worth for long-distance cruising. And when considering these high-power consumption systems, the cost of not just maintaining a diesel generator, but factoring in the eventual replacement of said unit must also be weighed into the total ownership costs. And finally, you should give some serious thought to how you wish to be spending your time while afloat and exploring the world. Do you want to be tied to a monthly maintenance schedule of complicated and time-consuming systems or would you rather be hiking, or snorkeling, or exploring a new city, or visiting a remote village? Simplicity in your cruising home will almost always translate to more free time and less overall expense.

Engines are a big potential expense and that's why some veteran cruisers from decades past chose to sail without an engine. But an engine can be an extremely valuable piece of safety equipment and can allow you to reach many places that would be difficult or impossible to reach without one. For example, entering tropical atoll lagoons with narrow channels or making a safe port in light winds a few hours in advance of a strong storm system are just two things a reliable engine can offer.

A well-maintained marine diesel can last many decades while a poorly maintained one could fail you the day you take delivery of your boat. So having a thorough understanding of the potential maintenance issues and costs you may encounter and factoring them into the ultimate cost of your boat is as important as negotiating the actual price you pay for it.

At the same time, all too often people replace perfectly good engines or 'rebuild' an engine that doesn't need it—all because of misinformation or bad advice from a person or company that may be looking out more for their own profit margin than your best interests. As a broker or surveyor, I have seen it all too often: owners of a new (to them) boat get 'tricked' into replacing or rebuilding an engine that may have only needed minor maintenance. So if your knowledge base isn't strong with engines, be sure to get some trusted advice before you proceed with the purchase of a boat or decide to rebuild or replace an entire engine.

The drive trains of engines can be a huge expense too. Prop shafts wear out and transmissions have a lifespan. And even if those two critical items are okay, factor in the cost of eventually replacing them down the line. Do note however that in many cases rebuilding a transmission is an acceptable solution as compared to replacing it. Rebuilding a transmission is not very expensive and much less problematic than rebuilding an engine. Even a worn prop shaft can be reused if you can change the area where the wear is bearing on the packing or cutlass bearing by using a drive saver or a longer or shorter shaft tube hose. Alternatively, a used shaft may be acquired at a fraction of the cost of a new one.

One place where savings can rarely be realized though is in the case of V-drives. If your 'soon to be yours' boat has one of these systems, be sure to cost out a replacement and keep that in the back of your mind when it comes time to plan your cruising budget, because one of those babies can be a $3-$5K surprise plus the cost of shipping to some far off port!

Electronics are one place where you can spend a *lot* of money and if your potential secondhand boat has a full complement of the latest gear, this can be a huge plus. At the same time if, as is often the case, you are looking at a boat that has a ton of older electronics that are showing signs of age or not functioning, be sure to point out to the seller or broker that the cost of replacing aged equipment is often more than the cost of installing new because of the labor involved in removing what is already there. And just because a set of older electronics is working at the time of your inspection of the vessel, it may quit on you the very next day! For example, a 25-year-old radar may work now, but in the first bout of bad weather may give up the ghost due to water intrusion into the radome, and an old autopilot that works well on the sea trial in calm weather may shred its gears or blow a seal once subjected to heavy conditions. And finding parts for old units can be hit or miss. Just imagine these scenarios and while this doesn't necessarily mean you have to plan on buying all new gear, you need to keep these potential expenses in the back of your mind as you move from the looking to the negotiation stages of buying your future vessel.

At the same time, remember that many long-distance cruisers don't spend fortunes on electronics, and in this modern age, it is arguable that simply having a tablet computer with a charting program, a wireless radar (if you feel the need for one), a basic depth sounder, a mechanical windvane, and a small autopilot that can operate the vessel in light winds while motoring may be an acceptable alternative to buying a whole new suite of expensive state-of-the-art electronics. For centuries, sailors have navigated with the stars and inshore using coastal piloting methods including the use of a leadline for depths. A set of ratlines up the shrouds can in many cases be better than a many-thousands of dollars forward-looking sonar. Try to keep your sights on what's important to you for the electronics you plan to use on your boat. Don't go overboard (so to speak) on buying new units, but do keep replacements and eventual upgrades in mind as part of the final cost of your future home.

Sails and rigging can be a big expense and require a careful inspection while shopping for your new sailing home.

It is unfortunate but often true that many surveyors these days make blanket statements about rigging based upon their desire to absolve themselves from accountability in the event of a failure. Often you will see a recommendation to 'have the rigging inspected by a qualified rigger.' Well, finding a truly qualified rigger that isn't profit-motivated is a challenge, and even if they aren't out there to sell you new rigging, it's not their money being spent; so all too often a rigger or surveyor might recommend replacing standing rigging that is perfectly fine just because it would be *nicer* if it were new. While this may be true, it's your hard-earned money being spent and so getting a true assessment of what's good and what's not is vitally important and can have a many-thousands of dollars impact on what you ultimately invest in your boat before you take off to go sailing long distances.

The same holds true for sails. If you follow a typical surveyor's 'pass the buck' recommendation to 'have the sails inspected by a professional sailmaker,' you may be told that all the sails are shot and need replacing when in fact they only require some re-stitching or a few small patches over wear areas. Racing sailors and cruising sailors often have quite different criteria for sails and what a racing sailor might consider 'worthless' could be just fine for a cruising sailor to use for a few more years. I once found a sail in a dumpster that had been tossed because the owners had been convinced to buy a new set of sails before they headed off into the blue waters. We used that sail for our mizzen for four years and ten thousand miles of sailing. Still, good high-quality sails are a terrific investment and are well worth the expense if you are heading far, but even here, big savings can be realized with careful shopping.

Take into consideration how you are going to be using your boat. If you are only going to cruise the ICW to Florida and jump over to the Bahamas for the first couple of years, or if you only plan to cruise the West Coast or Sea of Cortez for a couple of years, investing in new sails might be a waste of money. There are many very good used sail dealers and oftentimes great secondhand sails can be had from one of them for a fraction of the cost of a custom-built sail. Don't be afraid of a good used sail. If it has a decent shape and is offered by a reputable loft, it's probably okay. Years ago I read that world-renowned sailor and multi-circumnavigator Hal Roth once took one of his old drifter sails into a used sail loft and they turned it down because it was 'too worn' to be worth anything. So Roth took it back to his boat and proceeded to use it sailing... around the world. That 'worthless' sail carried him most of the way across the Indian Ocean.

Keeping all of the above in mind while boat shopping can be a huge help in avoiding unfortunate surprises down the line and that your 'dreamboat' doesn't turn out to be a financially draining nightmare! And it might also possibly save you tens of thousands of dollars in unnecessary expenses while outfitting your cruising home.

If all of the above makes it appear as if I am dodging the question of 'How much does a good cruising boat cost?' Consider that in my many years of sailing I have encountered single-handers who spent less than five thousand dollars for a boat on which they have crossed oceans. I have met countless cruisers out sailing the world on boats that only cost them ten- or twenty-thousand dollars, boats that were all up and ready to sail. I have made major voyages on boats which cost between twenty-five and fifty thousand dollars total investment including (used) watermakers, life rafts, windvanes, and cruising chutes, and that as long as you follow the guidelines in this book, you too can cross oceans or cruise long distances on a shoestring budget.

And What About a Catamaran?

Now that you've come this far into this book you've probably noticed I've made no mention of catamarans. As a former yacht broker and charter yacht captain, I do know of a few types that represent good values, but as a marine surveyor and offshore sailor, I have a hard time recommending any catamaran under 42'. Because of the cost of a decent catamaran in that size range and above, I feel like cats fall outside of the subject matter of being 'bargain boats.' However, there are a few types that one could consider. My problem with cats is basically they can go inverted and stay that way. Simple as that. I know that bringing that subject to light will also risk vehement reactions from people who have convinced themselves that catamarans are 'safe enough,' but as a marine surveyor who has personally inspected many cats that have gone upside down and in some cases even tumbled before landing up hillsides during hurricanes, I can't think of any good reason for considering a cat when that type of catastrophic event is possible. Some catamaran enthusiasts think that going inverted is unlikely and it may be true with typical coastal sailing and with total 24/7 vigilance offshore that a small cat can be kept on her feet. But should really bad weather come along, once you get into waves taller than the

beam of a cat you are out there asking for trouble. The fact is, it is indeed possible and if you cruise long enough it is even eventually likely that you may find yourself in waves of up to 20 or so feet. If you are in a good monohull, this is not a problem. With a cat in strong changing conditions, this type of seaway can allow wind to get under a hull and with some help from a breaking wave, can easily cause them to go inverted.

Modern cats almost always have 'escape hatches' under their bridge decks or in the hulls to allow supposed access to the outside of the boat should they indeed become inverted. But imagine that scenario at 3:00 a.m. in fifteen to twenty-foot waves and forty to fifty-knot winds and only starlight to assist you? A nightmare for sure! Even if you do safely escape, trying to stay aboard a slippery, awash, inverted hull is an iffy proposition at best in any kind of seaway.

One of the arguments for cats is that with proper flotation, they won't sink, and that's a good thing. But most cats are so lightly built that once they are filled with water and in a seaway with many tons of water crashing to and fro inside the partially sunk boat, it is only a matter of time until watertight bulkheads are breached, and in any case, what good is a ¾ sunk boat that's upside down in a big seaway?

I suspect I'll hear screaming and disagreements galore, but I contend that most smaller cats are not safe for long-term offshore cruising with a family and that even larger cats are a questionable choice for ocean sailing on a long-term basis. Sooner or later nature will throw a spat of bad weather at you and unless you handle it just perfectly, you could be in real trouble. Case in point: In November 2016, a large Atlantic 57 catamaran was on a delivery to the Caribbean and ran into a strong cold front north of the Dominican Republic. Onboard was a three-person very experienced catamaran crew, but the wind shift came so suddenly that they couldn't spill the mainsheet in time and the boat went over. And these were professional sailors! They spent ten hours clinging to the overturned hull before being rescued.

In 1992, we were hunkered down in a harbor in the eastern Bahamas while a late-season extra-tropical low developed and gave us 40-50 knot winds for several days before it meandered to the north. Around that same time, two 39' catamarans left Fort Lauderdale bound for the Virgin Islands with professional crews onboard. They intended to make a direct run for the islands. Both boats were never heard from again.

In that same system, before we made landfall, we had spent part of one long night hove to, sitting comfortably below, or with stints in the cockpit. Friends on a Pearson 424 took a knockdown and tore a jib but had no other damage. Of the eleven monohulls we knew of in that area, I don't know of a single one that got into serious trouble as that system went over. But the two cats just… disappeared. Do you really want a cat?

People generally choose catamarans because of space. Simple as that. A cat typically has multiple sleeping cabins and this has a huge attraction to families so that each child can have their own 'space.' And they are shoal-draft which is great if your intentions take you into skinny waters. If you are only going to be cruising the Bahamas or the Caribbean and are careful to watch the weather, then why not? Indeed, there are a few smaller cats that fall into the 'bargain boat' category and if even after considering all the negative aspects of cruising on a cat you still decided that's what you want, the Privilege 39s are well made and are good values as are the older Fountaine Pajot Athena 38s. The older TPI-built Lagoons however almost always have extensive moisture intrusion into the cores and oh yes, did I explain that the whole premise of catamarans is that they are lightweight and therefore almost all have very lightly constructed cored hulls? The laminate schedule on these boats is so lightly built that even bumping a dock can hole them and even if you lightly ground a typical catamaran on a shallow reef, the odds are that the boat will be a throwaway or at the very least require extensive repairs.

So consider carefully what I have said before you look at catamarans. We used to say in the charter industry that there are three types of people out there on the water: There are sailors, there are power boaters, and then there are those catamaran people.

Chapter Four

Where are the Best Places in the World to Shop for a Boat?

It has for many decades been a known fact that you can sometimes buy cheap boats in places like Panama, Hawaii, Fiji, and Southeast Asia. Upon reaching these areas, sailors are faced with the decision of whether they will carry on sailing, which might mean crossing a vast ocean, continuing around the world, or worse yet, having to sail their boat back upwind or through high latitudes to reach home waters. The alternative method of shipping a boat or having it delivered from somewhere far away can in some cases cost as much or more than the value of the boat. This realization leads many sellers to decide to part with their vessels at bargain prices and to just board a plane and fly back home.

While the above may be true, good buys can be found almost anywhere. However, some places are more fun and interesting to spend time at while searching for boat bargains, and the following is a breakdown of the pluses and minuses of the various areas where I have found great deals and what you are likely to find.

New England and the Mid-Atlantic

Generally speaking, while it's true that the northeastern USA is a great place to shop for a boat, prices for 'ready to go' sailboats in the mid-Atlantic and New England Coast are rarely bargains. However, the vast numbers of boats in these areas allow for the possibility that with diligent searching, a good buy can be found. And if you're looking for a smaller cruising boat or a fixer-upper, then the backwaters of the Chesapeake Bay are one of the best areas to go searching. Hundreds upon hundreds of disused or lightly used boats are stored in small boatyards all over the region and sometimes the best way to find one is to simply get in a car and drive from boatyard to boatyard asking the managers or owners if they know of any boats for sale (or boats whose owners are way behind in storage fees).

Sometimes the boatyards themselves have seized vessels for nonpayment and although these are oftentimes near basket-cases, occasionally a true bargain can be found. Also, check the charitable organizations as they often end up with donated boats that can be had at very reasonable prices. Even if a particular boatyard manager doesn't want to share information about the status of any late or unpaid tenants, if you see a boat you like the appearance of and it's looking a bit neglected, a search of Coast Guard records online or a call to the state's boat registry department may turn up an owner's contact details. Send them an email or call them and see if they may be interested in selling!

With the ever-increasing costs of storage for yachts on land, it is not uncommon to find boats being virtually given away just to rid the owner of the costs of storing them. Be sure to check on Craigslist often and search the local online ads as well as bulletin boards in yacht clubs, boatyards, and marinas.

The Carolinas, Florida, and the Southeast, Including Texas

In the good ole US of A, these parts of the country are where the highest number of true bargains can be found. Check around northeast Florida which has the largest number of cheap sailboats I've seen anywhere in the US. As with the mid-Atlantic and New England, marina and boatyard prices have soared in recent years all across the southeast except in this area of Florida and also to a lesser extent along the gulf coast of Alabama, Mississippi, and Louisiana. So people with cheap boats who have the wherewithal to do so have moved their vessels into these areas of the country to save on storage fees. Even so, many of these boats reach the point where they have been abandoned or are for sale at low prices just to pass the responsibility on to someone else. Shop carefully but if you are looking for a cruising boat at the lower end of the price spectrum and don't want to venture outside of the US, this area of the country is where you might have your best chance of finding it.

The West Coast: California to British Columbia

Tens of thousands of sailboats dot the harbors from southern California to southern British Columbia. As a general rule, West Coast boats are almost always 10-30% higher priced than comparable sisterships in Florida and can be twice or more as expensive as a similar boat being sold in some remote area due to circumstances. That having been said, sometimes even here, good buys can be found.

While West Coast boats aren't typically equipped for offshore sailing and the marina and boatyard prices are exorbitant, careful shopping may turn up a bargain. While there are some inexpensive commercial yards in mainland British Columbia and a few scattered down the coast, if you do find a good boat at a reasonable price and need to do a haul-out and refit, take a careful look at where this could be done affordably. Your great deal may end up costing you a small fortune if you have to spend a few months hauled out and paying thousands of dollars a month in storage fees! We were quoted at one boatyard in San Diego $4 per foot per night for a boat at the work pier and another $1.50 per foot for the mast plus the same for the boom to lay alongside. So for a 47' boat, that would have run up quite a bill in short order—$8,000 a month! With careful shopping, I found a boatyard nearby that was less than one-third that price. By contrast, I had hauled that same boat at a boatyard in North Florida earlier that year that only charged us $20 a day for the boat in the work area and the mast storage was free!

The Eastern Caribbean

Many thousands of boats are kept in the Eastern Caribbean and hundreds are sold each year in this area. It is generally acknowledged that late-model production boats that have been in the charter trade in this region may sell from 10-40% below what that same boat might command back in Northern Europe or mainland US and this is mostly because each year the major charter companies bring new boats into their fleets and so the older boats, like those that have reached five years of age, must be sold to make space for the new arrivals. Because of the sheer number of late-model ex-charter vessels that are yearly flooded into the market, great buys can be had. For example, if you are the owner of one of fifty identical five-year-old charter boats that must be sold, how could you make sure your boat sells? Easy—make sure it is the lowest priced one of course! So these 'price wars' develop that last as long as it takes for all of these sisterships to sell. Once that's happened, often the prices creep back up on particular models again, and then ten or fifteen years out, the boats that are from a different area that were never chartered have gradually depreciated whereas the vastly depreciated boats from the charter fleets have in many cases appreciated from their 'bargain closeout' prices.

When a boat gets to be ten or fifteen years old, what drives the price on these vessels more than age is condition and equipment, period. Most of the larger charter fleets only allow new boats to stay in their fleet for four to six years and at the end of that time, they must be retired. What many people don't realize is that while the big name brand charter companies do of course make money from chartering people's boats, where they really make their money is from selling new boats into their fleets! So these fleets must 'kick-out' the five- or so year-old boats to sell new boats into the program.

Another phenomenon is the scenario where a couple or family brings their boat to the islands from Europe or North America and spends a year or two sailing around and then decides to return to work. They might keep the boat hauled out during summers and still use it seasonally, or even just a few weeks of each year, but eventually, many of these boats end up going on the market. In many cases, people run short on money for maintenance and though some of these boats may require fairly extensive refitting to return them to full oceangoing status, the good news is that at the more popular yachting centers in the Caribbean, getting parts and services is as easy, or in many cases even easier than doing so up in the states or back home in Europe. This is because thanks to the charter industry, contractors and service people are geared toward the idea that 'right now' is what is normal and required. For example, when I first moved back to the Caribbean after an absence of twelve years I had become used to being based on the East Coast of

the US where in places like Florida or Maryland, one must become accustomed to sometimes waiting for long periods of time—weeks or even months—to get a skilled worker to fit you into their busy schedule. In the Caribbean, thanks to the 'right now' requirements of the charter industry, getting a skilled worker onto your boat is almost always easier. Here's an example: years ago I had purchased a staysail schooner in the British Virgin Islands that we launched after a speedy refit on the island of Virgin Gorda. Once we were back in the water, we realized that the main alternator on the engine was kaput. We were on a tight schedule to bring this boat up to the Chesapeake and needed to get to Puerto Rico to pick up crew and so at 10:00 in the morning I called the big alternator shop in Road Town, the main settlement on the island group, and told them that I had an alternator problem and needed a tech to help. The harried-sounding British man on the other side of the line said, "There's no way I can get anyone out there right away, but I can get a tech there by 2:00 p.m." Because in the charter industry, a breakdown on a charter vessel that has guests arriving the next day, or already has them aboard, can cost a charter operator thousands or even tens of thousands of dollars, these contractors are geared toward the concept that 'right now' is what is required!

The most active markets for boats are, in descending order, the British Virgin Islands, Saint Martin, Martinique, and Antigua with Grenada also becoming more active in yacht sales. But any of the eastern Caribbean islands may be harboring your future home. For example, on a recent stop in St. Kitts, I saw quite a few vessels that appeared to be somewhat neglected sitting in the boatyard there that I'm sure could have been for sale if I had asked.

Pacific Mexico

Some very well-priced cruising boats do become available in the Sea of Cortez area and on the mainland down south as far as Puerto Vallarta. I have personally boat-searched there twice and found the La Paz area on the Baja Peninsula and San Carlos on the mainland to harbor some good values. The cost of living is low and public transport is reasonable, so you could afford to take your time searching there.

The scenario here is like many places 'downwind': People start out in British Columbia, Washington/Oregon, or California and equip their boats to 'sail around the world' but by the time they get as far south as the Baja, they may decide that they've had quite enough of blue water sailing; they become accustomed to the easy protected-water sailing and predictable weather patterns of northern Mexico's Sea of Cortez and so after a year or two, maybe they store their boats on land for the summer and go back north to family or work. In the following years, they may come back and sail the boat some, but eventually, the boat isn't being used enough to justify keeping it and it must be sold. The problem here is the same thing that happens in the Caribbean and other popular cruising grounds where people can store their boats during the off-season: Once the boat has been sitting more or less idle or being sailed only sporadically, it begins to need updating, and things like new rigging, engine issues or chainplates and keel bolts may need renewing, so sailing the boat onwards, or even just back to home waters is out of the question. Instead, these boats often end up being sold at bargain prices because to attract a buyer to this somewhat remote area, the prices have to be substantially lower than similar boats would be in easier to get to locales. Be prepared to do some work, but with diligent shopping, you may find your great buy already sitting in this wonderful cruising area, ready to continue providing adventures for its new owners.

Panama, Trinidad, and Rio Dulce, Guatemala

I am grouping these together because they have one thing in common: they are all in areas where it rains often and almost incessantly at times. These destinations are all at what is sort of the 'end of the road' for many people's cruising dreams.

Trinidad was for many years, back in the 70s through the 90s, the best place to get work done inexpensively in the Caribbean. In recent years prices have risen, but it is still a good place to get major work done. Because it is considered by most insurers to be out of the hurricane belt, lots of people elect to leave their boats hauled out in one of the yards in the main yachting center of Chaguaramas. Because of the sometimes nearly incessant seasonal rains, when boats are left there for any great length of time—a year or more—without someone tending to them, things can go downhill quickly. If you are handy and don't mind relocating to take on a big project, sometimes bargains can be found there.

While not quite as rainy as Panama or Trinidad, the same is true for the Rio Dulce. 'The Rio' as it is locally known is all the way downwind in the Bay of Honduras and so people may end up there, having sailed down from the states or up from the southwest Caribbean and find that life is easy and the cost of living is so low that they never leave. One thing can lead to another and many of these boats end up on the market but may need rigging, engine work, or other maintenance to sail in the ocean again, so these boats can often represent a tremendous value for a handy boat buyer. Sometimes boats that are in great shape that need hardly any work also come on the market and because the Rio Dulce is a fairly difficult place to get to by airplane and taxi or bus, to attract a buyer, the prices on one of these vessels must be quite low. In general, boats in the Rio Dulce can offer a lot for the dollar.

Panama is another place where it rains a lot and it is also one of those places where boats arrive going east or west and the owners of these boats may elect to stay on for extended periods in either Colón, the San Blas Islands, or the Bocas del Torro area where yachts congregate to enjoy beautiful cruising in protected waters and an ultra-low-cost of living. After a few years of sitting idle, many of these boats begin to require maintenance that becomes difficult or unaffordable, or the owners eventually decide to go back home, wherever that is. They just don't feel up to the task of taking their boats back with them. It is a long way upwind and against the currents to sail back to California or the Pacific Northwest from Panama, and departing the Caribbean coast of Panama going east can be a major undertaking too—straight into the teeth of the Caribbean trade winds, which in the area north of Colombia can often blow 25-35 knots for weeks at a time. So for one of many reasons, these boats come on the market and often sell for bargain prices.

Each year services and facilities for yachts in the Panama area improve and it *is* possible to leave going east without having your backsides handed to you as long as you are patient and willing to move on a weather window rather than on a personal schedule. Getting from Panama to Cartagena, Colombia can be relatively easy, and if you wait for a lull in the trade winds, going north from there to Jamaica, the Windward Passage, the Bahamas, or east via the South coast of Hispaniola is possible in moderate conditions. Every year boats do make the passage from Panama to the Yucatan Channel as well. From there, getting back to Europe or the States is straightforward.

Heading north on the Pacific coast out of Panama is also not too difficult as long as you take your time and work the weather. But then again, once you get your bargain boat all sorted out, why leave to go back 'home'? There's a great big ocean just to the west. French Polynesia may not be an inexpensive cruising area, but when you continue to the west... the Cook Islands, Tonga, and Fiji are all quite affordable areas to cruise and Fiji can be darn right cheap to spend time in. With over three hundred islands, Fiji is a spectacular cruising area. The upshot of all of this is that if you find a boat in one of these areas like Guatemala, Trinidad, or Panama, maybe think in terms of getting the boat fixed up and just starting your cruising lifestyle from right there. But who knows, you may just like it there so much that you never leave!

Tonga, Fiji, and the lesser Pacific Islands

Each year work obligations or family responsibilities cause people to elect to leave their boats at one of the anchorages, marinas, or boatyards in Fiji or Tonga. Sometimes yachts come up for sale in such unlikely places as the Marshall Islands, the Cook Islands, or even Kiribati! If you decide to pursue one of these boats in the far-flung Pacific, be sure that the owner or broker is willing to provide hundreds of up-to-date photos and an accurate assessment of its current condition. Flying halfway around the world to a remote island to view a boat that five minutes into your inspection turns out to have insurmountable issues would be an unfortunate waste of time and money. But bargains can be found! I sold one of my own boats, a Flying Dutchman 50, while it was based in Fiji. It was in great shape and I sold it for well under market value because of its location and my need to get back to work in the Caribbean. Good friends of ours sold their immaculately maintained Camper Nicholson 32 there for a bargain price simply because they needed to move on to other things. Keeping your eyes open for a terrific buy on a boat in the Pacific islands may be a way to start your cruising in an area that many people spend years trying to get into a position to sail to, or never even reach! The Pacific islands are, to me, the ultimate cruising area. Keep in mind though that with thousands of islands and over 62 million square miles of sea separating them, services and supplies in the remote islands of the Pacific can be difficult to obtain. Friends of mine developed a problem with the fuel injection pump on their boat while anchored in Suwarrow, a remote uninhabited atoll in the western Cook Islands that required a qualified mechanic. They had to sail their crippled boat 450 miles to American Samoa to effect a repair. If the vessel had required a haul-out, the closest facility would have been another 400 miles away!

Fiji has a decent but small infrastructure for yachting and the main island of Viti Levu has good services. Tonga also has a small yachting infrastructure thanks to the charter fleets in the Vava'u group, but in the Cooks, Samoa, or Kiribati, even accomplishing a haul-out to check the bottom or change a through-hull may be impossible. So if you are pursuing a boat in one of these outlying island groups, the boat had better be a real bargain or the risk and hassles are just not worth it.

And don't forget French Polynesia. There are a few good haul-out facilities there and usually several boats to look at too, so an open-ended ticket to fly to Tahiti, Raiatea, Viti Levu, Fiji, and V'Vau, Tonga might just turn up your dream vessel, already at anchor in a fantastic cruising area.

New Zealand

New Zealand is a sailor's paradise. Hundreds of bays and thousands of miles of deeply indented coastline offer some of the best cruising in the world. It has been said that almost every Kiwi is a sailor or has a good friend who has a sailboat. While this may be true, the majority of boats in New Zealand are smaller coastal cruisers. However, every year hundreds of cruising boats from all over the world arrive, and often quite a few of these come on the market. Usually, the larger brokerage houses will list the more expensive ones, but many of the smaller or lower-priced boats change hands via many of the Internet sites for owners selling their boats themselves. Even just flying down and bumming along the waterfront on North Island will likely turn up some good deals. From New Zealand, you are only a little over a week's sailing away from some of the best cruising areas of the South Pacific with Tonga, Fiji, and Vanuatu just to the north. Services and supplies for yachts are plentiful and the cost of living is reasonable.

Australia

Lots and lots of boats are for sale in Australia. For two decades, as Australians became more affluent, there was a shortage of newer, modern sailboats. Through the early 2000s, you could buy a cruising boat in the Med, or a Caribbean ex-charter yacht, sail it to Australia and make enough of a profit upon selling it to pay for your whole year away sailing. But times have changed. After the influx of thousands of boats, there is now a glut of some models on the market and with a slowing of the Australian economy, prices have fallen dramatically so even despite the high taxes and VAT, occasional great bargains appear on the market—especially with not so well-known brands and so cruising through the listings on Tradeaboat.com.au or YachtHub.com may turn up just the boat you've been looking for.

Thailand, Malaysia, and Indonesia

For decades Thailand and Malaysia, and to a lesser extent Indonesia, have attracted sailors who become enamored with the well-developed culture, outstanding food, and unbelievably low cost of living. Boatyards have cropped up in the more popular areas and now thousands of boats spend time in some of these more popular harbors. Langkawi and Phuket often have many bargain boats available and this is an area where simply showing up and living cheaply on land while you search for that great deal you've been hoping for would not cost you a fortune. Like Panama and Trinidad, these places are the end of the line for many boaters' dreams and so if you are looking for a well-equipped project boat with abundant cheap help available, Malaysia, Thailand, Indonesia or even Singapore could be your ticket.

Turkey and Greece (and Croatia)

Western Turkey on the Aegean Sea and the Adriatic Sea Greek Islands offer many places to store boats and lots of Europeans maintain a yacht in these waters as their 'summer home'. Americans generally can't stay in the EU for more than 90 days, so you'll find many ex-pat boats being stored over on the mainland of Turkey. Don't listen to the news about the dangers of traveling in Turkey. The coastal areas are heavily reliant upon tourism and are very safe. The boatyards are huge and many good buys can be found here. European brokers are notoriously terrible about supplying accurate photos, so be careful about this before you spend a bunch of money flying to look at one boat, but if you can line up several to look at, your chances of success improve.

As a side note if you end up wanting a late model ex charter yacht, then the lowest prices in the world are typically found in Croatia. This is because Croatian charter fleets get a lot of use and often will run a yacht with very poor maintenance well past the time when it should have been retired. So in general, the poorest maintained ex charter boats are found there! But this is not always the case. Good buys can indeed be found and so planning a trip to the Adriatic may be worth the effort.

While it's true that the odds of finding a bargain boat are best in the highlighted areas described above, bargains can be found anywhere with diligent searching and many hours spent researching the market, maybe even in your own backyard! A couple of perfect examples of this are when after I had lost my sailboat in Hurricane Irma, I searched all over the world and even flew to New Zealand searching for something that met my needs. I ultimately found it twelve miles away in a boatyard on Virgin Gorda. Several years before, after I had sold my boat in Fiji, I'd flown halfway around the world to Europe and then all over the mainland of the US searching for a suitable vessel, but ultimately found a good buy just 200 miles from home in Antigua.

Chapter Five

The Role of a Broker, and a Surveyor, and For Sale By Owner (FSBO) Boats

In my early yachting career, like many people, I erroneously thought for quite some time that the best buys for a used boat could only be had by buying directly from the owner. After buying and selling many boats and eventually ending up in the brokerage end of the business, I realized that this is not accurate. In many cases as a buyer, I got a better value by purchasing through a broker, and here's why:

Many owners overvalue their boats. A good broker will educate a seller as to the realities of the marketplace by demonstrating comparable recent sales information. If he or she is an established and knowledgeable professional, they will usually refuse to accept an overvalued listing because trying to market an overpriced boat is a frustrating and usually fruitless effort. This means that in most cases the boats they represent are likely to be a good value for a buyer.

When it comes time to make an offer, it is much easier for a buyer to place a low (but realistic) bid through a knowledgeable broker. As long as the reasoning for the viability of the offer is made clear and is accurate and you can demonstrate your logic to the broker, in most cases, he or she will work hard to convince the seller of the viability of the offer. And then when a survey is undertaken, if additional problems arise, a good broker will help negotiate a satisfactory resolution and will also assist a new buyer with the logistics for registration and insurance and point them in the right direction for reasonable storage, repairs, or haul-out facilities and in

many cases can pass on industry discounts for equipment and upgrades.

That all having been said, sometimes it seems that there are only a handful of really good brokers out there! Word of mouth and making a lot of calls or sending lots of email inquiries will likely lead you to a good one. In general, a broker who takes the time to answer all your questions and goes to great lengths to get the information you need is probably the one to work with. Most brokers work within a multiple listing system similar to real estate brokers and so if you find a broker who has liveaboard or offshore experience and who is willing to put the time and effort into answering all your questions, suggests viable options, and goes to great lengths to assist your quest, remember that they can also show you boats listed with other brokers and act on your behalf as a 'buyer's broker' to reach a successful conclusion to your quest.

I've heard the argument that brokers will try to drive a price up on a boat and in some cases, this may be true. You don't want to work with those people and in the long term, this way of doing business is shortsighted. If a buyer overpays for a boat and then comes back in a year or two to resell, only to find out that they overpaid, that broker has an unhappy client. Word gets around and those types often do not survive in the business for long! However, if a good broker has helped you to reach a fair 'eyes wide open' value on a boat and if you've done a good job maintaining it, reselling will almost assuredly be easier with a broker who already knows the vessel and its history.

FSBOs or 'for sale by owner' boats can also be good values if the seller is realistic and easy to work with. In many cases, if you can have a meeting of the minds and go over the boat carefully and respectfully address the issues you find that need attending to, a seller will see the logic of a realistic offer and work with you. One obvious thing to mention here that unfortunately seems to be overlooked more often in recent times is that one should never be insulting or disrespectful and always try to be positive and forthright in your observations and statements. But of course, this will only work if the seller is being honest and forthright themselves! If a seller is trying hard to 'sell' you on the boat, pointing out only the good points and glossing over or denying the obvious faults then be wary! But in an ideal situation, a reasonable seller will be easy to work with, and provided you are also being realistic and reasonable, a good value may be arrived at. But what about writing a contract or making a deposit?

Many people feel wary of leaving a large deposit on a boat with a private party and so the solution here is to hire one of the many title/documentation agencies. Almost all of these types of companies offer escrow services to take care of holding deposits and disbursing funds at closing. A documentation/title agency can be easily located on the web and in addition to holding the deposit and handling the final closing transaction, they can also ensure there are no outstanding liens on the boat or encumbrances that may prevent a clean transfer of ownership. This is particularly important if you are dealing with a vessel registered in a different country or if it is an estate or divorce sale. Hiring a documentation and title agency may cost a few hundred dollars, but this is often money well spent and may give the seller greater confidence as the sales process unfolds as well.

The Role of the Surveyor

A marine surveyor is a professional who is in virtually all cases hired by the buyer and whose job it is to examine the potential purchase on behalf of the buyer to assist them in reaching an informed decision as to whether to proceed with the sale or not and in many cases can provide an educational experience to the buyer as he or she goes through the vessel. If it is possible for you to be present during the survey, a good surveyor will welcome his client following them during this process and many important details will surely become evident during the inspection.

In short, the surveyor's job is:

1) **To provide an expert set of observations without undue alarm, coloring, or opinions based on personal bias.**

   For example, if you end up with a surveyor who is so opinionated that he or she appears to have an 'attitude' regarding a particular design or based simply upon the initial appearance of a vessel as they approach it on the dock or onshore, you may have hired the wrong person. I've met surveyors who seem to carry a chip on their shoulders and feel the need to be overly pessimistic and alarmist, often finding 'faults' even where none exist simply to make their opinions appear more valuable. One fellow in particular who used to work in the mid-Atlantic would write either a good report or a bad report mainly based upon the mood he was in on that particular day! And I know of a female surveyor who nearly prevented a knowledgeable buyer from owning a boat he had been trying to find for years by writing a heavily colored report that made it impossible for him to obtain the financing he needed to complete the purchase. And this was a very nice boat! Although the boat had virtually no appreciable findings and was in rare, ready to go condition, she undervalued it by tens of thousands of dollars and ignored the market comparables and recent sales data in favor of her 'gut feelings' which were, in fact, ultimately wrong. The buyer was an attorney and had to threaten legal proceedings before she agreed to review her data and reissue a correct valuation based upon the realities of the market and comparable sales.

However, one should also be cautious of a surveyor who is overly effusive with the attributes of a particular vessel. While in some cases this may be genuine, there is always the chance that the surveyor may be being overly kind about the vessel because he or she is either a friend or acquaintance of the seller or broker or simply because they are nostalgic or overly favorable to a particular design or model of boat. The latter is not necessarily a bad thing, however, as long as it is accompanied by a clear and concise evaluation of the state of that particular vessel.

We've all heard the urban legend stories about marine surveyors who were 'in the pocket' of a broker and should therefore not be trusted. In my many years working as either a broker or as a surveyor (at different times!), I have found that this is almost always untrue. Sure, the surveyors may know the brokers fairly well; the waterfront community is pretty small. But if you've picked your broker with care, you might well find that he or she will be following the surveyor around to make sure they don't miss things and even points out concerns or issues they or you, the buyer, may have noticed on the initial inspections. Hopefully, you've chosen a surveyor who is not offended by this and takes the time to inspect any of these additional areas of concern on your behalf. However, in-the-pocket surveyors do exist, and in fact, I accidentally hired just such a fellow a few years back. I was interested in a vessel in New Zealand and reached a contract with the seller through his broker. But before I flew down to survey the boat myself, I hired a local surveyor to look it over—mainly to save myself the time and expense of flying halfway around the world in case it turned out to be less than what was presented by the broker and from the photos the broker had supplied. The local broker recommended a surveyor and I hired him to look it over. The report looked great, although it was missing some key items to my way of thinking. When I reached the surveyor by phone he assured me it was a fantastic vessel and even went so far as to say that if he were looking for such a vessel that he would probably buy it himself! That's quite a recommendation and although he wasn't a member of an association I subscribe to, I thought it safe to buy the tickets and fly down to see it myself. Eight thousand miles of flights later it took me less than a half-hour to see that the surveyor had glossed over the biggest defects and missed others altogether and that the boat was going to need a major refit before it could be put into use. The flights were a waste of time and money and so instead I made use of the time I had allotted for buying a boat and preparing it to sail north to Fiji by renting a car and touring the north and south islands. Was there a lesson learned there? If the survey you get looks too good to be true, double-check the surveyor's references. Upon more research I learned that this fellow got the majority of his work from local brokers and was indirectly in their pocket, I'm sure!

2) **To explain findings to a buyer (and/or owner) in a manner that is objective, clear, and concise.**

A good marine survey will outline key systems and structures in such a way that a quick scan of the document should present a clear picture of the vessel's suitability and condition. Always ask for a sample report from the surveyor you are about to hire. Beware of 'essay' type reports that may often be mostly 'boilerplate' full of excessive disclaimers and little substance. Once while working as a buyer's broker, I was trying to help my buyer with a boat he found in Honolulu. He hired a local surveyor and the ensuing report issued was quite long with lots of photos and basically said... nothing! No substantive information other than what was already known from the listing information supplied by the broker was in the report and it made us wonder if the fellow had even visited the vessel! At the same time, the majority of reports I've read by reputable marine surveyors do present detailed descriptions of the vessel and their findings. Look for references to specific requirements such as USCG or federal requirements and also references to 'voluntary compliance' organizations citing standards as issued by organizations such as the ABS, ABYC, EU, and Lloyds. These are often of note only and don't necessarily become causes of concern unless they are so excessive or expensive to put right that the decision to proceed with a purchase must be reassessed. A clear and concise survey report will however give you a good 'punch list' to work with as you prepare your 'new-to-you' vessel for your intended use.

3) To not make 'blanket statements' or generalizations

A good surveyor won't make generalized comments or broad-brush statements. For example, to say that "All of these boats have mast step problems" or "The decks on these are always bad" when in fact the vessel he or she is about to survey may have had the decks replaced and the mast step rebuilt. At the same time, a good surveyor will be aware of potential issues to look at and can save you a lot of time and trouble finding out things that may be commonly known in the marine industry. For example, if a boat has internal ballast with separations in the keel, a good surveyor will likely recommend opening those areas up to make sure no water has intruded and will make you aware of the potential issues that can come about from delaminations in cored structures or deficiencies in a vessel's wiring or tankage. Another example: older Hallberg-Rassys and Oysters, both very pricey brands, used untinned wiring and non-marine grade terminal blocks which corroded and caused resistance in older models, and being aware of a potential major cost of putting new tanks or replacing built-in chainplates on a boat that has these items could help you to negotiate a reduction in price for the eventual repair of these design or build faults if it was not already known and discussed as part of your original offer. Any huge expenses on the horizon should be pointed out in your report and a good surveyor should make you aware that these challenges may be coming about during your ownership. In short, a surveyor's job is not to scare you away from owning a boat but rather to make sure you are entering into the process with 'Eyes wide open'.

4) To lay out in a written report a set of findings that are prioritized, with accurate descriptions of specific faults or observations.

Having a good handle on what's needed to make your new-to-you boat ready for cruising is important and a good survey report will prioritize things in regards to safety or necessary importance for proper operation and also give you a good idea of what's needed for your ongoing ownership, pointing out things that should be watched or addressed promptly or as they become evident later on. For example: if your vessel needs two through-hulls replaced and the heat exchanger serviced to prevent overheating, those are safety items and should be addressed immediately. But if it's noted that you need to monitor the condition of the water tanks or to periodically red-bed deck hardware to prevent water intrusion into the deck core, these are things you would do on almost any vessel and are just good to know, but not necessarily of utmost importance to begin using your "new to you" vessel. Your survey report should provide a 'punch list' of prioritized items of maintenance needed to keep your boat in tip-top shape

5) **To be available and ready to answer questions or clarify points either via email or phone with the client or associated parties (IE broker, contractor, or even the seller).**

Questions will come up and your surveyor should make him or herself available to answer those for you. Remember that these people are busy professionals and so getting a list together before a call or sending a detailed and concise email may be the best way to get the answers you need without wasting time or causing repeated interruptions. Still, you have a right as a client to have your questions answered and if something isn't clear in the report, call or email your surveyor and get that addressed right away. Make sure in advance that this will not be charged for and if you feel something was missed or glossed over or that a second follow-up is required, most surveyors will have no problem with this request.

6) **To promptly present a written report that accurately reflects the condition of the vessel, her systems, and some of her positive aspects along with the issues that need attending to.**

A survey report shouldn't just be all about defects and potential problems but should paint a balanced picture of the vessel without any 'coloring' or bias. When you read your potential surveyor's

sample report, be sure that he or she isn't painting an ugly picture and only focusing on defects and shortcomings. Some surveyors believe that unless they find lots of problems or potential defects that they aren't doing a good job and this is just not true. A good survey report will present a true representation, showing both the good as well as the not so good issues that are found and keep in mind that this report will also likely be used to secure insurance and possibly marine financing, so while a report that only addresses problems and makes the boat appear to be a floating wreck may help you to renegotiate the price with the seller to address the findings, it may also almost assuredly make the vessel uninsurable and unsuitable for any marine financing as well! Resist the temptation to seek out a surveyor known as being 'the toughest' or 'the deal-breaker' because although these people may think they are doing their clients a favor by writing gloomy, depressing sounding reports full of multitudes of horrific findings, the reality is that in many cases these types of surveyors miss important big issues while ranting about what may be smaller problems and in general come across as 'know it all' individuals who love to pontificate and are often short on real experience in the industry. They will kill your deal for you and maybe hope you will rehire them for another survey because they were 'tough.' I've heard of people going through three or four surveys on boats with the same surveyor only to find each one falling miserably short of their surveyor's standards. Many of these vessels may only have minor issues and so someone else ultimately gets to own them while the prospective buyer who has been intimidated so badly by so many bad reports may just give up on the whole idea and not go on to own a boat at all.

Summing things up: a good survey report should be an accurate 'snapshot in time' of a vessel showing her just as she is, including her good points as well as her blemishes and defects, and provide a (hopefully) shortlist of deficiencies that need to be addressed before putting the vessel into service

7) **To never assume that a buyer, owner, or broker has access to technical details or knowledge of the specifics of any technical issue or has a background that allows them to fully understand the significance or insignificance of a specific finding, or to assume that what is common knowledge within the industry is known or understood by a client or associated parties.**

In short, a good surveyor will explain things in layman's terms and be patient and mindful of making sure that their client understands the findings as they are described. They will be available to answer questions and may even be able to explain how best to tackle necessary repairs or to find help for repairing or servicing issues that need attending to that are beyond the abilities of the buyer to undertake. As an industry professional who is hired to look out for your best interests, your surveyor should also be your go-to source for advice and recommendation as you undertake any of the large projects you may be signing up for on your new-to-you boat. Many surveyors will encourage you to keep them on retainer for consultations and may offer a discounted fee for issuing a follow-up report, if or when needed.

Making an Offer

Over the years I've often heard opinions that there is always some automatic or assumed immediate discount from an asking price such as "offer 10% less" or worse the yacht club bar 'experts' who will tell you, "No matter what they're asking, offer half!" The reality is that no such simple formulas exist.

The best way to ascertain the value of a boat is to have a surveyor assist you or to ask a reputable broker to present why he or she thinks a particular boat is well priced. If you have taken the above considerations into account on the ultimate costs of a boat versus the buying price, then you can look at what other sisterships of a type may be asking and a good broker should be able to show you sales data of what other similar vessels have sold for. Then look at how these other vessels were equipped and, if possible, carefully scrutinize any photos or write-ups to ascertain the condition of the boat and equipment they have and compare them to the vessel you are looking at buying. Run the numbers to see what it takes to make the comparable vessels equal to your prospective purchase so that you can calculate what might be an appropriate offer.

If you are working with a seller directly, oftentimes you may need to agree on a number that works for you both and then get the survey done, and after the survey is complete, go over any new findings with the seller to discuss the costs you are likely to encounter to make it suitable for your intended use. In many cases, as long as you aren't trying to exaggerate the numbers or make up unnecessary repairs, a seller will have no choice but to concur with you and to agree on a realistic value for his or her boat. Do what I try to do when dealing with a seller who is reluctant to 'own up' to the realities of what his or her boat may be worth; just ask them to forget that they are the seller and instead to just pretend they are a prospective buyer and looking to buy this boat. Have them add up all the items needed to set it right and ask them what they feel a good value is. This is almost always a surefire way to come to a meeting of the minds

The rules I always abide by when making an offer on a boat are:

1) Be polite and honest.

Remember that for most people a boat is a very personal thing. Boats often represent an effort to fulfill emotional needs and so often hold fond memories and were the promise or realization of their owners' dreams. If a boat is in poor condition or shows neglect, a seller may be somewhat ashamed of that and so when pointing out things it needs or obvious flaws, be sure to do it in a way that doesn't make them feel defensive. Stuff happens in people's lives and in many cases, by the time a boat comes on the market, the seller knows very well that he or she has been remiss in dealing with the boat's needs and issues. Rubbing their faces in that could antagonize them. And in some cases, the boat you may be looking at is in terrific shape and might not need much at all, so complimenting them on their upkeep, explaining that you acknowledge what it took to do that while also expressing concerns about what it's going to take for you to get things the way you want them in order to be able to use the boat as you wish may help to convince a seller to accept your offer.

2) Do your research and show what you have learned so that your offer has a justification.

If you are making an offer substantially below what is being asked, be ready to explain why and show, documented on paper or Internet links, data to justify your offer. Even if your explanation is only that to accomplish what you are hoping to do with the boat means you have to offer perhaps a little less than she might be worth to a wealthier person. If the seller (or broker) likes you and if you can get them to see things from your perspective, you have a chance of coming to a meeting of the minds.

3) Place yourself in the seller's shoes so that you can see things from their perspective.

Remembering that the likely reason why the owner had the boat in the first place is that they had huge aspirations for adventures or just plain good times with family and friends. Recognize that unlike a car or an airplane, and even more so than a house, a boat often carries with it a certain mystique and perhaps an illusion of freedom, adventure, and promise that are always an undercurrent when a seller is considering an offer. In some cases, a seller has financial obligations that must be met that are precipitating the sale, or they may simply be changing 'tacks' in life and deciding to do something else with their time or money. The funds they will receive from the sale may play a big part in whether they can meet those obligations or realize their next goal. But if you feel the boat is overpriced and can justify it to the seller, use the example of the stock market. When the market falls, no matter what you might have bought that stock for, it is only worth what the market will bear. And boats are not typically appreciating assets.

4) Be upbeat and hopeful.

Along with being polite and mindful of a seller's feelings and commitments, a buyer's attitude plays a far larger part in how a negotiation comes to fruition than many people realize. If you are hopeful and optimistic and keep reinforcing your dreams and aspirations for the boat, talking about all the things you will be doing to fix up the boat, or augment its equipment or systems may help even a hardened seller to soften to your cause. Enthusiasm and an upbeat attitude go a long way in almost any business negotiation!

Chapter Six

What is Most Important to Look for When Shopping for a Cruising or Liveaboard Boat

What Can I Afford to Own, to Live on, and Sail Long-term?

As you begin your search for the perfect vessel with which to embark on this life-changing experience, one of the first things you'll likely do is look online at all of the For Sale websites offering what appear to be beautiful vessels that could take you across oceans to the destinations of your dreams.

The reality is that there has virtually never been a vessel built that doesn't have at least some problems to solve. This is just how boats are. Even if an owner thinks his or her boat is perfect, I can promise you that I, as a marine surveyor, could go aboard and find present or future potential problems that were previously unknown to them. But does this mean we shouldn't go sailing? Of course not! What you must always keep in mind though is that you should only proceed with the purchase of a boat when you have made a thorough assessment of all of the things you can find that it will require to get it to the condition level needed to ensure that it is safe and seaworthy for your intended use.

Secondly, but just as important, is that you can see the clear and straight road to not only repairing or refitting the vessel in a satisfactory manner but to be able to do that within the budget and time frame you have to work with.

You will notice while going through my list of recommended boats at the end of this book that there are certain brands I have omitted and also that by no means is my list limited to the *only* boats suitable for long-distance sailing or long-term liveaboard cruising! You will also see a few boats on my list of great boats that may have potential complex repair issues that may or may not have been addressed during their ownership and so here is a list of some of the bigger things to watch out for on any older vessel, regardless of the brand or age, that should be carefully assessed before making the dive into boat ownership.

Things to Watch Out for When Used Boat Shopping

It's appalling to me to see these days so many 'new to the lifestyle' cruisers out there looking at buying 45-55' sailboats that are thirty or more years old and expecting to safely sail away forever on a shoestring budget. It is folly to expect everything to go perfectly well all the time, so if sacrificing a bit of 'elbow room' to instead own a boat that won't break the cruising budget to maintain and thereby allows you to have the freedom to stay out sailing long term, then why in the heck wouldn't you do that? I mean, if 'space' is that important to you, why not just stay in a house?

It's really easy to fall into a trap of looking at boats that are too big or will require too much money to get them truly ready. Many of the ads may say 'ready to cruise' or 'turnkey', but in my experience, very seldom do you run across a cruising yacht which is truly in this condition. Everyone's idea of 'ready to go' is different too. For some people, a one-burner stove, a bucket to pee in, and an Igloo cooler are plenty with which to take off and sail the world, while others will require air conditioning, watermakers, bow thrusters, and electric winches! And the irony is that the amount of fun you can have cruising on your 'dream boat' has very little to do with how big it is or how it's equipped. The people on the minimalist cruising yacht may be in the same state of bliss as the older couple on the tricked-out 50' yacht with all the gadgets. The key to happiness on a cruising yacht is having a boat you can afford to maintain so there are no worries about dealing with the maintenance and running costs while you are out there sailing the world.

Since what's required for comfort and happiness afloat is such a hard thing to pin down, let's assume some basics: First of all, if you are out there sailing on savings and running the boat as cheaply as possible until the next bit of money comes in, then to allow for as much freedom as possible, it's important to spend as little as you can on running costs. This is obvious but sometimes forgotten. If you have a big boat with too many systems, or with older equipment that is always breaking down and needing repairs, then your time away from ports or an income stream for repairs will be shortened considerably versus how things might have been if you had a smaller, simpler, easy to maintain boat with all the gear in top-notch condition.

For an older couple with some retirement savings, the perfect boat for them might be fairly comfy and have more systems that may periodically need to be replaced, but provided this is within their budget, who cares? The most important thing to look at while choosing your boat to take off and sail the world is simply to carefully calculate how long you expect to be out away from an income stream, or what your income is, and how much you'll have to work with each month or quarter to visit the places you want to go, take care of your personal needs and to keep the boat you are considering in top-notch, ocean-worthy condition.

Because to me, it is obvious that the real reason so many aspiring long-term cruisers never make it past the second or third year is that they failed to assess the longer-term maintenance costs of the boat on which they have decided to go sailing.

Please at this point indulge me to let you in on a little secret. As a general rule, boats are very expensive to keep in top condition! And the real reason why most cruises come to an end is that the boats start requiring so much work and investment that the owners can no longer afford to keep them in a safe or reliable enough condition to take them offshore. You will see this evidence all over the world where a boat has come in from its last long passage and the owners KNOW it needs several expensive things done if they were going to continue, but instead of paying for these things, they decided to just cruise locally. Eventually, the boat gets to the point where it really can't even be taken sailing at all. It then lives at anchor or in a slip and only sails near shore in light conditions and even then, eventually, some critical system goes down that is prohibitively expensive to rectify, and that's the end of the lifestyle. The boat is sold for what appears at first glance online to be a bargain price with tons of cruising gear. But the reality is that most of the equipment is obsolete or in need of replacement and the crews retire to an RV or lodgings onshore. The way to avoid this trap is to own a boat you can afford to maintain. This aspect is far more important than having a boat you can afford to buy, but which will bleed your finances down until it is no longer possible to go sailing on it.

There is good news though. A little later we'll talk about how to keep a boat in top condition WITHOUT spending a fortune at the marine stores or boatyards.

Why are People Often Impressed by Larger Boats?

Sitting in the window seat of the Boeing 737 as we banked out over the blue waters of the Pacific, I was bound for North America and a return to the USA to visit my aging parents in Arizona. As the island of Oahu receded into the distance, I settled back in my seat to read when the woman sitting next to me, noticing the sailing magazine I had opened said, "Oh, are you a sailor?"

I told her that yes, I owned a sailboat and had been cruising in some of the remote areas of the Pacific and had just left my boat in Fiji so that I could return to the States to visit family. She asked me, "How big is your boat?" When I answered, 50 feet she said, "Oh wow, nice boat!"

This is such a typical response from land people who like to ask, "How big is your boat?" as a first question as if the size of the boat somehow tells a story of who the sailor is, or about how interesting or impressive their story might be.

Many sailors also have this flawed idea that bigger is better and that when they see a really big boat that this is somehow interesting and special. Do we as sailors all have size envy and do most sailors lust after larger boats?

As a person who has spent a large portion of my life sailing, and who has worked in the yachting industry for decades as either a broker or a surveyor, I can tell you that in almost all cases, when a person is selling their boat, they are doing so to 'move up' to something larger.

Moreover, in almost all cases when a really large sailing yacht arrives from far away, it becomes a topic of conversation among the smaller cruising yachts' crews. "Wow! Look at that yacht! She's quite impressive! They must have a crew of fifteen!"

My question is this: Why is that impressive? What about that single-hander on the 28' cutter that just arrived from Micronesia after seventy-two days hard on the wind? And what about that 38' steel cutter with the middle-aged couple aboard. They just got back from cruising the Aleutians, and later spent three months at sea sailing down to the Chilean Fjords nonstop so they could accurately judge the differences between the two high-latitude cruising areas. What about them? Are they not more impressive sailors than the crew of the bigger boat? Chances are the CEO who owns the mega sailing yacht doesn't have half the seamanship skills that the smaller yachts' captains have and the 'professional' crew of good-looking twenty- or thirty-something know-it-alls think they are the coolest boat in the anchorage and are virtually unapproachable in the same way that the roadies and entourage of famous rock bands stay aloof from mere fans.

I guess that after so many years of sailing and working within the industry, I have developed a different attitude toward the fancy big mega yachts. I say "Who freaking cares about the big boat, the snooty crew, or the super-rich people who own these gigantic abominations?" They are often just wannabe sailors who are spoiled, and in many cases lack the courage and the skills to sail far on a smaller boat and so need the security of a professional crew and a large boat to feel safe.

Okay, so maybe that's a bit harsh, and certainly, some of the large yachts are very special and require very skilled sailors to operate them, but for the average person to lust after a large boat like this is, I think, misguided. In fact, in most cases, a smaller boat is eminently safer, more flexible, and practical. Looking back at history, the reason why big ships were necessary for exploration was that there were virtually no supply ports in the remote unexplored regions of the world and so everything a crew would need had to be brought along. And a large crew was needed because casualties were not uncommon at sea in those days and the sail handling and anchor work was all done without modern winches or furling systems or hydraulic or electric windlasses. However, even on Captain Cook's famous explorations on the relatively small *Endeavour* and *Resolute*, he often employed the much smaller ship's yawl boats for the actual coastal piloting and charting. Because these vessels were handier and more agile, they made superior vessels for exploring the little inlets, bays, and islands while the large mother ship was only able to safely sail by from a distance.

Smaller boats are much better for coastal sailing, and now that the modern world has made it possible to get things like rigs, engines, sails, and electronics in almost any part of the world, the need to carry these things along with you is diminished. In the old days carrying extra spars to make new masts and booms and hundreds of yards of sailcloth was considered prudent, but when is the last time you saw a cruising yacht that carried such spares?

Another reason why people choose a big boat is that they say they want more space. What is this space for? If it is to accommodate additional crew, then certainly, an extra cabin or two makes a lot of sense, but if it is just to have a bigger living area, one has to ask: Why? I have found in all my years of cruising that to be truly happy and comfortable on a long cruise you need a good place to sit in the cockpit out of the weather, a nice place to read a book down below, maybe a place to watch a movie on a flat-screen, and a workable galley that is big enough for two cooks, but not so large that you have to move around a lot while preparing a meal, plus of course a

comfortable bed for in port and a secure berth for when you are at sea. Beyond that... what is all the other space for?

Of course, storage space. I have heard it said that one can never have too much storage on a yacht. While a few cruising yacht designers allow for this, an all too common design flaw in newer boats built for 'cruising' is a virtual lack of large volume storage lockers. You see this all the time in evidence when these light displacement boats are weighed down with all the necessary stuff it takes to go long-distance sailing and often the side decks and cabin tops are jammed with jerry jugs, spare sails, life rafts, folding bikes, kayaks, and surfboards. So often today you see boats being built that appear to have been designed by boardrooms full of non-sailors; they have huge wide-open spaces below, virtually zero storage, and lack adequate sea berths in favor of round dinettes, curved settees, and swivel chairs! These boats are built to feel 'light and airy' to sell at boat shows to people who have never really been long-distance cruising.

I was recently looking at boats with a couple who wanted a more modern design but wanted enough storage space to bring all the things they felt they needed for their family of three children and to get this in a modern design, we were looking at 54' sailboats! Thinking back to my many years of sailing with kids onboard, we did it with five people; three kids and two adults in only 39' on deck and in a hundred-year-old design aft cockpit double ender at that! We carried everything we needed and only had our dinghy and life raft out on the deck. But of course, the boat weighed in at nearly 30,000 lbs which is what a typical 50' boat weighs these days.... Back in the 90s, we did a lot of long-distance sailing with two kids onboard in a boat that was only 32' long. But again, she weighed 20,000 lbs, had 47 storage lockers, and she was not 'light and airy' below. But she did have great sea berths, a couple of super reading spots, and a comfortable bed when in port. And the kids could watch movies at sea without me worrying about them being thrown across a wide cabin by an errant breaking wave!

Smaller boats are also easier to handle. Sure, it is possible to sail a big boat shorthanded with the right sailing gear and electric or hydraulic assistance but think about what happens when something goes wrong. Case in point: we were sailing a 53' single headsail ketch along the south coast of Martinique a few years back, beating into 30 knots of wind, and the headsail lashing parted, sending the heavy working jib tumbling down to the deck and much of it over the side into the sea. It took my 110-pound sailing partner and me all the strength we had to drag that wet sail back to the cockpit and stow it. Resetting another huge sail would have been exceptionally difficult in those short and confused head seas, so we motored the last few miles into port with just a reefed mainsail. On a smaller boat, this would have been a relatively simple job to reset a sail. On our old steel brigantine, the hydraulic windlass quit working at one point so it was left to just the three of us to bring the 110-pound anchor and half-inch chain in by hand with a lever, link by link. If it had been a 40' boat, we could have just pulled it in with our bare hands.

Sure, a bigger boat is, in theory, faster. That's the argument I've always used when trying to talk myself into buying a bigger boat, but the reality is: all sailboats are darn slow! If you want to get somewhere fast, take a plane. It's also true that most prudent sailors slow down at night anyway to lessen the chance of sustaining significant damage if an object is struck. And most smaller boats move out better in lighter winds than bigger sisterships, so a much bigger boat is only faster under ideal conditions. In reality? The difference between a 55' boat and a 40' boat on a long passage might only be a day or two. And the 35' boat might be another day behind. A few years ago in the mid-Pacific, I met a family cruising on a steel 36' cutter that had just come in from a 2,400-mile passage from the Marshall Islands and I asked them what kind of speed they made on passages. The captain said, "We try to go slow. We like it better when the boat isn't heeled over so much and it's easier on the kids too. And we sleep better when we are going slower. We like it out there, so what's the rush? It's out at sea where the really special things happen. Plus in ports, you only spend money." Well said.

And that brings up cost. Of course, in general, smaller boats are less expensive to buy than big boats, and it is inarguable that smaller boats cost less to operate.

Many marinas and boatyards have a sliding scale of haul-out and storage fees. Dockage rates for boats under 50' are almost always quite a bit less and under 40' there is often another price break. Years ago I owned a 52' Farrington schooner and we decided it might be fun to splurge for one night and check into a marina in the British Virgin Islands. Upon tying up we learned that the charge for nightly dockage was $1.50 per ft per night, up to 50'. Above 50' it jumped to $3.00 per ft. Ouch! We took on water and went back out to the anchorage for the night. Of course, most cruisers don't go into marinas very often, but haul-outs and bottom painting, yard storage, and all the rest of the things like sails, engines, rigging, and systems are, generally speaking, much more expensive on bigger boats.

We met a cruising couple a few years back on a heavy ketch-rigged 52' fiberglass yacht who were trying to live on a limited retirement budget. They had bought the largest boat they felt they could afford but had failed to consider the 'big ticket' items that were on the horizon for them if they were to continue cruising. We saw them again a couple of years later in the southern Caribbean and they were broke. There had been some 'unexpected' expenses and the boat had eaten through the rest of their cash reserves and despite this, the boat still needed more money spent on it to bring it back to seaworthy condition. They were living like hermits in a bay and couldn't even afford to go out to a beach bar to meet up with friends or take a bus into town to buy groceries. They said they were going to have to sell the boat for a much-reduced price and were through with cruising. I couldn't help but think that if they had gotten a smaller boat that had been more affordable to maintain that they could have still been out sailing, without the stress of running out of money.

If you can bring yourself to simplify your life and do without some of the 'comforts' you think might be necessary, you might be happier in the long run without them. And the less money you have to spend maintaining your boat, the more money you will have for sailing to exotic places. The simple lifestyle of cruising lends itself well to washing clothes by hand, hanging laundry in the rigging, and doing maintenance yourself rather than hiring workers in a yard. On a smaller boat, you might be more likely to keep up with all the jobs needed to keep the boat looking good and running well but on a larger vessel, it might be more likely that special technical helpers or day laborers could be necessary simply due to the sheer volume the work entails. All cruisers spend a portion of each month maintaining their boats, but if you are on a smaller, simpler boat, your days of work will be proportionally less than those of the crew on the larger, more complicated boats. It's an obvious fact too often ignored.

For any of you who want to believe in your heart of hearts that smaller boats are perfectly capable of making long passages and multi-year cruises in total comfort and safety, but just aren't sure, just take a look at some of the epic voyages of the great sailors of yesteryear like the Pardeys, the Hiscocks (who circumnavigated twice on a 30' boat, then went bigger and finally went smaller again later). And look at sailing greats like Hal and Margaret Roth or Herb Payson and John Guzzwell. All these sailors have made long world voyages on boats under 40' and in the case of Guzzwell, he did his circumnavigation on a self-built 20' wooden yawl!

If you are thinking of stepping up in size or perhaps buying your first cruising boat, maybe you should look long and hard at some of the great older designs out there or at some of the well-made newer boats that might be a fair bit smaller than what can be bought for the same money as a larger, light modern production design. You will see that the heaver, better-made boats typically have more storage, are more seaworthy, and offer less long-term maintenance issues than the more modern, lighter boats. Prudently assess your budget, your cruising plans, and your needs and desires and consider this question carefully: Is bigger really better?

Chapter Seven

Fixing Up an Old Boat: Knowing What is Possible and What is a Lost Cause

Even if you have owned a few boats or grew up sailing with your parents, searching out and locating the right boat for your needs from the tens of thousands that are available on the used market can be a daunting proposition. Surfing the net for the perfect vessel can often lead to a surprising conclusion: Once you narrow your parameters to your specific needs and a set budget, you'll likely find that there are only a handful of boats that come even close to meeting your requirements and that each one of them has a different set of challenges or numbers of deferred maintenance or outfitting issues that must be assessed and solved to satisfy your needs.

I wonder if in 1942 when Ray Greene built his first fiberglass sloop in his Toledo, Ohio shop he had any idea what a revolution to boating he had precipitated!

During World War II, many different materials were experimented with for constructing boats and ships. Laminated plywood was a revolutionary material that allowed for the quick and inexpensive production of thousands of patrol boats and launches. Ferrocement was experimented with and was best known as the material used to build many of the Liberty Ships which carried troops to Europe for the buildup that led to D-Day and the ultimate retaking of Europe from the Axis powers. Glass reinforced plastic was also incorporated in the construction of smaller vessels and out of this technology sprang the use of the material with the general public for both smaller commercial vessels and pleasure craft after the war.

In 1947, Carl Beetle introduced a fiberglass catboat to the public and by then Ray Greene was already building a 16' daysailer called the Rebel and released a 25' cruising sloop in 1957. By late 1956, Coleman Boat & Plastics on the West Coast began building a 41' Phil Rhodes designed cruising yacht of this new material, and finally, at the New York Boat Show in 1959, Everett Pearson introduced the general public to the Triton, which was to become the first highly successful design to be built of this new material. She was a 28' cruising sailboat made entirely of what was coined 'Fiberglass' which at first met with some skepticism, but by the middle 1960s the use of the material had virtually taken over yacht and small shipbuilding in both the US and in Europe. Just to show what a revolutionary building material this was, it's probably safe to say that a large percentage of the original fiberglass sailboats built during these early years are still sailing the world's oceans today and of those that have fallen into disuse it can further be said that the problems these derelict boats have stems from poor ownership and maintenance and that it is more than likely the wooden parts and ancillary equipment that has made them unusable, not the fiberglass hulls and decks which in most cases are probably still basically fine, or at least repairable!

As addressed below, there are many aspects of fiberglass boat construction and design that need to be assessed and considered when searching for a long-term home on the sea, and keep in mind that often the architects and engineers who designed them had little or no cruising experience and few had ever lived aboard for any length of time, if at all. Compound this 'highbrow ignorance' with builders who were often left with quite a bit of creative license in how these designs should be built produced sometimes mixed results, which can be seen scattered all across boatyards and backwaters of the world. The more successful of these are still sailing while many of the failures are growing weeds out of their cockpits, hulls filled with rainwater, collapsing under their own weight on their jack-stands or lying half sunk in the mud of an estuarial creek.

As we shall be looking into further on, fiberglass construction has so many variations and innovations that each of these will have to be addressed individually, but suffice to say that the single biggest saving grace of this material is that a vessel built of it, even if left neglected for a decade or more, can often be brought back to seaworthy, safe, and attractive condition, given enough time and energy!

Within the body of the following pages we will address how to narrow your parameters and locate a good bargain vessel that has the potential to be the vessel of your dreams and without breaking the bank and destroying your marriage (or soul) in the process!

Let's go over the potential issues likely to be encountered on an aging fiberglass sailboat and how these problems can be assessed and solved.

The Hull

One of the most common issues you may be faced with on an older sailboat is blistering and osmosis of the wetted surfaces. Ever since the early 1980s, when the phenomenon of fiberglass hull blistering became widely apparent, the dilemma many boat owners face is: When is blistering a problem, and how bad does it have to be before a repair is necessary? Thankfully one of the most amazing things about fiberglass boats is how easy it is to undertake extensive repairs and have the results of these repairs leave you with a hull that's just as strong, or even stronger, than when the boat was new.

One of the most controversial issues you are likely to encounter is how to properly undertake a blister repair. The controversy stems first because these hull repairs are often precipitated by negotiations during the sale of a boat and secondly from many misconceptions about the implications of osmosis and the resultant degradation to a laminate's structure.

The condition of the bottom is frequently an issue that prevents an older fiberglass boat from selling after a survey and sea trials have been completed. If the pre-purchase survey report points toward the need to undertake a proper and potentially expensive repair to a bottom due to osmosis, this finding may be challenged by the broker, the owner, the buyer, or the contractor. The conflict is likely to be about the best way to accomplish a suitable repair. This difference of opinion can ultimately lead to compromises that result in an ineffectual repair being undertaken.

If a blister repair is done incorrectly, a badly degraded or weakened laminate may result which can lead to excessive flexure of the hull, may allow the osmosis to continue to degrade the laminate and in some cases can weaken the structure of the hull even more than having left it alone while leading the boat owner to believe he or she has "fixed" the problem. To put it another way, an improperly repaired bottom may ultimately cause what was in reality only a cosmetic repair to become a much bigger problem for the owner years later. However, if a repair is properly accomplished, there is no reason a hull cannot recover all of its original strength and rigidity or become even better than new through the use of state-of-the-art materials and procedures that were not available when the hull was originally built.

Osmosis is a term used within the marine industry to refer to the ingress of water molecules into a fiberglass laminate structure. The resulting chemical breakdown of the laminate creates a blister through a process known as hydrolysis. Blisters may form between two layers of gelcoat or between the gelcoat layer and the first layer of laminate. Blisters of this variety could, after ensuring that the laminate is dry, be dealt with by a simple cosmetic repair. Often these blisters are tiny, the size of a pencil eraser at most, and can be widespread over the wetted surface of a hull and yet still not significantly affect the vessel's structural integrity.

Left alone, however, small blisters can lead to a breakdown in the underlying layers of laminate. At this stage, slightly larger blisters may form, up to the size of a dime or so, usually only in the first layer of laminate.

Typically, beneath the gelcoat of a hull, the first layer of laminate on most fiberglass hulls is chopped strand mat. This is used because it has excellent "hiding" properties so can lessen the possibility of print-through to the gelcoat finish from subsequent layers of woven roving as the hull ages and the resins shrink. Unfortunately, chopped strand mat is a less-than-perfect 'sponge'. If not well wetted-out during layup, years later a close inspection may reveal that it is full of small air voids that through osmosis have become full of water. Chop strand mat, unfortunately, exhibits a propensity to transmit any moisture present within its structure to the laminate below. Even at this stage, this first layer is largely non-structural and—in many cases, providing that the hull was heavily built and that the mat has not significantly degraded—it may be possible to remove the gelcoat, thoroughly dry out this first layer, spot-fill any blisters and voids with mat and epoxy filler, and then simply recoat with a barrier coating and bottom paint.

Even if the first mat layer is heavily compromised, but the underlying structural laminate turns out to be sound, in some cases removing this first thin mat layer and making sure that new exposed laminate is dry and fair may be enough to provide a suitable foundation on which to apply a barrier coating and bottom paint. This may be all that's necessary for a satisfactory repair.

Sometimes, however, removing this first layer reveals a more advanced stage of osmosis: additional pockets of moisture and compromised, or hydrolyzed, laminate. In this case, provided that the damage is localized to a reasonable number of specific areas, it may be acceptable for these blisters or voids to be ground out, proper laminate replaced (not with body filler or epoxy putty!), and once thoroughly dry, the bottom can be barrier coated.

The bad news, particularly with vessels that have spent many decades in the water, is that after removing the first layer of mat there could be many areas of high-moisture content. These have formed because air voids within the woven roving layers that were not properly wetted out during the construction process have become filled with water. In this case, a laminate profile should be taken to determine the extent of the ingress of moisture and the progression of the resulting osmotic degradation.

A laminate profile is accomplished by carefully grinding a small area of the bottom and removing layer by layer until good, undamaged laminate is found. Once the number of layers of damaged fiberglass has been determined, a repair can begin with the removal of those layers with a fiberglass planer, or peeler. It's a simple job to cut out and lay up new layers of cloth to restore the hull to its original thickness and structural integrity. Using some of the new biaxial cloths and vinyl ester resins followed by an epoxy barrier coating should provide a decades-long or even better-than-new repair.

We've all heard that proud boat owner in the boatyard who claims, "My old [such and such brand] boat has never had a blister." However, if you take a look at some older hulls, you're likely to find massively crazed gelcoats that are unable to form a blister because they are so thin and brittle and have an underlying laminate structure that's so porous, a blister simply cannot form. Years ago I saw a 1960s Camper and Nicholsons sloop that was having a laminate profile performed by a reputable yard to determine how far hydrolysis had progressed. As each successive layer of glass was removed it was finally discovered that there were no areas of the bottom of the hull that had escaped osmotic degradation and that to restore the hull to its original integrity, a complete relamination of the entire bottom was necessary. This is not typical, but can happen!

It's important at this point to bring up some misconceptions that seem to continue to float around the waterfronts of the world.

Misconception #1—"These old hulls were built so thick you could lose half the glass and she'd still be plenty strong." Or similarly...

Misconception #2—"These old hulls had [twice, thrice, pick a number] as many layers of glass as they needed. They just overbuilt them because they didn't know how strong the stuff was."

Most older fiberglass designs indeed had fairly thick hulls but it's not because the architects or builders didn't understand the material, it's because these boats were often patterned after wooden boat designs which, because of the nature of the structural dynamics of wood as a building material, had to weigh a lot. The architects and engineers had to stipulate the use of many layers of laminate so that the weight distribution would be similar to the wooden designs they were mimicking because this is what the buying public was accustomed to seeing. And so—*to float correctly on their lines— they had to weigh as much as their wooden sister ships.* Because the architects and engineers knew that the structural characteristics of the laminates were substantial, they would often leave out such later developments as cores, ribs, or stringers in the belief that the thickness of the laminates alone, combined with a few full or partial bulkheads, would provide enough rigidity.

When these hulls were new, and if the hulls were provided with no large flat sections or unsupported panels, they could indeed prove to be quite stiff. As time went on and the material was better understood, however, it became evident that fiberglass laminate structures, even if not compromised by osmosis, when flexed many times began to become "softer" and less rigid over time. The use of cores made of balsa wood or foam helped control flexure considerably. Other manufacturers addressed this problem through the use of longitudinal stringers and 'floors' (transverse stiffeners) rigidly glassed into the hull structure to bring the flexible nature of fiberglass better under control.

Some manufacturers 'floated' bulkheads in the overhead (deck or cabin top), allowing the hulls to flex and move within a fairly wide range. The development of the internal grid structure so common today was a mass-production-driven development that allowed a builder to make a hull even thinner by using the interior furniture and cabin sole supports (transverse floors and longitudinal support members) as integral parts in the structural stiffness of the hull.

What does this all mean relative to the structural significance of osmotic degradation to a hull? On an older hull built with thick laminates and with no significant flat sections, the loss of structural integrity of some of the outside layers of the hull might be considered insignificant. If a bottom on one of these boats was developing minor blistering of the outside layers of laminate, in many cases a thorough drying of the structure and spot repairs made to the areas of the hull where blisters formed, followed with a state-of-the-art barrier coating could likely be enough of a repair to be considered structurally sound. On a more modern, thinner hull or one of cored construction, however, the rigidity of the structure must be more carefully considered when making a plan for a proper osmosis repair. In many cases, a peel and relamination of the hull is the only acceptable solution.

Misconception #3—"Moisture intrusion into a balsa or foam core in a hull will always be localized and won't allow moisture to intrude into the adjacent core, even if holed."

If the hull is a cored structure, then it is vitally important to confirm that moisture has not migrated into the core material of the hull. Despite all of the engineering papers put forth in the early years of the development of cored hull construction that claimed water would not intrude laterally in a cored laminate, it has been proven through time that if water molecules do indeed infiltrate a cored area, particularly one of organic materials such as balsa, that moisture can travel extensively throughout the adjacent areas via kerfs or voids built-in during the construction process and may, depending on the extent or severity of the ingress, lead to a very expensive repair. Because of this potential complication, if a cored hull is being considered for repair, in addition to performing a laminate profile, in some cases core samples should be taken as well to ensure that an accurate assessment of the integrity of the underlying structure can be made.

Misconception #4—"If a cored hull has isolated (or even extensive) damp or delaminated areas, especially below the waterline, you should not buy the boat because it will be impossible to repair in a cost effective manner."

In most cases, this is absolutely not true. A vessel with a cored hull showing moisture intrusion or even some areas of delamination (separations of the core from the outer skin) can in many cases be easily repaired. The beauty of this type of construction is that areas of separation can typically be mapped out simply by tapping with a plastic hammer and using a moisture meter and in most cases the outer skin on a cored hull is thinner than the inner skin, so if an area of delamination or excessive moisture is found, the area can be opened up by carefully cutting the outside skin off to reveal the core. If it is indeed compromised, it can simply be chissled out and then lightly faired and a new piece of core put back in place of it. This is how deck recoring is done. But the beauty and simplicity of doing this on a bottom of a boat, for example, is that a deck usually has a textured non-skid pattern that will need to be reestablished, and getting a perfect result on a partial deck recoring is more a job of dealing with the cosmetics than with the relatively simple structural aspects. On the bottom of a boat, all that needs to be done, once the wet core is dried out, or the degraded core is replaced, is to relaminate the section, fair it smooth, barrier coat it and bottom paint it. So in reality, even an entire 'bad' core on a bottom could, depending on the size of the boat, be redone over a period of a few days or weeks by replacing sections piece by piece. But of course, the chance of finding a boat with an entirely degraded core is unlikely, and you probably wouldn't buy it anyway. What is more likely to be found might be water intrusion around a through-hull that has allowed some moisture intrusion resulting in possible core degradation over decades in some areas of the bottom and as I said, if the core is only a little damp, but not degraded, simply allowing it to dry over time with either exposure to air, or with fans and heat lamps, and then relaminating the bottom to its original thickness in that area should make for an effective repair. And if time is of the essence, the damp core can be removed, and then new core put in and relaminated which can often be accomplished over just a few hours at a time spread over a few days. So if you find a terrific boat that happens to have a few areas of damp or separated core and if the price make sense, you can certainly effect a proper repair and the cost of this can be surprisingly low compared to making a major repair on a solid laminate hull, mainy due to the fact that core material helps reestablish sufficient laminate thickness in the structure quickly; one of the main reasons builders use it in the first place!

Misconception #5—"Those little cracks in the gelcoat don't mean anything."

While it is true that, especially on some of the older heavily built boats, that a gelcoat crack may not necessarily point to structural weakness and that as gelcoats age, they often shrink and produce cracks, with many of the newer hulls that have large flat sections, such as many powerboat hulls and certain sailboat designs, taking a laminate hardness profile of the hull that is demonstrating extensive gelcoat cracks or crazing on its wetted surface is vitally important. In many cases if flexing is occurring, telltale cracks may develop in the area of bulkheads, stringers, or transverse 'floors' and on more modern boats, the internal grid units (IGU) may become separated or show spiderweb cracks on the inside surfaces where the grid unit joins the hull. All of these things may point to the possibility of a softening of the laminate structure due to osmosis. In cases like these, the only way to restore structural integrity is to remove the weakened laminate and replace it with new.

When trying to determine the structural integrity of the fiberglass laminate you have exposed for repair, there is a valuable tool called a Barcol hardness meter which is used in the quality control aspect of fiberglass construction to determine the rigidity of a laminate structure. This instrument has a tiny metal probe that is forced against a laminate to give a reading of the laminate's relative hardness. Readings of less than 25 on the scale of the instrument are generally considered to be too soft; readings of above 45 are often considered to be brittle. This is an oversimplification, as certain types of resins and composite structures have characteristics that could hedge the higher 'cutoff' figure, but the lower figures are of the greatest interest to note when deciding where to stop when 'peeling'

a boat for a relamination with new cloth. Even if low moisture readings are encountered after removal of a layer or two of laminate, a Barcol test should be performed. In some cases where a boat has developed a severe case of blisters or even just hydrolysis without blisters forming, as is the case sometimes with older boats that have lost much of their resin content over many decades of immersion and are then left to dry for a long time in a boatyard (several years); even though the material may read 'dry' on a moisture meter, laminating on top of this heavily degraded material would be a waste of money. If financially viable, all compromised or weakened laminate should be removed before relaminating when trying to restore a hull's structural integrity.

Thankfully, water absorption through the layers of an underwater surface due to osmosis is so slow that it can take decades before extreme procedures are necessary. It is not unusual when performing a laminate profile to find that immediately under the gelcoat the laminate looks whitish and has high moisture content with low Barcol readings. A layer down from this the laminate may be much darker and moisture content may have fallen significantly. Often the layer under this shows moisture and Barcol readings that are all quite normal and so a fairly non-invasive repair may be sufficient.

After conferring with contractors and surveyors about the best way to undertake a proper repair and to ensure the best possible outcome, it is very important to be certain that no matter what method or to what extent the issue is addressed that the result is a dry, hard, and fair bottom with no structural weakness. Using state-of-the-art materials such as biaxial cloths and vinylester or epoxy resins will help ensure a long-lasting repair. Under no circumstances should one be happy with simply grinding out wet blisters, filling them with putty, and slapping a barrier coating over a bottom that is not thoroughly dry and sound.

If the vessel you're looking to buy has blisters, you may be lucky enough to find that the boat needs only some drying out, spot repairs, and a barrier coating. Less luckily, you may learn that it needs a full peel and relamination. In either case, however, provided that you follow proper procedures and accepted industry methods, your money will be well spent and you will be secure in the knowledge that you have restored or even augmented your boat's original structural integrity.

Misconception #6—"External ballast is best because the metal will absorb the impact of a grounding and thereby save the hull."

This is one that has been floating around in various publications for decades and was a carryover from the days of wooden boat construction when vessels often carried internal ballast in ingots or 'pigs'. The concept that an external keel would 'absorb impact' was based on the premise that the ballast would be lead which indeed would deform somewhat on an impact, but even still, the thinking here is flawed, and here is why: External keels of course must be attached with bolts. There are typically two types of bolt attachment types for lead keels and generally only one for iron keels with a few exceptions.

Let's start with Iron keels. Most of these have threaded holes into which a stud or a bolt can be installed with nuts to draw it tight. The advantage of this type of attachment is that when the keel bolts require replacement (and this is inevitable), they can simply (or sometimes not so simply) be withdrawn and new ones can be installed. This is how most of the French boats are built and in many cases, keel bolts can even be installed while a boat is afloat if done one by one and torqued properly. Some of the early fiberglass production boats using iron keels had the bolts cast in and these are much more difficult to replace. But iron is pretty stiff so one could redrill holes to be tapped to allow the installation of new bolts. While not easy, it is not impossible.

Lead keels are another issue altogether and these are the keels that were being touted as preferable for external keels by the yacht building elite in decades past because of their supposed impact absorbing characteristics and of course,

because lead is more dense than iron, it allows for a lower center of gravity. The problem here is that there are typically only two ways to install a bolt in a lead keel. The first is that what you might find on older wooden boats where a cavity was created in the lead keel casting so that a nut could be inserted and the bolt could be threaded unto the nut and then the cavity was filled in. This cavity could ideally be later opened up when it became necessary to replace the keel bolts. No problem.

Unfortunately, there is a much easier, cheaper, and faster way to build a lead keel and that is to install J-bolts, permanently cast into the lead. Using this method, the bolt stays put very well and offers little potential for movement, but what happens when it is time to replace the bolts?

Keel bolts don't last forever! With the recent increase in disasters at sea where keels have separated from the hulls of yachts, more than ever it is time to pay attention to this important issue. This is why you won't see me recommending many of the older designs that have external lead keels. External keels of iron, if built with threaded studs, are okay because these are relatively straightforward to replace, but cast in J-bolts in a lead keel are a nightmare to replace and that is why vessels like Valiants, Hylas 44s, Lafitte 44s, Saga 43s and many otherwise fine vessels are not in this book as recommended vessels. While these are excellent designs, the cost of replacing keel bolts with an external lead keel is so prohibitively high as to put this out of the scope of a 'budget cruiser' and similarly, we cannot recommend getting involved with a boat that has thirty- or forty-year-old keel bolts for the obvious reason that should they break, the consequences are beyond bad. They are catastrophic.

Some of you may say, "But these can be replaced!" And that's true. Keels can be unbolted, crated, and sent back to one of the handful of manufacturing plants in North America where new bolts can be properly cast in place, but this is a very expensive procedure that could cost tens of thousands of dollars.

One other super expensive thing that is often overlooked is built-in permanently installed chainplates. Years ago we were seriously considering buying a Hylas 44 for our personal use. These are beautifully constructed vessels but have two fatal flaws. The first is the above-mentioned cast-in J-bolts for the lead keel and the second is glassed-in permanent chainplates that cannot be accessed without removing virtually all of the port and starboard interior of the boat and grinding out the old chainplates! This is another tens of thousands of dollars or many hundreds of hours of labor proposition and certainly would put any boat built like this out of the 'bargain boat' category, no matter what the purchase price.

However, if you find a boat with internal glassed-in chainplates, and if they are oriented fore and aft rather than athwartships and just on the inside of the hull, in many cases the existing chainplates can be cut off at or just below deck level and new external chainplates can be bolted to the outside of the hull using the old internal chainplates as backing plates.

The Deck

One of the most common issues you may encounter when purchasing an aging sailing yacht is decks that have become compromised through the degradation of the core material used to stiffen them.

An old surveyor friend of mine once said, "Ninety percent of the problems we find on fiberglass boats are with the ten percent of wood used to build them." While a few production sailboats have been produced that do not have a core in their decks, such as the CSYs, some of the older Moodys, and a number of the early Bruce Roberts designs. The fact is that most decks are stiffened with some type of core material. With boats built after about 1970, the most common material used was end-grain balsa wood. Laminated inside of the deck structure as edge grain cubes, this material is lightweight, bonds well to the adjacent polyester resins and in a properly engineered laminate structure provides tremendous panel stiffness... until it becomes wet and begins to degrade. And not all 'Balsa cores' are the same! One popular brand name is Baltek. This is what you will find on most American-built production boats and a few of the higher quality boats built in Europe or Taiwan, but the majority of Taiwanese boats built that advertised balsa core decks have no-name unbranded materials which are often of questionable quality and so on any boat with a 'balsa core', great care must be taken to ensure that no significant moisture intrusion or delamination of the core material has occurred.

The second most common material typically used to stiffen deck structures, especially on Taiwanese boats from the 70s and 80s and some older American production boats from the 60s and 70s is plywood. These are the most typical decks that exhibit serious issues over time. Note however that even here, there are differences in build quality. Westsail, Islander, and a few other US manufacturers used Douglas fir plywood as a core material which is quite rot-resistant and many boats with balsa cores will still use plywood in high-stress areas such as cleat attachment points or outboard of mast partners because the plywood has far more structural integrity and resistance to compression loads than mere balsa wood. But some manufacturers, particularly of lower quality Taiwanese boats, used lauan mahogany for deck cores. Luan is not true mahogany and is very prone to rot if allowed to remain wet for any great length of time. The glues used to join the layers were also often water-soluble and so the layers can separate if allowed to remain wet for long. If you are looking at a boat with a lauan mahogany deck core and high levels of moisture are present, plan on dealing with deck repairs in the not-too-distant future.

The third type of core material one is likely to encounter is high to medium density foam. This can be a terrific material as it does not readily degrade from moisture intrusion. But it does lack some of the strength and stiffness that wooden cores possess. If you are looking at a boat with a foam core deck, such as the Downeaster, some of the Hylas, and C.E. Ryder boats, even if you find delaminations or separations of the core, repairs can be as easy as finding the extent of the affected area, marking it off, drilling some small holes at the extremities of the separations and injecting an epoxy resin to stiffen and re-bond the laminate. Care of course must be undertaken to be sure the areas are dry, and if any distortion of the skin fairness is noted you may need to use weights or possibly temporary bolts and battens to pull it back into shape while the repair is setting.

We've talked about hull blistering on fiberglass boats already but here are some things to keep in mind. If you look for boats in an area of the world where they are hauled and decommissioned for a good portion of each year, the chances of finding a bad case of osmosis are greatly reduced. However, with internally ballasted boats in temperate zone climates, if water should ingress into the skin between the ballast and the fiberglass, it can freeze, causing this area to separate. If this is allowed to go on for many years, you may find a keel with separations that have resulted in having virtually the entire keel laminate debonded from the encapsulated ballast, resulting in the total weight of the keel resting only on the bottom of the skin of the hull/keel shell! This is extremely dangerous and would require drying and rebonding of the keel skin to the ballast because a heavy grounding could result in the internal ballast falling out.

I've seen it happen! Another possible outcome can be that the ballast moves enough to cause fracturing of the connection where the top of the encapsulation joins the interior sections of the hull. This type of high-stress area can ultimately lead to a breach in the integrity of the hull itself and so should be carefully assessed on any older boat with internal ballast where extensive separations of the skin in the area of the ballast are noted.

Similarly, if you find a great looking boat with external ballast and a notable gap at the leading edge of the keel with rust (with iron) or green 'ooze' coming out of the hull to keel joint (with lead), this signifies that significant movement has occurred and that water is certainly migrating into the connection and coming into contact with the keel bolts. While many amateurs will tell you that stainless steel keel bolts are superior to mild steel, the fact is that mild steel bolts will show significant wastage and look quite terrible while still maintaining tremendous integrity whereas stainless steel can *look* great but may suddenly fail due to crevice corrosion. So making a careful examination of the keel bolts for corrosion and the adjacent areas of the hull for stress cracks or signs of movement is extremely important. Still, if you find an awesome boat that needs new keel bolts and you can adjust or figure the cost of undertaking this maintenance into the price of the boat, you would benefit from having a boat with brand new keel bolts that will likely be good to go for the next twenty-plus years. Even if you have a lead keel with the cast in J-bolts, Mars Keels in Canada and Durokeel in Mexico City can replace these for you and although it isn't cheap, if the rest of the boat is a great buy, it may well be worth the investment of removing the keel and shipping it to them for rebuilding.

Hull/deck joints are another area of fiberglass boat construction that can exhibit real problems as time goes on. You will read in many books and blogs that a through-bolted hull/deck joint is the best, but this is just another oversimplification. The best hull/deck joint is one that doesn't allow for moisture intrusion or movement. Amel uses fiberglass to make this joint 'one piece' with the hull. Some manufacturers use bolts or screws and an adhesive sealant such as 3M 5200 while others, especially Taiwanese builders, may lay fiberglass over the joint on the underside to keep water ingress caused by aging bedding compounds from leaking into the interior. If you see this type of joint, be ultra cautious! Often lower cost builders will use inferior stainless steel as fasteners and when (as is inevitably the case) water gets into the area around the fasteners where it's encapsulated by fiberglass, the steel will 'rot' and you may be left with a hull/deck joint that is only being held together by aged, dried out sealant, and one thin layer of fiberglass!

A similar and potentially very difficult repair is when you find boats with raised bulwarks where the stanchions or genoa tracks are bolted or screwed into the bulwarks with no access to the nuts or backing plates. On designs such as the Peterson 44 and Liberty 458 as well as many Taiwanese boats like some Tayanas, Island Traders, Hans Christians, early Ta Shings, Vagabonds, and many others, this area may be filled with chunks of lauan or other types of 'filler' wood and the tracks or bulwarks may just be simply screwed into this! Similarly, bolts may be threaded into nuts that are then glassed into place to 'hold' them before the area is covered over underneath with fiberglass and so when moisture migrates under the stanchions or tracks and corrodes the nuts and bolts (which will inevitably happen), leaks will eventually rot the wood and the only way to properly repair this will be to open these areas up with either a series of holes from the outside or from underneath which, of course, requires extensive destruction to the interior; so it is super important to keep in mind when looking at vessels with this type of construction. Should that put you off buying one of these types of boats if all other things were good? No, but I'd be sure I had a plan for how I was going to fix it eventually or even just arrest it in the short term or this could end up causing a real heartache later on.

Internally 'glassed-in' chainplates that are inaccessible for inspection are one of the potentially more expensive repairs one can come across on an older vessel. Fiberglass boats are ultimately completely repairable of course, but when one has to disassemble large portions of the interior of a vessel to gain access to make a repair, it becomes a pretty big project! And to me, it represents a certain type of arrogance within the boat industry that some builders (or designers) feel it is 'okay' to design and create something that might last twenty or so years and then will become a huge expense to repair. Their attitude might have been *The original owner probably won't have the boat by then anyway, so who cares*? If that wasn't the thinking, then what on earth would compel a builder to create something that is basically irreparable without huge expense when just a little more time and attention to detail might have allowed for easy replacements of chainplates, tanks, or engines?

The good news with all of this, however, is that if you are handy, clever, and full of energy, a boat with problems in inaccessible areas might be a super buy—provided of course that this all comes out before the sale and can be calculated into the purchase price!

Another area to carefully examine on any older sailboat, wood, fiberglass, or steel, is the mast step. On deck-stepped masts, the cabin top or deck should be carefully sighted to look for depression or changes in the shape of the underlying structure. It is quite common for inexperienced owners or riggers to overtighten rigs which over time can cause a downward deflection in the area around the mast step. While a slight deflection may not be a 'death warrant' for an older boat, significant depression in the area around the step surely points to changes in the overall shape of the hull itself and your detective skills should immediately be exercised looking at the compression post/bulkheads or underlying support structures for rot or broken support members. While repairing a depressed mast step area on a deck-stepped mast can be accomplished, it can turn into a big job and may require a lot of careful thought and labor to come up with a suitable solution.

'Keel-stepped' masts are often thought of as being superior to deck-stepped masts, but this is another case where giving an overly simplistic answer to a complex issue may lead to conclusions that are not entirely accurate. While it's true that stepping a mast to the keel or (better yet) to a support structure that spreads the load of the mast step to a large area of the hull is indeed potentially a great way to secure a rig. If a heavy section mast is stepped on a cabin top or deck that is substantial enough to support the load, the deck-stepped mast will be perfectly fine and offers some advantages of its own. Reputable builders of offshore sailboats such as Hallberg-Rassy, Westsail, some Tayanas, and many steel ocean worthy boats used deck-stepped masts. But a well-designed keel-stepped mast is a great system and in my mind is superior to a deck-stepped one... but only if it is properly engineered!

When looking at a keel-stepped mast, remember that not all installations that call themselves keel-stepped are properly engineered. On some of the older Morgans, Bristols, and Tartans (all great builders, by the way) we often find aluminum or steel mast steps installed with lag bolts into the underlying lead ballast and set in such a way that water cannot drain away. Keel-stepped masts, of course, will in most cases allow some water to migrate down the inside of the spar to drain to the keel. This is usually just rainwater and if it can drain away easily, is not a problem. But in some designs, the water just sits there. Then as the bedding compounds for the mast step bolts age, water can migrate into the ballast encapsulation and if some bilge water mixes with it and is allowed to sit long enough, the bolts or the mast and step itself will eventually corrode. So take a close look at the condition of the metal on the mast step and the mast itself where it comes in contact with the step. If you find excessive corrosion, note it, but don't necessarily run away. Negotiate a price reduction and then simply pull the spar, cut off whatever amount is damaged, and have a new elevated mast step created by building up the area under the step to the height

that compensates for the amount of the mast that was removed. The support for this new step on a smaller boat could just be a dense piece of hardwood or even epoxy-impregnated plywood, but using a strong, inert type of material like Extren plate or any type of solid fiberglass would be better. Deal with this type of problem properly and you will end up with a mast step that will outlast even you.

Over-tensioned rigs can cause big problems. I once bought a boat for a very good price because a rigger had accidentally over-tensioned the rig and caused a significant hull distortion. The boat was a Taiwanese Flying Dutchman 50 with ½-inch V1 shrouds (the section of 'uppers' that goes to the first spreader), and then the remainder of the uppers, called the V2, were 5/16-inch wire. Most cruising boats are tuned so that the uppers would want to have approximately 15% of the breaking strength of the wire as their static dockside load tension. So this rigger looked at the ½-inch wire, consulted his tables, and thought, *Hmm, breaking strength of half-inch wire is 29,700 lbs, so 15% of that is 4,455 lbs...* and he proceeded to crank the turnbuckle that tight. What he *should* have done was to look aloft and note the diameter of the wire aloft and tensioned the rig for 15% of the 5/16-inch wire's breaking strength (12,500 lbs) which would have been 1,875 lbs—big difference!

The owner trusted the rigger and the boat, at least initially, handled the excessive load. The owner sailed off to Hawaii, French Polynesia, and back, and after a year and a half had gone by, the hull in the area of the chainplates had dimpled visibly on both sides, because fiberglass is basically plastic, even with the tension on the shrouds released, the dimpling didn't go away. I fixed it by using hydraulics to push the hull back into shape and building in a set of stringers to better distribute the load of the chainplates and when I re-tensioned the rig (properly this time) the problem was solved. It cost me about $5K to repair and that more than offset the $40K price reduction I had gotten because of this defect!

Look at the rigging and tensioning carefully on any boat you are considering buying. In many cases, older fiberglass boats have over-tensioned rigs and this can be simply, as in the above case, because of an inexperienced rigger or owner making a mistake, but it can also be because as fiberglass boats age, they often become more 'flexy'.

Flexing of the hull in the area of the rig is a common problem on older boats and in particular on newer, more lightly built designs, or on boats with cored hulls that have been structurally compromised by damage, delaminations, or moisture intrusion. If a boat's hull is too flexy, getting the rig to stay in column may be difficult or even impossible and so achieving even a 15% rigging tension might put too much stress on the structure. If when sailing your prospective boat you notice excessive slack in the leeward shrouds, look very carefully at the cause of it and for this reason alone, a good sea trial in strong conditions should be high on your list for your due diligence when buying an older fiberglass boat. Chances are if the boat is one of the heavily built designs of the 70s and 80s, it will be fine, but if it is a newer or more lightly built boat, achieving proper rig tension may be difficult. And the telltale signs are, as I said, an over-tensioned rig while dockside, visible dimpling of the hull sides or distortions in the area of the chainplates, a depressed mast step area, or all of the above. Be careful here! Even with designs of great reputation and with heavily built solid hulls and stringers, years and years of immersion can lead to the hull softening and allowing excessive flexing. I once surveyed an early 70s Swan 43 in Antigua with a hull that was so hydrolyzed that in between the stringers and frames the hull had been distorted simply by the weight of the boat and the pressure of the water it was sitting in. When hauled, you could see every frame and stringer and bulkhead 'printing through' with visible dimpling in between these rigid structural members! Needless to say, she was a flexy boat and the rig would not stay properly in column, even with the stays and shrouds super tight when at rest.

Another area that deserves careful inspection is the bulkhead tabbing where delamination at the bonds of various structural bulkheads and furniture has allowed these components to shift.

If the vessel you are considering is fiberglass, chances are the bulkheads are made of some variety of plywood and may have a veneer of some type covering the actual structural component. Morgan yachts used Douglas fir plywood, heavily tabbed into the hull sides with woven roving and then covered the fir with a thin teak plywood veneer. This allowed for a very clean 'finished' appearance down below but makes it exceptionally difficult to inspect the tabbing. One good way to tell if there is any separation is to get a soft rubber mallet and after wrapping it in cloth, bang fairly solidly in any areas that you suspect may be loose. Place your hand against the bulkhead or adjacent hull and you may feel movement. Using a moisture meter may also show if there is an elevated reading where the bulkheads meet the hull which can be a sign of rot or delamination. On a sea trial, you may see or feel movement when you tack. While this may sound nit-picky, confirming that the main and partial bulkheads are well-secured means that the hull is probably still fairly stiff and should give you the confidence to move forward with further inspection.

Another defect you may see, and one that is sometimes found on Taiwanese boats, in particular, are delaminations in the structures under the cabin sole. If water has ever gotten into the boat and been allowed to sit for any length of time, the end grain of the base of bulkheads can absorb water and in the case of many lower-quality designs, there may have been interior grade plywood used for these structural members. I've seen many examples of extensive delamination in bulkheads which are at first invisible because they are below the cabin sole and not showing any signs of discoloration above the sole. A repair to a defect like this may be as simple as determining and solving whatever caused the ingress of water and then drilling a series of holes in the wood, injecting epoxy, and screwing or clamping the wood back together again, or it could mean a much more invasive replacement of all or part of the compromised bulkhead... a big job in most cases!

Many of the more modern boatbuilders have tried to eliminate the potential for the above issues with the introduction in the early 1980s of what is called an 'IGU'. As I mentioned earlier, this stands for 'Internal Grid Unit' and is a quite common building practice these days. Installing an IGU is done by molding a complete stiffening structure into the hull which in many cases includes the bases of bulkheads, stringers, frames, and sometimes even a complete internal liner which is placed into a 'green' partially cured hull while still in the mold to stiffen it and provide an easy base on which to install the interior bulkheads, furniture, and cabinetry.

While this concept was first engineered in the 1970s, by the late 80s it was becoming more and more common and was eventually adopted to some extent by most manufacturers worldwide. It allows for significant time savings during construction and better overall quality control on the finished product. The problem with this type of construction is with the bonding that is used while installing it.

Some builders resisted this trend and prided themselves in using traditional individually glassed-in bulkheads and stringers and 'floors' (transverse members that support the cabin sole and spread the torsional loads of the keel and mast loads). While this was an admirable effort, many manufacturers used laminated plywood for the floors and solid wood for the stringers which was fiberglassed over. When water would get into these floors, stringers, and frames they could eventually rot which is another fairly big project to overcome. So an all fiberglass 'grid' that can't rot seems like a great idea, right?

Well, technically, if properly done, it is indeed a great idea. Hallberg-Rassy uses this method and individually glasses a heavily built grid into their hulls to a good result, but other builders, like Beneteau, Hunter, the new Jeanneaus, Bavaria, and others attempt to simply 'glue' the IGUs into the hull using a very thick, filler heavy, polyester goop which sometimes doesn't bond in all places

and in other cases, when struck firmly, as may be incurred as a result of a heavy grounding or impact, cracks and separates from the hull skin because as anyone who works with fiberglass knows, the resin itself with no reinforcing fibers is quite brittle!

So when looking at boats with IGUs, carefully inspecting the internal grid's bond to the hull in all areas using percussive soundings or in some cases, infrared imagery can tell you if any movement or separation is going on. Another much easier way to see if there is movement is simply to look for hairline cracks in the gelcoat or resin visible on the inside of the hull, typically in the bilge in the area of the keel. If you see a lot of small cracks, movement is surely occurring!

Repairing a separated IGU is not impossible but must be carefully assessed on an individual basis when contemplating buying a boat with this type of construction. If you are clever and can come up with a satisfactory solution for re-bonding a separated IGU, you may be able to negotiate a significant price reduction and still end up with a 100% sound hull at substantial savings.

Leaking hardware and tracks are an often glossed over issue that almost all older boats suffer from to some extent.

When looking your prospective vessel over, be sure to spend some time looking at the underside of the decks where tracks, cleats, and stanchions are secured. If you see discolorations on the bolts or nuts, there is leakage. This needs to be arrested or crevice corrosion will surely occur and the actual cleat or track or stanchion base may eventually crack and need to be replaced. All too often this type of defect is overlooked when boat shopping and yet re-bedding a significant portion of the deck hardware on an older boat can be a many-day project and should be calculated into the cost of purchasing. It is also likely that when the bolts or screws are removed that you may find degraded fasteners and replacing these may be necessary. Add this cost too into the eventual price of your dreamboat.

Even despite all of these areas of concern to be aware of while shopping for a fiberglass boat, it is still an amazing material and in most cases is totally, infinitely repairable. Have fun looking and keep all these considerations in mind and you will surely find a boat that satisfies your needs at a price you can afford.

The Case for the Steel Yacht

We've all seen them at anchor, the French or German boats, or maybe a Canadian or a Dutch flag flying from their sterns. The designs are often not easily identifiable. They are boats we don't recognize. They are in many cases built of steel.

In a world of cookie-cutter production designs and with the abundance, or perhaps overabundance of fiberglass yachts available on the new and used market, prices have never been lower for owning a fiberglass boat. We see them everywhere, sailing on all the world's oceans, and the vast majority never experience any significant problems. Hunters have been sailed across the Pacific, Catalinas around the world, and in the South Pacific. Beneteaus are now as common as Westsails and Tayanas once were. So why then do some people still choose steel?

The obvious reason is, of course, strength. On a recent very windy crossing of the Caribbean from the Virgin Islands to Panama on a steel yacht, I passed about 80 miles off the mouth of Colombia's Rio Magdalena. Due to recent torrential rainfall, the river was disgorging billions of gallons of muddy waters mixed with trees and floating debris, we did not stress unnecessarily about this because I knew that if we did strike an object, even at eight to ten knots as we rolled downwind, that a dent was likely to be the worst damage. When sailing in the confined and murky waters near the coasts of Belize or Panama, knowing that a grounding would not necessarily fatally damage the boat is a definite advantage of a steel hull, in my mind.

Others choose steel because it is inexpensive to work and maintain. Although indisputably steel is a higher maintenance material than fiberglass, when a major repair or change is undertaken, the costs of doing these things are often much less than on a fiberglass boat. One can reduce maintenance costs even more by hauling out in yards accustomed to maintaining workboats. Many smaller commercial boats are steel and the yards that work on them are generally much less expensive than 'yacht yards' which cater to shiny 'rich people's toys'.

Another reason to have a steel boat is the desire for a custom design. Having been involved in the yachting industry for over four decades, and having worked with many discerning owners, I realize that the older and more experienced people become, the less a production yacht is likely to fill their needs. A steel boat can often be built as a one-off for little more than building it as a production design. If you want something built in your own special way, steel allows for that at a moderate cost. On the used market, some very well-maintained, brilliantly conceived custom steel yachts sometimes become available. These are often the result of an owner's many years of experience and interestingly enough, these custom boats are typically no more expensive than a lightly equipped modern production boat. It seems that within the less experienced sailing populace, there is a fear of owning a custom boat and a general set of misconceptions about steel.

Let's briefly address the three major concerns typically expressed about steel yachts.

Rust: Modern coating systems have virtually eliminated the problems of rusting associated with older steel craft. With the latest three-step coating systems available, keeping a steel boat rust-free and looking great is easier than ever. Still, careful attention to the coating systems, particularly on the inside of the boat and in areas that are not easy to see, is vitally important. However, with careful attention to detail and through the use of a modern coating, keeping a steel boat rust-free is not nearly as challenging as it once was.

Low resale: While this is truer now than ever and steel boats can present themselves as tremendous values and often sell for substantially less than a similar production fiberglass design, a properly built and maintained steel boat will always attract a following. The longer and farther people sail, the more they come to appreciate the high tensile strength and peace of mind that having a steel hull under them provides.

Unfamiliarity with unknown builders or unfamiliar designs: Although many reputable naval architects have designed boats in steel, many of these designs are built by amateurs with varying degrees of success. If you are considering a design you are not familiar with or a boat built by a home builder or unknown yard, consult a qualified marine surveyor well acquainted with metal boats and get his or her opinion before proceeding further. Disqualifying a boat because it was not built by a big yard is foolish; many one-off builds or even home-built vessels can be far superior to production or semi-production boats. But a poorly built hull finished out by an inexperienced or ignorant builder can offer nightmares and even if purchased for a low price may be costly or even impossible to put in good order.

On the plus side, lastly and most importantly, a steel boat is often unique. In a world of increasingly similar-looking sailing yachts where it is becoming more and more difficult to maintain your own identity, sailing into an anchorage crowded with identical-looking white sloops and cutters, I find it refreshing to see an esoteric custom yacht at anchor. These are often steel boats of which each is unique, sometimes unusual, and refreshingly uncommon.

What About Wood?

For hundreds of years, and up until the 1960s, if you were shopping for a sailboat, wooden vessels made up the vast majority of what was available on the used market. By the 1970s and 80s, if you were searching around for a good inexpensive cruising boat, invariably you'd consider a wooden one. The bargain prices on some of these lovely-looking designs seemed almost too good to be true and oftentimes were. Occasionally, however, a terrific wooden boat did come up for sale and because of the huge shift in perceptions of the yachting scene in favor of relatively maintenance-free fiberglass during this same era, it seemed that all wooded boats were devalued to a level that made them quite attractive to a sailor on a budget.

Today, because wooden boats do not tolerate years of neglect, most of the large number of such yachts that we typically saw sailing in the final days of the twentieth century have now gone to pieces. Wooden boats are for the most part no longer being produced, and the ones that remain from earlier times have usually had significant money invested in them over the years to keep them viable. The limited number of wooden boats still available on the used market today seems to have caused them to come up in relative value to compare with many fiberglass or steel yachts of similar vintage. That having been said, often a wooden boat with some potentially serious issues or vessels that have been allowed to fall into cosmetic disrepair can still offer quite a potential bargain on the used market. For example:

A 50' wooden ketch from South Africa that had been built in the early 1980s appeared on the market in the Virgin Islands a few years back. This boat had originally been constructed for the crewed charter yacht industry and was quite nicely appointed for her time, but as the crewed charter trade became increasingly competitive through the end of the last century, her older looks and dated accommodations made her unpopular compared to the newer catamarans and large custom yachts that appeared on the charter scene in the Caribbean in the late 1990s and onwards. This vessel was then sold to a liveaboard who let the maintenance slide and then she was resold for a loss to a fixer-upper fellow who hauled the boat and started working on her, but then lost interest and moved back to the continent. She sat for some time on land in a yard in the Caribbean where unbeknown to her owner, she picked up a colony of termites. She had by then been sold again to some young cruisers from Holland who sailed her for a few years, but when they discovered that she had gotten termites in her deck area, the owners panicked. There is probably nothing that scares a wooden boat owner more than the thought of bugs eating his or her hull out from under them, so the boat was sold for a mere $25K to an enterprising Englishman who also happened to be a shipwright. He simply tented the boat and fumigated it twice, eliminating the termites, and then went about repairing the relatively minor damage done. Once completed, the boat was almost as good as new and he sailed the boat across the Caribbean and eventually crossed the Pacific to New Zealand with few problems.

Another similar story involved an ex charter vessel that had termites in the deck. This was a more extensive issue and the owners finally just walked away. She was sold for her yard bill of $13K and the new owner fumigated the boat and sailed it just as it was to Trinidad, removed the old deck, and built an entirely new one. The hull was fine. For less than $40K he had a well-outfitted 53' sailboat and as far as I know, he is still sailing her today.

At the other end of the spectrum, there is the story of a Hinckley Standard I was involved in selling many years back. As one of the first true production line boats during the 1950s, Hinckley built the Standard 35 to be a cheap, easy to produce boat for the average family. This was in the days when Hinckley was more synonymous with what we might think of as a Hunter or Catalina quality vessel—A decent boat, but certainly not top quality. Compared to similar custom wooden boats of her era, she was cheaply built. This particular boat, when I first encountered her in the late 1980s, was in the possession of a professional boat builder who was out on a two-year cruise with his wife and two young boys. He had already replaced several planks, the transom had been rebuilt and the aging engine had been

doctored to keep it running. At the end of their cruise, they sold the boat for $17K. The new owners then replaced the keel bolts, had several more planks replaced and added new sails, and after a 20K additional investment, sold the boat a couple of years later for $20K. The next owners then replaced the engine, bought all new canvas, had her decks rebuilt, and refinished the hull for the umpteenth time, selling her a year and a half later for $25K. She now had owners who wanted to 'do her up right', so they took her to a boatyard on the Eastern Shore of Maryland and told the yard manager to make her perfect. $40K later they had a nice-looking boat which after two years was sold for $35K. Finally, she was purchased by a very wealthy family who spends on average $25-$30K a year maintaining the boat to a condition that might make her worth $40K on the open market should they ever sell her. So if you think about this, for all that was spent on this little wooden boat, one could have taken that same amount of money and purchased a brand new 35ft sailboat with a warranty and been sailing this whole time, rather than overseeing major overhauls... but then again, she was a HINCKLEY.

Wooden boats have a lifespan that can be long if significant money and labor are invested in their upkeep, but they can also have a very short lifespan if neglected. It's as simple as that. If you have the skills and are knowledgeable enough to know the difference between a real problem and a cosmetic one, then by all means consider a wooden boat.

Some excellent examples of well-built wooden yachts are still being produced in places like New Zealand and Canada, but great care must be taken in choosing one. Unless you are an expert yourself, hiring the best crotchety old marine surveyor who specializes in wooden boats is a must before taking the plunge into wooden boat ownership. While it is true that a properly built wooden boat can be easy to take care of, and with good basic skills most work can be done by a motivated amateur, it is important not to allow yourself to 'fall in love' with a boat's history, its pedigree, or its looks. It must be SOUND or only have problems that you can <u>easily see your way to solving</u>. If you see problems that you can't see a financially viable way of resolving, no matter how beautiful the vessel is, or how low the price, you should walk the other way, briskly.

After all of these somewhat scary stories, I do have to say that it is true that a properly built wooden boat can be a good choice for cruising. Good examples of some things to look for are boats that were built with single skin carvel planking and hefty framing. Cold-molded boats can be quite good as well but great care must be taken to ensure that no moisture has penetrated the kerfs between planks where it can become trapped, causing rot. I have seen perfectly sound-looking cold-molded hulls with a small soft spot on the inside of the hull that when opened up, revealed a six-foot area of the hull that had completely rotted the middle layers! Not a good thing to think about when you are plunging to windward into steep, short 8-10' seas! However, repairing that type of problem is not that difficult. Even remolding an entire section of a cold-molded hull is relatively easy and inexpensive if you do the work yourself. It is knowing about it first before buying that will give you the confidence to undertake the project and not get fleeced in the process.

Strip-planked boats were quite popular in the 1950s and onwards as it was easy to use a single male mold to build multiple hulls, thereby bringing production costs down. However, a strip planked boat can be one of the most difficult boats to repair. If considering one of these hulls, checking around the keelson, stem, and transom for soft wood will tell you whether to look any further. Find a problem there and your life of misery will only be starting.

Also generally to be avoided are boats that have, after the fact, been 'sheathed in glass'. This is typically done when a boat is too leaky to keep afloat any other way. What happens however is that once the skin is applied, any moisture trapped in the joints and voids, which invariably results in such a process, encourages pockets of rot to develop and it can spread like cancer underneath your pretty, shiny new exterior sheathing. If considering a boat that has been sheathed, know that you will always need to be wary of any separations in the outer skin from the planking and that these areas will need to be addressed immediately. And also consider that if the hull was weakened enough before the sheathing process that she was leaking badly, then there may be deeper problems that should have been addressed but are now covered up and difficult to assess. There are cases however where sheathed boats have lasted decades and occasionally you still see them out there today, but buyer beware.

One case however where a fiberglass skin on a wooden hull is not a bad thing is if it was applied at the time of original construction to a proper marine plywood or cold-molded hull. This final touch to a sound building process adds dimensional stability to an already strong hull and if you encounter a boat of this construction, it can last as long or longer than a similar fiberglass one.

When perusing the listings of boats for sale, if you encounter a wooden vessel that sounds promising, don't immediately dismiss it just because it is built of wood. Using the guidelines above, carefully assess whether it is worth looking into. If properly built and maintained, and if you have the skills and knowledge, and a desire to see yourself as the owner of a wooden vessel then by all means pursue it. Hire the best surveyor around and make sound decisions. You may just find yourself out there sailing in a vessel admired by almost everyone you encounter that takes you far and does so in safety and comfort. Be smart, be frugal, and shop carefully!

And What About the Rigging?

Whether your new-to-you boat has a fiberglass, metal, or wooden hull, in almost all cases it will have stainless-steel standing rigging.

Standing rigging can be quite costly to replace and as I said earlier, all too often surveyors will condemn perfectly safe and sound sets of standing rigging simply as a way of absolving themselves from the potential for liability. Checking around large boatyards for cast-off rigging wires sometimes yields perfectly good rigging and in many cases, thrown away fittings that can be reused by a bargain boater. I have seen perfectly good standing rigging removed and thrown away simply because the new owners of a boat wanted to start with new rigging or perhaps an owner was leaving on a major voyage and chose to replace the rigging just for the peace of mind this can provide.

Standing rigging is almost always replaced when the swaged fittings begin to show pitting or cracks, but in many cases, the actual wires are still fine, so locating older wires in good condition and cutting the fittings off, replacing them with Sta-Lok, Hi-Mod or older recycled Norseman fittings may allow you to re-rig a boat for pennies on the dollar and as long as common sense and careful periodic rigging inspections are carried out you may get many more years of service out of rigging wires that were considered 'throwaways'.

Furling gears are all too often replaced because they are getting older-looking or because of some simple defects that can in many cases be resolved, so when on a super tight budget, if you can't afford to just do a complete rerig or justify buying a new furling system to replace aging gear, consider this: Many of the quality old roller furling gears such as the Hood Seafurl IIs and the older NC series Profurls or older Harken gears can become very stiff to operate and in the case of the Hood gears, might develop small cracks at the pre-feeders that look scary but are inconsequential. These issues have caused many owners to have these units removed and discarded so new furling systems can be installed. In many instances, such as with the old Hood systems these bearings, which were stainless steel ball bearings in open races, can be washed out and will operate perfectly and the cracked pre-feeders can be cut off and re-spliced with no problems. Install a new stay wire or even a good used wire and you may have a perfectly serviceable gear for almost nothing. The same holds for some of the old Profurls which used simple easily-replaceable low-cost bearings and the older Harken gears can usually have bearings cleaned and even new toggle fittings installed to make them as strong as new. So finding a secondhand furler for little or nothing can sometimes save you thousands of dollars when upgrading your bargain cruiser.

Chapter Eight

How Safe is it Out There, and is it a Safe Place to Raise Children?

Having raised my kids to experience both sea and land-based life, I can honestly say that the years we spent cruising with the children and homeschooling them were much more productive and stand out in their memories far more so than the years we spent stuck in port while they attended land-based schools. I have a personal opinion that is based on observations from my many years of cruising, that children who are raised on a sailboat while cruising from country to country, living in close proximity to their parents and forced simply by availability to become friends with not just other children their ages, but with children of almost any age or culture as well as adults too, seem to have a much more self-confident way of carrying themselves when they reach adulthood. It seems to me that many kids these days spend too much time exclusively within their peer groups and devote much of their free hours to social media, while little time is spent doing important and useful jobs that are abundantly available to a cruising kid on a boat. That many of these children raised in our modern land-based society reach adulthood with very few life skills to draw upon, and are uncomfortable carrying on conversations with people who are from vastly different backgrounds, or who are much older or culturally different is a sad reflection on our current educational system.

Not so with cruising kids. Visit any anchorage anywhere in the world where cruising yachts with kids aboard are present and you will find well-adjusted, outgoing adventurous people. Firstly, the parents have to have been that way themselves to take on this lifestyle in the first place, but when living on a boat it is virtually impossible to just sit around watching TV or playing games for hours on end when there are so many jobs to be done and so many interesting activities to be involved in. Hiking, swimming, touring new cities, sailing overnight for days or weeks at a time all give children a wider sense of awe and wonder of the world around them. Just a single night watch shared with a parent at age nine or ten can give an opening to speak about many worldly things. Kids require constant input and that great big world out there is full of experiences that would be missed if they were living in a land-based setting with TV, homework, school, and after-school activities as their only diversions. Assign a thirteen-year-old the watch at night on a breezy passage and you will see their confidence soar. Trust them to take other kids out alone in the dinghy and to make wise decisions about safety and planning and you may observe a close mirror of your own decisions and actions.

I've heard some parents lament that they would like to take their kids sailing but felt that it was too dangerous. These dangers could be addressed in two groupings: civil dangers and natural dangers. Let's talk about civil dangers first.

While many people living in cities and larger communities have come to believe that they are only safe within the confines of their familiar surroundings, cruising teaches you that this is not so. I've found on our wanderings about the globe that life in some of our so-called civilized countries is far more dangerous than in the smaller, out of the way places. In general, I think it is safe to say that people tend to become numb to the dangers to which they have become accustomed and that once you make the break and head out into the wider world, you see that human nature is the same all over the world. From my observations, people are inherently predisposed to be kind and friendly, and only when you get in areas of the world where there are huge wealth disparities or overcrowded living environments and extreme poverty does crime and desperation cause people to become unkind, dishonest, or vengeful. My motto is to avoid these places altogether. I like to sail to small countries with relatively low population densities. On our wanderings in the Caribbean and across the Pacific I always tried to visit islands that are bypassed by most cruisers and even in the Caribbean, by visiting islands that are not so popular, you will likely find that people are often friendlier and kinder than the locals you may meet in the major tourist centers.

Having kids along really helps when making friends ashore! Kids are your best ambassadors to a new place. They often make friends easier and sometimes within a short time ashore I'd see the children playing with local kids or being given a tour of the village by a troupe of youngsters. My daughter's blond hair was often a huge sensation ashore when every child wanted to touch it and feel its texture.

One time we were in Caribbean Mexico and had just pulled into an anchorage where there were about a dozen boats with children aboard. These boats were from all over the world and we were the only American boat in the bay.

Within two days and after a few trips to the beach, a group of eleven children had formed and because we had sort of a 'pirate shippy' looking boat, they all wanted to come over. So the next day we had eleven children ages six to fourteen aboard speaking six languages. The only child who could speak and understand all the children was a six-year-old Swiss kid named Urs whose parents had raised him since a baby aboard their cruising catamaran as they sailed around the world. He became the interpreter for all the children and they had a fabulous day swinging out on the rigging, jumping in the water, playing hide and seek, and other games.

But what about piracy? When you tell some of your landlubber friends about your plans to sail the world, one of the first things they may bring up is concerns about piracy. How prevalent is it really and what can be done to minimize risk?

First of all, only three times in all my years of cruising to 37 countries have we run into anything which seemed dicey and the first time was in Apalachicola, Florida in 1988. We were tied up in a disused commercial basin which has since been renovated but at that time it was a free dock and we were preparing to head offshore across to Tampa the following morning.

It was early evening and a group of 'good old boys' came in on a pickup truck and parked not far from our boat. They were noisily drinking and laughing and started making lewd comments about my pretty wife and it was looking like they might start to cause some real trouble. I decided that was an excellent time to get my shotgun out and oil it down, I did this in the cockpit in a very visible manner and after a double-take from the guys, it didn't take long for them to decide to go have fun somewhere else.

The second time was while offshore between Nevis and Montserrat. We had left at 2:00 a.m. to arrive off Montserrat early enough to stop but still have enough time to sail on to Guadeloupe if conditions were favorable. However, it was a pretty windy night with a good six- to eight-foot seaway running when at about 4:00 a.m one of the (at that time) very prevalent bright orange inter-island wooden freight boats was closing us on a convergent course. I altered course to give better clearance and they changed their course to close with us. As they got closer still, I once again changed course and they again changed course until they were getting quite close. I now saw that there were about fifteen guys on deck and they were moving around to get on the side closest to us. As they closed to within shouting range, I yelled loudly at the top of my lungs to my sleeping wife below "Get me the shotgun!" I did this loudly enough so that it could be heard on the freight boat which was now only about 20' away and I slammed the tiller over to turn 90 degrees away. They passed us just a few feet away and continued into the night. To this day I wonder if they might have just been coming by to say hello or to ask for their position, or to offer fish in trade? But it seemed dicey at the time. It's also possible that they had just been opportunists and who knows what their real intentions were, but I sure didn't want to find out!

The only other incident I have had was off the northern coast of Venezuela in 2010. This was at the height of a period when several cruising boats had been attacked and so we were already on high alert but had planned to sail to Puerto La Cruz despite the dangers on the belief that the odds were in our favor and that we would be fine.

We spent a pleasant couple of days anchored at Los Testigos, a small group of islands about forty miles east of Isla Margarita which was the closest port we could clear in at and we had gotten an early start that morning. At about 10:00 a.m. my youngest son, then seventeen, was alone at the helm, and the other three crew members and I were all resting below. My son called me from where I was resting and when I poked my head up through the scuttle, he motioned with his head to starboard and said, "These guys have been following us for about ten minutes. What do you think?"

I looked over at the boat which was about 200 meters off our starboard stern quarter. It was a 30' or so panga-type open boat with a big outboard (a type commonly used for fishing nearshore waters) with three men onboard. As I looked at them through my binoculars, they huddled and then put bandanas over their faces and turned to speed directly toward us. I immediately yelled down below to the crew, "Everybody up on deck. Now Now Now!!"

As my sleepy crew all cambered up into the cockpit, the panga drew alongside but upon seeing so many people aboard, the panga crew hesitated, again briefly huddled, and then abruptly stopped their boat and turned for the coast. Was it an averted pirate attack? Possibly. But we were certainly asking for trouble sailing in waters that we knew to be potentially risky! Would I sail to Venezuela again? Probably not. But these three instances are the only dicey situations we have run into in all our years of sailing to 37 countries, and the first incident was in the United States!

In 2011, we were about a hundred miles off the Pacific coast of Colombia on our way to Ecuador when a lone fishing panga approached us from seaward. As it drew alongside we were addressed in good English. "I saw your flag and wanted to see if you would like some fish!"

He had been tending to the nets for several days and was eager for company. After a short exchange, we gave him some beer and we got some fresh fish and waved to each other as we parted.

We were anchored in a remote area of the Turks and Caicos when three men in a small boat approached us and asked if we were fishing and reminded us that taking conch was not legal here. When we said we were aware of that, they asked us how many people were aboard. When I told them we had six people aboard, they huddled and then handed up a bag of six cleaned conchs, wished us a good day, and sped away.

While I honestly believe that the Venezuelan guys were up to no good, we could have avoided that situation entirely if we had just not gone to an area where there was a known danger of piracy. In the case of the good old boys in Florida, they probably didn't present a real threat and were just being loudmouthed. And to this day I wonder if the orange freight boat was just lost and needed a position to get pointed back in the right direction. In those days it was not uncommon for local freight boats to navigate by line of sight and charts or even a simple compass were sometimes luxuries absent aboard those vessels!

All in all, in my forty-plus years of cruising the world's oceans I would say that in general, safety from predators is not a major concern. Stick to spending your cruising time in areas that are known to be safe and remember that most people, deep down, are good by nature.

The 'natural' dangers many land-based people think about are typically not of concern on a boat. We rarely deal with high speed traffic for example. But of course, ocean sailing with children onboard does require careful planning and certain safety precautions. There are many excellent books on the subject of preparing a boat for cruising with children and in most cases, common sense is the most obvious element. We always netted out boats completely when the kids were young and insisted, even on daysails, that the kids have a safety harness on and attached. Kids can be impulsive and it's just not worth it to risk seeing a little one slip over the side when an extra few seconds to be sure they are safely clipped-in takes such a small effort. But when sailing in calm waters or in port we rarely made our kids wear a life jacket on deck once they had proven their ability to swim.

Because addressing all of the concerns and issues that a cruising family may encounter while sailing the world's oceans could easily take up an entire book of its own, I strongly recommend Behan Gifford's excellent volume entitled *'Voyaging with Kids—A Family Guide to Life Afloat'* in which she provides fabulous insights and recommendations from her own family's many years of world cruising.

World cruising with children is to me the most exciting and wonderful upbringing any parent could ever provide for their children. The many years I spent sailing with my kids stand in my memory as the best years of my life and when I ask my now-adult children about their recollections of their school-age years, the most vivid memories certainly seem to be of the many countries we visited and of the natural wonders we all witnessed

Chapter Nine

What Can Go Wrong and How Can I Prevent It?

One of the biggest aspects of the cruising lifestyle that keeps people from ranging far and wide is the realization that there are significant potential dangers out there and that preparing for these eventualities is a daunting and sometimes bewildering task. Much of the apprehension that comes to the surface stems from two areas: experiential, and preparatory.

As far as experience goes, it might be said that there is simply no better way to learn than to go out and just try. Like the star of the early nineties sailing movie, Captain Ron said, "If anything's going to happen, it's going to happen out there!" But of course, good judgment dictates that having a basic understanding of the mechanics of operating a boat is essential and these skills can either be learned incrementally on your own in a safe area (hopefully on a small boat), or more quickly by taking a sailing course, or better yet and more in keeping with our goals of staying within a tight budget, by sailing with friends that can show you the ropes.

Nathanael Herreshoff, the legendary yacht designer often referred to as the 'Wizard of Bristol' and who was also the father of one of the first cruising yacht designers, L Francis Herreshoff, once said (and I paraphrase here): "One should learn to sail on a small centerboard boat, and then never set foot in one again." This is because a smaller boat will respond very quickly to trim and handling and will let you know right away if you are doing something wrong. An ever-increasing trend we are seeing these days is for people to go into big boat sailing with a knowledge base of zero, buy a boat based on reading books or watching Youtube videos and attending boat shows, then try to learn to operate it on their own or with just a few days practice with a captain or friend. This may be okay in some cases, but especially with larger boats, learning this way can lead to potential problems should things go wrong. And so this brings us to the second aspect of being prepared, and this is all about maintenance and preparations.

Entire books could be and have been written about what you can do to maintain a boat properly and one thing I can say with certainty is that if you wish to become a budget cruiser and to live a lifestyle far away from the infrastructures of modern shore-based society with their marinas, mechanics, and boatyards, then keeping your boat as simple and easy to maintain as possible is of the utmost importance.

Too many times in my world travels I have seen people stuck in a port waiting for some critical part that is needed for a system the owners of the boat have decided they can't live without like a bow thruster, diesel generator, a watermaker, air conditioning, or a washing machine and the more complicated a boat becomes, the more often you are likely to be dealing with maintaining or replacing these systems regularly.

It goes beyond the scope of this book to get into how one learns to sail and operate their boat, but along these lines, being prepared for eventualities in many cases has to do with knowing your boat well and having a good understanding of how to repair things and keep them operating smoothly. And if you're going to accomplish this on a tight budget, this means scrounging for spares when the opportunity presents and by doing maintenance and repairs yourself.

I can't tell you how many tens of thousands of dollars I've saved over the years by going to marine consignment stores and shopping on eBay or even checking boatyard dumpsters for cast-off equipment. Checking Facebook 'Treasures of the bilge' sites or posting 'parts wanted' can save a lot of money in the long term while outfitting a boat. It's also important to carry critical spare parts. While it may be true that while cruising in areas like the Bahamas or Eastern Caribbean it is possible to find parts fairly easily, in many areas of the world it can be exceptionally difficult to find spare parts and so on especially vulnerable or esoteric systems like pumps, hydraulics, rigging, or electronics, finding spares for some of the more critical components and carefully cataloging them and storing them aboard can turn a potentially disastrous breakdown into a minor inconvenience. Imagine losing your autopilot's computer brain halfway across the Pacific and having to hand steer for 2,000 miles when, if only you had been prepared in advance, it could have meant just a half-hour spent changing out the computer module to have you back on your way? Or how about finding a cracked fitting in your rigging and needing to jury rig for thousands of miles until a spare part could be procured when a little planning might have allowed for a simple repair resulting in 100% integrity? Or how about losing your pressure water pump and having to suction or foot pump water for a few months until a spare could be found when careful planning might have allowed you to just replace the bad unit in a short time?

Being prepared means not only knowing your boat is in good shape, and understanding how to service its systems, but it should also include anticipating what could go wrong and being prepared for this by carrying extensive spares onboard.

Getting along well with your crew is a vitally important aspect of making your life afloat more enjoyable and safer too.

A little over a decade ago I found myself the owner of a 64' brigantine and ended up in Central and South America, cruising on both the Pacific and Caribbean coasts. With the last of my children now grown up and out on their own, the 'free labor' to help me run the ship was gone and so we had to resort to finding a crew to assist in the operation of the boat. With nine working sails and only two tiny winches, the chore of raising and lowering the heavy gaff sails using block and tackle and the furling and unfurling of square sails and topsails was a lot of work for a crew of four and darn near backbreaking for a couple, so we began to take on various adventurers and charged them a nominal amount for 'room and board' while we sailed from country to country. Because we had a virtual revolving door of these mostly younger people aboard, I found that posting a set of shipboard guidelines to refer to helped tremendously and I wrote the following specifically for that little ship's crew, but most of what is here will translate easily to almost any vessel, and even with a crew of just two, may provide some valuable insights to help promote shipboard harmony.

Common Sense Shipmate Guidelines

For those of us who undertake long offshore passages or extended coastal voyages aboard sailing vessels, our highest priorities are that the times we spend aboard be as pleasant and safe as possible. To that end, a captain may want to write down a few basic guidelines to provide to new crew members which, if followed, should allow for a good experience for all. Over the years and while running our old brigantine *One World*, which carried on occasion crews of up to nine, we developed some basic rules that contributed tremendously toward a better overall environment for all those onboard. Although

common sense is certainly the basis for any guidelines aboard an offshore cruising yacht, we have found that some of the specific key points that should be addressed with any new crew as they come aboard before a cruise of more than a few days are as follows:

1) On a vessel that has only one main common area, privacy is important. For this reason, when someone is in the head or their cabin, or even in a pilot berth just a few feet away attempting to read or rest, do not speak to them. If it is imperative to do so, knock first if there is a door or tap gently on a nearby bulkhead to get their attention and await an answer. Do not speak through walls unless invited to do so. Although mostly an illusion, the privacy that a few feet and a bulkhead can provide goes a long way toward improving shipboard harmony. If you're in the head and make noise, the illusion that maybe others can't hear you helps preserve dignity. In no case should comments ever be made about sounds or disturbances that happened 'behind closed doors' unless they are brought up first by the person or people responsible, and then perhaps pretending you didn't hear might be a nice way to help them relieve any embarrassment or unease. In the Caribbean charter industry, there is an 'urban legend' that we've all heard. It's the story of the four couples, all best friends, who show up for a charter and take a small four-cabin sloop out for a week. A week later the eight former best friends fly home, never to speak to each other again. This could very likely be because this first rule was not observed.

2) If you get it out, put it back. With several people aboard, putting things back where they go is imperative. With a larger crew, losing important items can be frustrating, or in some cases even dangerous. A misplaced stuffing box wrench or spare bilge pump handle might be a good example. If you use a tool, put it back. Drink a cold beer, put a warm one in the fridge. Run out of toilet

paper, put in a new roll. If you empty the water pitcher, refill it, and so forth. If you dig a sail or some other piece of gear out, put it back in a neat and organized manner. Keeping the boat tidy and shipshape makes for a more pleasant and safer environment for everyone.

3) In the galley: If you are cooking, be neat. Put things away when possible, when not in use. Keep the galley sink clear and walkways unencumbered. When doing the dishes, the dishes are not done until all flatware, silverware, and cooking utensils are put back where they belong, and the counters and stovetop are all clean. The heavy washing up should perhaps be done using a saltwater tap or on deck with saltwater in a bucket unless there is enough water to use fresh for this.

Knives from the knife block or main knife drawer do not leave the galley, ever. If you need a knife on deck, there should be at least one for this purpose. Ask if you cannot find it.

4) Plates and cups brought up to the cockpit or on deck during your watch do not stay out in the cockpit or on deck after your watch. Stepping inadvertently on a plate or cup carelessly left in the cockpit or on a side deck can cause an injury.

5) Laundry: do your own. Maybe coordinate this with what else is going on so that there are no issues of hanging clothes getting caught in running rigging and so that wash or rinse water can be shared. Be sure to plan early on choosing your laundry day. Undertaking a large scale washing might not be such a great idea if squally weather is anticipated, numerous sail changes or many course alterations are in the works, or on the final day of a passage when many other things may be occurring on deck at the same time.

6) When showering, clean the shower drain screen and wipe down the shower area after your use. There is nothing worse than cleaning out someone else's hair from the drain except for one thing: seeing a dirty toilet bowl! Remember, when showering, to wet down, then turn off the water and lather up, then rinse off. This saves a lot of water. If the toilet bowl is not clean after your use, use the brush or toilet paper to wipe it out. Be sure to close the intake valve on the toilet if flooding can occur and never put toilet paper or anything else (like tampons) in the toilet. On many marine toilets, even a small piece of paper can clog the valves and make it necessary to disassemble the dirty toilet to repair it. Not a pleasant job in port and much more unpleasant when in a significant seaway.

7) Running rigging: Always put it back on the cleat or pin or line organizer designated for that line, and always do it the same way. Never take shortcuts or just hang it on the cleat or leave it in a loose coil next to a winch. If a squall comes up or it is forgotten, it could end up over the side and wrapped in the prop or rudder. We never want to see the sheets or halyards lying in a pile on deck. Halyards need to be coiled or flaked and put away immediately after use. This is just good seamanship.

8) Dinghies: If you put a kayak, rowing dingy, or SUP (Stand Up Paddleboard) in, or launch the inflatable; when you are done with it, put it back! You can pass this responsibility on to someone else if arrangements are made in advance and they want to use the craft after you. No exceptions. In advance of launching, make arrangements with the people who will help you put it back.

9) Switching water tanks: Never switch the water tanks unless you have cleared this with the captain and written it in the logbook. If we run out of water on a passage, we could all die. The captain must be informed before you switch tanks, not one or two or three days after! Unless previously cleared with the captain, the pressure water should not be used on a passage. We've seen entire tanks emptied because the weather was bad and a tired crew accidentally left the tap partially on. This happened twice on one passage years ago and five people were left with 17 gallons of water and a broken watermaker to last five days until port. Enough said.

10) Always wear your safety harness offshore at night or when under a downwind rig. A cruising sailboat can be very hard to stop quickly when under poled out sails or spinnaker rig. Wearing your harness on deck is a rule even in nice sunny weather when alone on deck offshore. Even on a clear day, if someone goes over the side, they can become quickly lost in the waves astern. If an hour or more were to pass before the missing crew was noticed, the chances of recovery would be slim indeed. If you go aloft on mast steps or ratlines, clip-on as you go up. We want you to stay alive and unbroken.

11) Use common sense with provisions. If you use up all the butter baking or most of any one thing on special non-essential foods, then we could run out. Save making special things for special occasions and when we are near re-provisioning points. In short, check with the Captain or First Mate before using large amounts of individual items or for use of essential staples or basic provisions.

12) Garbage: when on an offshore (not coastal!) passage or out cruising in remote areas where garbage disposal onshore is not an option, never put food or paper wrappers, coffee grounds, or anything that could spoil in the garbage. Throw it over the side. Plastics and toxins are the only things that

go in the garbage; all other things go over the side. Paper products should be cut up into small pieces and cans have bottoms cut out or crushed so they sink, but should never be disposed of in coastal waters.

13) Salty people: if you are salty, do not come below. If you are salty but your clothing is still basically dry, towel yourself off with a special towel that you have designated for this purpose. Saltwater is the enemy of a boat's interior and is death to electronics. Never come below dripping in saltwater. If possible, rinse off on deck with freshwater or towel dry with your special (salty) towel. The salty towels and clothing should be washed out with fresh water on deck or hung to dry and shaken before bringing them below.

To us, these thirteen points represent the most important issues to consider when sailing with a crew offshore. Following these simple rules may seem a bit silly to some, but through trial and error, we have found that following these guidelines can make for a safer, more relaxing, and harmonious experience for everyone aboard.

Chapter Ten

Where are the Least Expensive and Best Places to Sail?

While many of your land-based friends might imagine that world cruising is all about sailing off to Tahiti or the Mediterranean or cruising the Eastern Caribbean chain endlessly, sipping umbrella drinks on the beaches of fabulous resorts, and staying in fancy marinas, the reality of budget cruising is that while sailing these areas on a tight budget is certainly possible, staying around resorts and marinas will run up the expenses and these types of places must be avoided at all cost! There are still plenty of inexpensive places to sail in this world and some of them offer the most pristine and uncrowded cruising anywhere on the planet.

All too often sailing destinations that have become overly popular also become ultra-expensive and as soon as the charter fleets start to move into an area you can forget about it being affordable, or pristine. Overcrowding of harbors with private and charter vessels leads to indifference on the part of the locals and greed and capitalist ideals can often take the place of hospitality and friendly encounters.

I've heard many people who are cruising the Caribbean say they want to sail the Pacific but were not going because they'd heard it's too expensive and I've also heard people say that cruising the Caribbean isn't any fun; all the anchorages are too crowded. But we have cruised some areas of the Caribbean that are off the beaten path and have had entire bays to ourselves. And in the Pacific, most people take the same route across from Panama stopping at the Galapagos, Marquesas, Tahiti, the Southern Cooks and Vavau, Tonga, and down to New Zealand. But there are many other routes one can take!

We had been anchored at Niuatoputapu in the Niua Group, a remote area of northern Tonga for a few weeks and were the only boat in the anchorage. Because the Niua Islands are somewhat off the normal cruising routes, so far that year only nine boats had entered the well-sheltered lagoon. Suddenly one morning eleven new boats came in over just a few hours. These sailors were part of the 'Pacific Puddle Jumpers', a loosely run rally-type event that leaves yearly from the west coast of Central America. They were traveling across the Pacific as a 'group' and suddenly the character of the anchorage changed. When I spoke to one of the captains on shore the next day, I asked him how he liked cruising the Pacific so far and he said, "Well, I'm a bit disappointed actually. Everywhere we go is so expensive and the locals aren't friendly, and it seems like the anchorages are all too crowded."

We had just spent six months meandering off the beaten track in remote Eastern Kiribati and the Northern Cooks and had in several cases been the only boat to visit an island in months.

We had been invited into people's homes and there had been parties thrown in our honor, all just because we'd shown up! His statement made me realize that a world cruising voyage is truly what you make of it. They were choosing to travel in a big pack of friends to all the popular spots while we preferred to travel alone to areas less visited. I can guarantee we had a more authentic experience and I'm sure we spent a lot less money too!

Granted, if you want to visit the BVI, the Grenadines, or Saint Martin during the high season, the anchorages will be crazy busy and prices for things onshore will be sky-high, but there are many areas of the Caribbean that aren't so expensive and some that are darn right cheap to visit!

For example, Panama is still a very inexpensive area to cruise. With shores on both the Caribbean and the Pacific Ocean, there is a lot of coastline in Panama and quite a few offshore islands to explore too. The cost of living in Panama is quite low and the boatyards are generally much more reasonable than elsewhere in the Caribbean basin.

Guatemala and the Bay Islands of Honduras are great places to sail on a limited budget. Food and basic supplies are inexpensive, and boatyards and services are substantially less costly than first-world prices.

Even the Bahamas can be an inexpensive area to cruise provided you do significant provisioning in the USA, Puerto Rico, or St. Martin before you sail there. Plan on living on the hook, diving for your food, and avoiding bars and restaurants, (when you happen across one) and you can get by on very little for a good portion of each year. Granted, it's a good thing to support local businesses and we do often try to shop in the small outlying islands or visit a local bar or restaurant from time to time to give the small business owners a little revenue, but staying away from the bigger towns will almost always save you money in the long run. Many 'snowbirds' come to certain areas like Georgetown in the Exumas and anchor amongst many hundreds

of other boats, never leaving until the following spring, and yet you can sail just a day or two away to one of the far out islands and have the place all to yourselves. The fishing is still good in the more remote areas and since there's almost no place to spend money in the out islands, you can often get by with spending little or nothing.

While we haven't cruised in Indonesia and Malaysia, many of our friends who have spent years there report ultra-low prices, many pristine anchorages, and beautiful, friendly people.

In the South Pacific, Fiji has a very low cost of living and offers some of the most rarely visited, cruiser-friendly, English-speaking islands and villages in the world. With a population of less than a million that is mostly centered on the two main islands of Viti Levu and Vanua Levu, many of the outlying islands are sparsely inhabited or in many cases entirely devoid of people. The waters surrounding Fiji are navigationally challenging so have kept the bareboat charter fleets at bay and perhaps because of this, yachties are still welcomed where visits ashore are, in many of the more remote villages, a rare event. The area is so large that one could spend years cruising this vast archipelago without seeing every anchorage.

If you are an American and want a little taste of the good ole USA for a bit without leaving the deep South Pacific, American Samoa has a very good all-weather anchorage at Pago Pago on the island of Tutuila. Goods and services can be readily had there and it's a great place to spend a portion of each season before going back to Tonga or Fiji, just a few hundred miles away.

The Philippines are even more vast in scope and while more heavily populated, are also the cruising base for hundreds of yachties each year. Again, a super low cost of living and myriad islands are the attraction.

Mexico's Sea of Cortez, even after all these years and with the introduction of new yachting facilities and more and more boats each year is still a beautiful and inexpensive place to cruise. Costs there in many areas are about half of what it might be to cruise in the USA and it's still possible to have many anchorages to yourselves.

Mainland Ecuador only has a few anchorages but offers at least one safe and secure place to leave your boat while exploring inland. Shoreside costs are ultra-low and public transport is readily available and inexpensive.

Even in some of the most popular cruising grounds, it's still possible to spend little by provisioning well when prices are low on key items and buying from farmers and fishermen as opposed to stocking up at supermarkets. In many places, the public markets offer substantial savings and are lots of fun to shop at too. If you're on a tight budget and in a major country, many times you will find that the big supermarkets throw outdated food away. In virtually every case this stuff is perfectly fine, but once an expiration date is reached, it has to go. While we have not personally done this, we have met budget cruisers who have taken to 'dumpster diving' at some of the big 'first world' stores right after the shelves are cleared of old produce. A quick trip to a well-stocked dumpster can save hundreds of dollars and in many cases, the produce you might find will last just as long as the items you might have bought that very same day in the store.

While cruising, always try to avoid marinas. Even haul-outs can usually be done inexpensively if you bring your own materials and pull the boat at a small commercial yard as opposed to one in a major yachting center. With a cat or full keel boat in an area of large tides, bottom maintenance can often be done on a steeply shelved beach or alongside an old wharf.

Investing in good tools and proper work safety gear so you can easily and inexpensively do your own labor is the best way to go when taking on major jobs, but if you do need help on especially big projects, consider putting them off until you can undertake them in a country where labor rates are low. Many people save substantially by getting major work done in places like Mexico, Panama, Malaysia, or Fiji where local labor is skilled and inexpensive. However, even in the USA, relatively inexpensive boatyards and reasonable labor can be found by searching the net for other cruiser's experiences. Staying out of major yachting centers and away from big boatyards is almost always the best plan when cruising on a tight budget.

Chapter Eleven

Choosing Ocean Worthy Yachts That Represent Tremendous Value

The best used boat bargains of all time are out there right now. Thanks to the longevity of fiberglass construction, and the superior modern coating methods for metal hulls, more boats are out there for sale today than ever before. Knowing what to look for and what to avoid can be made much easier with the help of a good yacht broker or marine surveyor, but here are some guidelines and suggestions of what to look for, and what to avoid.

When you are concerned about value, a good place to start is to look at some of the well-made fiberglass production designs of the late 1960s to early 1990s. The early 1970s began what I often refer to as 'The golden age of fiberglass boat-building'. Along with a general awakening to the need for a clean environment and a popular movement to simplify one's life and 'get back to nature', small to medium-size sailboat production exploded all over America and Europe during this decade.

During postwar World War II years and until the late 1960s, most sailors who participated in offshore sailing were racers and so yacht design in this era was primarily driven by two racing rules. The CCA (Cruising Club of America) rating system for North America and the RORC (Royal Ocean Racing Club) rule for Europe, both of which encouraged vessels with long overhangs and short waterlines that were created to heel a lot and thereby increase their moving waterline length. But because these two rating rules fostered somewhat different design parameters, a general call for a true international offshore racing (IOR) rule was needed. This took a few

years to fine-tune and develop and so with the anticipation of the IOR racing rule for sailboats, many builders created racing boats that also proved to be excellent offshore cruisers. With shorter overhangs and generally wider beams, combined with high ballast to displacement ratios resulted (at least initially) in the creation of vessels like the Swan 40s and 43s, the American 'clones' such as the Tartan series or some of Pearson's designs and a general rush to fill the need for vessels with better overall seakeeping and sail carrying capabilities arose. It was through this rule, which penalized deck length, that the first reverse transom vessels began to appear. Although through later exploitation of the rule's loopholes, quite a few very ugly and even some unsafe designs were ultimately built and marketed, overall, the earliest vessels built to the new rule often made terrific cruisers once additional tankage and some interior modifications were made. Many of these early IOR designs have proven themselves on countless passages and long-term cruises.

Simultaneously, an emerging trend for certain sailors to want to go ocean sailing but not participate in racing created a demand for more ruggedly built and perhaps less svelte cruising yachts. So, boats like the Westsail 32, the William Garden type full-keel ketches and some of the traditional New England working craft inspired designs all became touchstone vessels that spawned an explosion of clones and copies, many of which are still sailing the world's oceans today.

Boats became lighter and larger below for their given size during the late 80s and many experienced offshore cruisers think that by the early 90s, most of the moderately priced models being produced were no longer as seaworthy or sea-kindly as their earlier cousins. With the exploitation and eventual demise of the IOR rule, racing boats were no longer as well suited for cruising as earlier designs and it appeared to many that yacht architects and builders created designs based upon decisions made by boardrooms and committees, concerned more with how a boat would look at a boat show dock than how it would stand a blow far offshore. Marketing decisions dictated the boat-building practices that became predominant in the industry. Today, with the cost of a new 35-40' boat settling in at the range of $250K or more, many people are looking into older, quality vessels that can be purchased at a fraction of the cost of a new boat and then refitted to serve their purposes.

Although there have been many 'so-called' advances in yacht design in recent years, you can't cheat the sea. Our forebearers knew the sea well and through hundreds of years of refinement, certain types of hull forms evolved that formed the basis for many of the cruising boats built during the 'Golden Age' of fiberglass boatbuilding. Today, however, many of the design attributes of modern buoy racers have unfortunately found their way into cruising designs and more often than not, interior layouts built for life at dockside have dictated the hull forms that carry them.

Most of the arguments for building lighter displacement, lower wetted-surface boats have been based on supposed performance advantages and yet, a Westsail 32, one of the most traditional and heavy displacement cruising designs out there has proven itself in many recent ocean races, challenging the myth of weight vs speed. In ideal conditions with small waves and light winds, a modern lightweight hull form is of course potentially much faster than a traditional heavy hull, but in a real seaway and a big breeze, all bets are off. In many cases, the traditional heavy boat, designed and developed to sail in real ocean conditions is superior, far more comfortable, and safer than a modern design and is more likely to deliver its crew comfortably to the next port. In a recent long offshore race, a Westsail 32 placed second behind an ultralight displacement all-out race boat and might have won had a gear failure not occurred. In the 1996 Annapolis Bermuda race, a friend of mine sailed to a win in his division on my own former Westsail 32, fully loaded down for cruising with a big dinghy on deck, wind generator and solar panels out in the breeze, and a windvane self-steering gear dragging off the stern, arriving only hours behind some of the all-out racers whose crews sat on the windward rail the whole way out, sailing boats stripped out with no cushions or doors below decks to save weight! It's no secret, veteran cruisers Lyn and Larry Pardey said it decades ago: If you own a traditional heavy displacement boat, keep the bottom clean and use big light air sails when they're called for.

I believe there is entirely too much time spent in books and magazines comparing keel and rudder shapes, oversimplifying yacht design as if looking at the side view of a hull might tell you how a boat will handle. The hull form is much more important than the shape of the keel! If you look at canoe and kayak designs, you will see that subtle differences in hull forms can yield quite different handling characteristics. Lake canoes will track straight all day long and yet are difficult to turn quickly whereas whitewater canoes can spin on a dime but are challenging to steer in a straight line. Canoes don't have large keels! To simplify yacht design with a statement like, "Full keels track better but are poor upwind performers," or "Fin keels sail upwind better and are more maneuverable," is overly simplistic. The main thing that makes a rudder more, or less, effective is how large it is and how far aft it's hung and what the hull form in front of it is like, not whether it is attached to a keel, a skeg, or is a separate spade.

Another argument for modern fin keel designs is that they are easier to back up in a crowded marina, which is usually true. However, in many cases, the increased lateral plane (wetted surface) of a full or long keeled boat can make it easier to back up than a fin keel boat with a flat bottom that prefers to walk sideways until way is on. And unless your chosen lifestyle will mean that you are backing and out of tight marina slips regularly, the perceived ease of maneuvering in a marina should hardly be a primary reason for choosing a particular type of hull design! While sailing fast in big seas, a skegged or attached rudder is also much less likely to stall at high angles of attack. Evidence of this is easily observed in the many photos and descriptions of spade rudder boats that have broached while reaching or running in big sea conditions after a helmsman overcorrected, causing the rudder to stall, or simply lost control surfing down a wave. Airplanes can take off and land at low speeds with wings that are still able to maintain lift at large angles of attack because of the laminar flow created by flaps extending off the main wing surface. Imagine this when looking at an attached, skegged rudder or full keel versus what you might have when expecting a spade rudder to remain effective when at a large angle of attack. Spade rudders will stall just like an airplane wing would if it has not deployed its flaps.

Another important attribute of the more traditional long keel or full keel yachts is that they are much easier to handle in lumpy, confused seas. High aspect ratio fin keel boats can become so difficult to steer in a confused sea state that an autopilot or windvane cannot handle them and they must be hand steered. This is not an acceptable scenario for a husband and wife team on a long passage. While possible, it is surely not an enjoyable way to spend hours and hours during inclement weather. Owning

a boat that tracks well under windvane or autopilot while the person on watch sits safely and comfortably tucked in under the dodger is a far better situation and leads to a happier, well-rested crew.

Let's talk about sea-kindliness. When was the last time you saw the term 'sea-kindly' used in a new boat advertisement? Many traditional types of boats have fairly complex 'wineglass' type hull forms; very difficult to design and very comfortable at sea as they typically do not present large flat surfaces to the waves in any one orientation. A comfortable, easy motion for your yacht should be one of the highest priorities when you are choosing your new cruising home. However, some of the more recent so-called 'traditional' designs have simplistically designed hulls which are nothing more than rounded or flattened bowl-shaped bottoms that roll and pound just like their lightweight fin keeled sisters.

The strength issue is rarely argued and even among modern light displacement proponents, you will hear a consensus that heavy boats are stronger. In recent years I've heard many newer lightweight boat sailors say that their boats are "strong enough." How strong is strong enough when you are in storm conditions, or if you hit an unlit adrift steel buoy, a partially submerged container, or a whale while traveling at eight knots on a pitch-black, new moon night? Steel is generally more robust than even the stoutest of fiberglass boats, but an older heavily built fiberglass hull, strongly constructed and in good condition can withstand incredible punishment. I have yet to hear a long-distance cruising sailor who has told me they wished their boat had a thinner hull and was less sturdy!

We've all heard the 'urban legend' argument that older fiberglass boats were built heavily because the designers and builders didn't know how strong the material was and so were reluctant to 'lighten up' the scantlings. This is not entirely accurate. Remember that typically, most designers and many builders were also engineers and certainly knew the structural characteristics of the materials they were building with. The simple fact is that when fiberglass construction was first introduced, it was a mistrusted material in many sailor's eyes and because most of the early designs that were built were simply fiberglass reproductions of popular wooden types, they had to weigh the same as their wooden cousins or they would not have floated on their lines! To many experienced sailors, it appears that because of budget constraints and marketing decisions made in boardrooms, modern boats have become lighter and flimsier, and advertising departments have sought to convince us that this is for performance and livability!

As anyone who owns a classic boat knows, aesthetics is a big part of a sailor's enjoyment. When other boaters photograph your boat, there is a pride of ownership that makes some of the aspects of keeping an older boat in great shape a little easier.

Aesthetics, sea-kindliness, performance, value, and strength are all great reasons to own an older, quality boat. Longevity is in your favor and there is little doubt that some of the purpose-built hefty cruising boats built in the '60s through the '90s will be around well into the end of the 21st century. Our grandchildren's children may well own a 100-year-old 1965 full keel cruiser on its fourth engine and sixth set of sails!

There are of course shortcomings with every boat type. Heavy displacement boats need much bigger hardware, sails, ground tackle, and rigging, etc., that cost more for overall length than they would for a lighter and larger boat. To reuse our example of the Westsail 32: those vessels have a rig as big as many 38-footers and the ground tackle you might expect to find on a modern 42' boat.

When you go shopping for one of these older boats, it is important to keep in mind that upgrading or replacing engines, rigs, sails, electronics, rebuilding interiors, or rewiring can drive the investment up well beyond the original purchase price. Even despite this, with careful shopping, you may well end up with a much

better, stronger, and more comfortable boat than you could have purchased new for even multiples of the amount of your investment. Shop carefully and have fun!

Here are some suggestions for some of the best bets where your investment of time and money could be rewarded with a strong, handsome cruiser at a very good value.

Following is a list of boats worth considering along with approximate price ranges in 2020s dollars. Assuming average condition and requiring the usual outfitting and improvements, these vessels represent particularly good values compared to other types but it should be noted that this is by no means a list of the ONLY great boats out there and even a full listing of all my personal favorites would likely miss many terrific designs. And of course, the area you are shopping in will likely yield locally built vessels that may be fantastic seaboats, but that may not be well-known on the world market. Sometimes these 'obscure' designs can be fantastic value simply because most potential buyers might pass them over due to unfamiliarity.

While you are shopping for your dreamboat, the best advice is to cruise the net, talk to a good broker (if you can find one!), and find a marine surveyor with offshore experience that you trust who can give you sound advice. Experts like Robert Perry, John Neal, Paul Exner, and others are available on a consultation basis as well and they will often supply you with their personal favorites as you go searching for your bargain cruising boat!

There are lots of great older boats out there. Begin with how you want your boat to be equipped, then work backward from the price of your complete cruiser and you should be able to make a logical purchase. Get out there cruising sooner! You may be happier, and will certainly be wealthier, and may own a better boat than if you had purchased new

Contessa 26

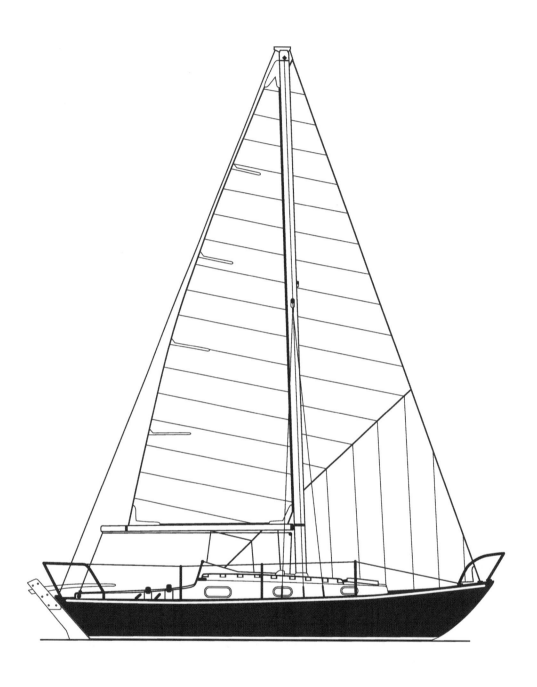

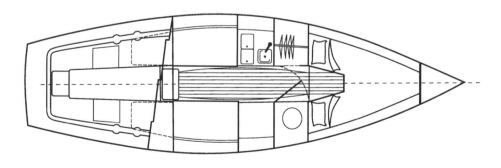

Chapter Twelve

Forty-Two Examples of the Best Bargain Cruising Boats of All Time

Boats Under 30 Feet

Contessa 26

The Contessas became quite famous when from 1985 to 1987 a plucky teenager by the name of Tania Aebi became the youngest woman to circumnavigate the world sailing one of these terrific able little sailboats. A few years later B.J. Caldwell became the youngest person to circumnavigate at that time in a sistership and many epic voyages have been realized aboard these svelte pocket cruisers.

Basically a hybridized Folkboat hull built in fiberglass, the Contessa was an enormously successful design with good sailing characteristics and generally fine sea keeping abilities. Originally produced in the UK from 1966 to 1977, in the late seventies J.J. Taylor of Toronto, Canada began production, building around 400 boats and these are typically what you may find on the used market in the USA or Canada.

A bit wet when going to weather, they make up for this by being relatively dry and comfortable off the wind. With adequate storage for a single-hander, the simplicity of the design makes for a low cost of operation. Don't expect to find refrigeration and solar arrays or below-decks autopilots on one of these basic little cruisers. The people who sail these will be used to living with the bare necessities. Although an inboard diesel was standard and aids in getting into and out of crowded harbors, it's arguable that it's not even necessary. They tack as quickly as some racing dinghies and go upwind as well as many racing keelboats.

With enough sisterships out there in the world market to allow for a decent selection, prices for these legendary vessels remain relatively low. Sub teens will likely find you a basic Contessa while newer pristine examples rarely sell for more than mid-twenties.

Tartan 27

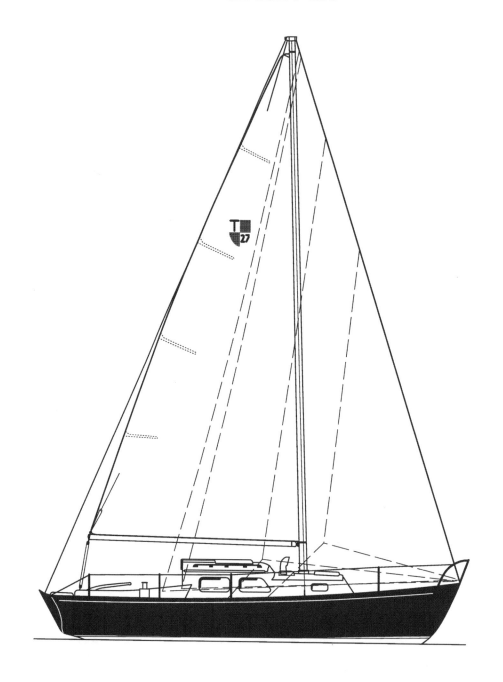

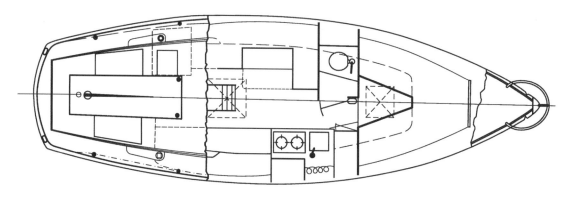

Tartan 27

With over 700 of these attractive little cruisers built over 19 years beginning in 1961, the Tartan 27 is surely one of the most successful cruiser/racers of her era and is a great choice for a pocket world cruiser.

Several design and construction improvements were undertaken over the long production run with the earlier boats built with external bolt-on keels, while after 1971 they had internal ballast, which is what I would be looking for if I were searching for a Tartan-27.

As one of, if not the very first fiberglass production boats designed by the world-renowned Sparkman & Stephens firm, this design is a thoroughbred in every sense of the word. She is a fast boat for her length and despite what is considered heavy displacement by modern standards, she moves out well even in light air and yet still retains good sailing performance, even when loaded down with months of supplies for your ocean crossing to Nuku Hiva!

A few years ago I met a single-hander on one of these boats down in Panama who had purchased his stock Tartan 27 in Texas for a few hundred dollars and left for Colombia with a Rand McNally Road Atlas as his only 'chart'! Missing Colombia by a couple of hundred miles, he instead found himself in Panama and when we met, he was on the rapid learning curve of not only learning how to sail but how to navigate too. I gave him a bunch of charts and sold him some small boat parts and lo and behold, four years later he sailed into a bay in Western Fiji and anchored right in front of me. He now had a pretty woman onboard with him and had become an accomplished sailor, having just traversed some of the most navigationally challenging reef strewn areas in the world.

With used prices on these boats ranging from a few hundred dollars for a fixer-upper to as much as low-teens for a very nice one and many available for under ten thousand dollars, the sturdy Tartan 27 can be your bargain-priced ticket to the world and is darn good looking too!

Things to watch for are centerboard issues on some of the later versions and of course older inboard gas or diesel engines that may have already been swapped out by now. Through-hulls in early boats were gate valves which should be switched out. The Tartan 27 is a super well-made American cruiser and is worth your time seeking out.

Pearson Triton 28

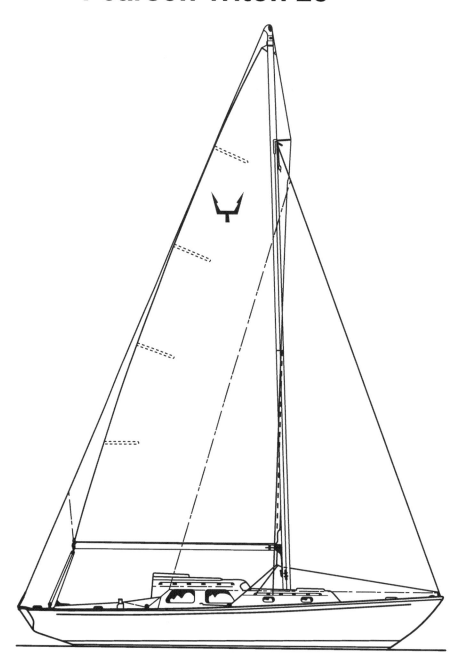

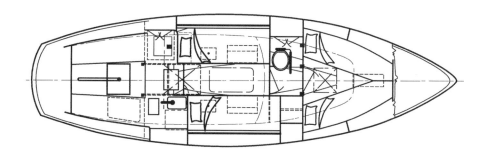

Pearson Triton 28

First produced in 1958, The Pearson Triton's introduction at the 1959 New York Boat Show made a huge impact on American yachting. It is argued by some that the Pearson Triton, while not the first fiberglass auxiliary cruising sailboat built in the US, was certainly the one that brought about a wide acceptance of fiberglass construction to the yacht building industry.

The Triton was a Carl Alberg designed four berth true auxiliary yacht that was capable of safe offshore sailing and the count has certainly long been lost on how many of these tough little yachts have crossed oceans or even circumnavigated the planet.

With a substantial solid fiberglass hull, plywood stiffened deck, and on older models, an attached bronze and wooden rudder, and a rather crudely finished interior of the hull and cabin overhead, these boats are certainly not built to the standards later designs might have enjoyed. But, the great care and attention to detail used during construction allowed for a well-made yacht and it's probably safe to say that most of the original vessels built are still in service today.

Storage is copious and carrying capacity allows for enough provisions and spare parts to allow a couple to cruise far and wide and yet, the simplicity of the design gives the potential for a relatively trouble-free yacht.

Prices for these can be sub $10K for a somewhat neglected one to upper teens for a nicely maintained vessel and enough were built that good examples can surely be found with a little searching.

It should also be noted here that some cousins that deserve mention and are also quite plentiful on the used market are the 32' Pearson Vanguard and the 30' Pearson Coaster and Wanderer. Also built in the same era, many of these have made epic voyages and the prices are typically not much more than a good Triton.

Southern Cross 28

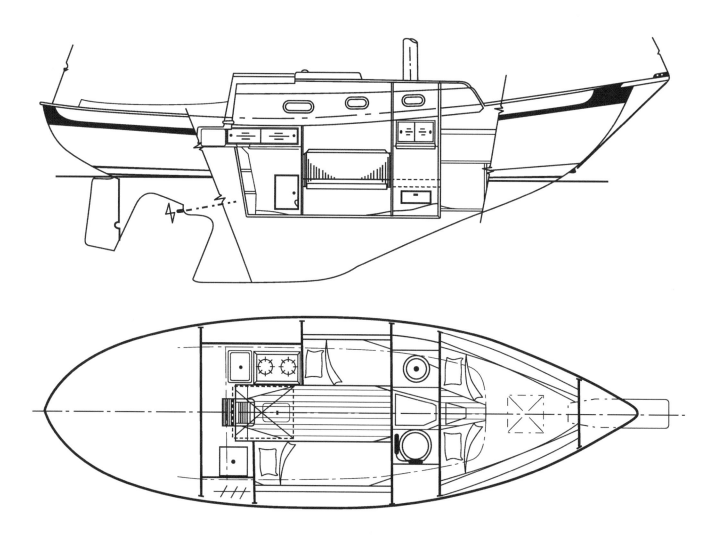

Southern Cross 28

A smaller sister to the very well-received Southern Cross 31, the 28 was created by Annapolis native Tom Gilmer, designer of the famous Pride of Baltimore and also the designer of the first fiberglass yacht to circumnavigate, the Allied Seawind 30.

The Southern Cross 28 featured a more modern keel and rudder shape than her older sisters and was originally available as a shoal draft version, but this was quickly replaced with a deeper draft model which is mostly what you will see on the used market these days.

Chosen for two single-handed circumnavigations, one via the five capes by Donna Lange, this able little vessel has surely been proven in some of the worst sea conditions on the planet.

Sturdily built and superbly sea-kindly, the Southern Cross 28 offers more storage and carrying capacity than you might expect for a vessel of this size. She has moderately heavy displacement and a stiff Airex cored hull.

With less than a five-foot draft and easily handled cutter rigged sail plan, this boat makes a terrific coastal cruiser too, and single-handing is easy. She has a secure-feeling, deep cockpit and a well-placed inboard engine. Originally available with a gas or diesel powerplant, most of the ones you will find at this point in history will have replaced the gas powerplant.

Things to watch for are mast compression issues and of course, aging chainplates and through-hulls but the sheer simplicity of these boats make checking one over fairly easy, and upgrading it probably won't break the bank either.

Prices for a fixer-upper one of these may be from the low teens to mid-twenties while a super nice one may command as much as the high thirties.

Eastward Ho 24

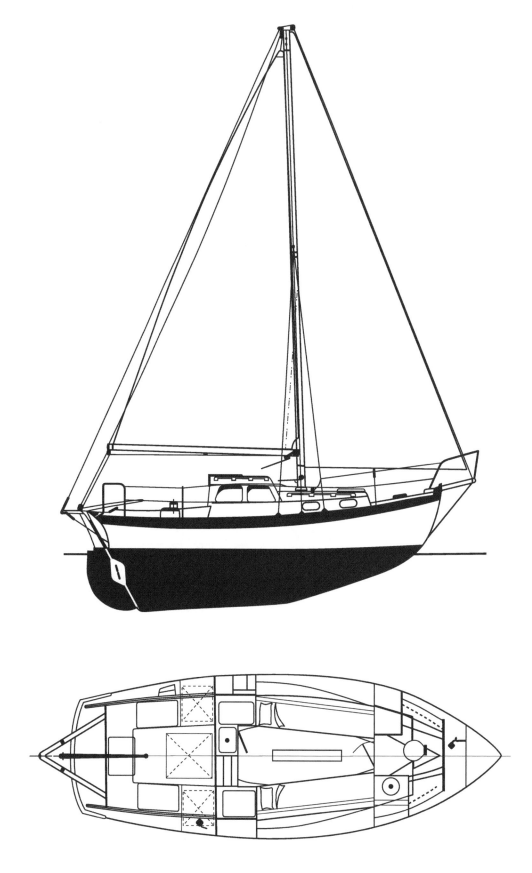

Eastward Ho 24

A super sturdy and able vessel that is little known to most is this Eldridge-McInnis design. Originally built in wood to a mid-50s design, in 1975, the Portsmouth Yacht Company in Rhode Island commissioned the hulls to be built by C.E. Ryder, renowned for their Southern Cross and Sea Sprite series vessels.

With 6' of headroom and a sensible seagoing layout, these full keel vessels are heavily built and sail quite well. I know of several of these that have completed major passages and one windy night crossing the boisterous Windward Passage between Haiti and Cuba, an Eastward Ho 24 kept up with our svelte 39' ketch almost the entire way across in 25-30 knot winds and lumpy ten to twelve-foot seas. The crew reported a relatively dry ride and while in the Cayman Islands I did some day sailing on this engineless cutter (the owner had removed the motor which he said was noisy and smelled). The boat tacked easily, pointed high, and felt like a sturdy vessel.

Standard with either a Palmer gas or Bukh diesel inboard engine, most will likely have been repowered by now.

Prices for these tough little boats can be anywhere from a couple thousand dollars for a fixer-upper to around ten or slightly more for a well-found vessel. A great bargain cruiser, a properly outfitted Eastward Ho 24 could take you far.

Baba 30

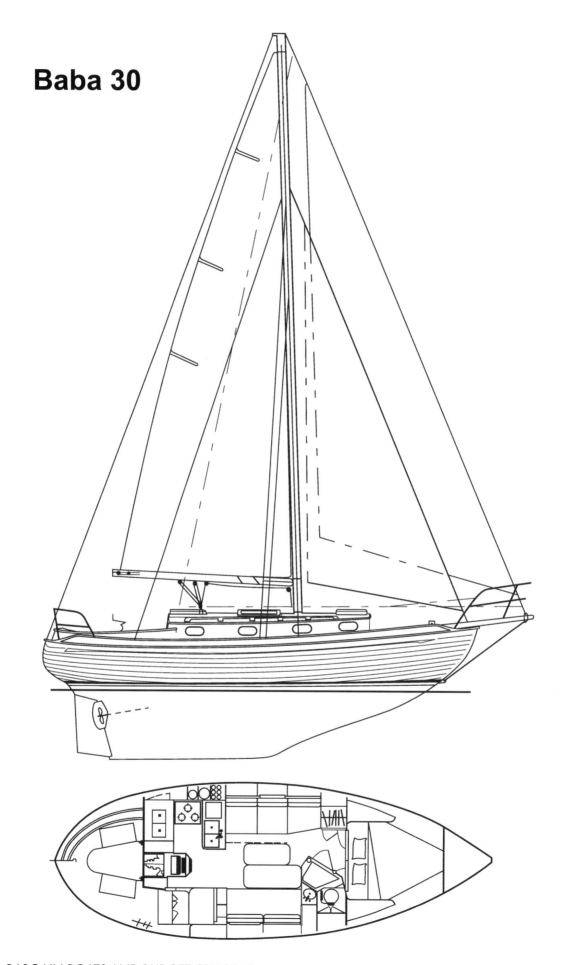

Baba 30

Built by the world-renowned Ta Shing Yacht Building Company in Taiwan, this able little cutter feels more like a big boat than a 'pocket cruiser.' The craftsmanship is superb and the materials used were the best of what was available in the Far East at the time.

A wonderfully balanced sail plan and relatively narrow sheeting angles give this boat good upwind performance. I remember sailing a Baba 30 out of Pearl Harbor, beating up the narrow channel to the sea (with an engine that didn't run) and three times being turned back by the Navy because a ship was coming in or going out. We must have tacked forty times on those three tries before we made it to the open sea and each time she came about smartly and quickly regained momentum. They are small enough to be super easy to sail and yet are large enough for a couple to sail around the world in relative comfort.

The accommodations are somewhat typical for this size boat as there's not much room for real creativity in 30 feet, but there are good-sized settee-type berths to port and starboard, a real sit-down chart table, and an amazingly workable U-shaped galley. Forward is a full V berth that is adequate for long-term living and abundant storage makes this a great little pocket cruiser and comfortable liveaboard home. Tanks are easily accessible in the bilge and storage is abundant. The side decks are wide enough for easy access forward and the hull form has an exceptional sea-kindly motion.

Teak decks were almost always ordered and so care should be used when assessing the condition of the deck core under the teak. Most had wheel steering although some had tillers. The fuel tank is in the bilge and should be looked at carefully but changing it out is not difficult and may be a good bargaining point if the boat you are considering hasn't already had this done.

Prices for these may run from the low 20s up to mid-50s and the later version of this same design called the Tashiba 31, is typically only a little more. A surprisingly sprightly sailer and quite pretty as well, if you are considering vessels in this size range, a Baba 30 is one to look at for sure.

Nor'Sea 27

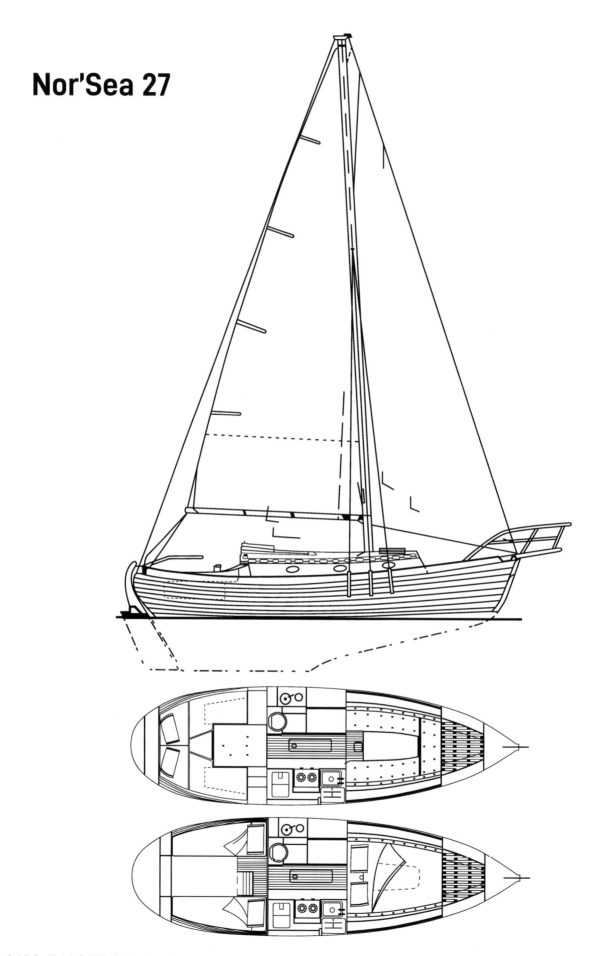

Nor'Sea 27

Another one of my favorite ocean capable designs, the Nor'Sea 27, was offered in both an aft cockpit and a center cockpit deck plan on a sturdy shoal draft hull. Designed by Lyle Hess to be a true offshore-capable, yet trailerable, auxiliary cruising yacht, the Nor'Sea 27 began production in 1977 and is still being made today.

These pretty little vessels are unusual in that they incorporate an imitation 'lapstrake' planking which, while salty and attractive, is not so much done for appearance as much as for the tremendous stiffness it provides for the already fairly thick hull. The added advantage of this lapstrake design is that the cockpit tends to stay drier in a seaway than you might expect on a vessel of only 27' on deck by deflecting light spray down and away from the decks.

Most of the Nor'Seas you will find on the used market are the more popular center cockpit layout and although arguably, designing a center cockpit on a vessel of such a size can hardly be practical, many owners make use of this space for the tremendous additional storage it provides, and I've heard of some owners using this cabin for guests or children too.

Add to all of these attributes the fact that many have crossed oceans and even circumnavigated the earth, if you have a heavy-duty tow vehicle, you can load the boat on a trailer and take it across the country and cruise the Bahamas one season, then Puget Sound the next, and the Sea of Cortez the following season, all without ever needing to do long offshore passages or an expensive Panama canal transit.

With prices for these starting in the low to mid-teens for an older model up to as much as the cost of a new boat, there is almost always a good selection of these out there and one to fit your budget will, with a little searching, surely come along.

Bristol 29.9

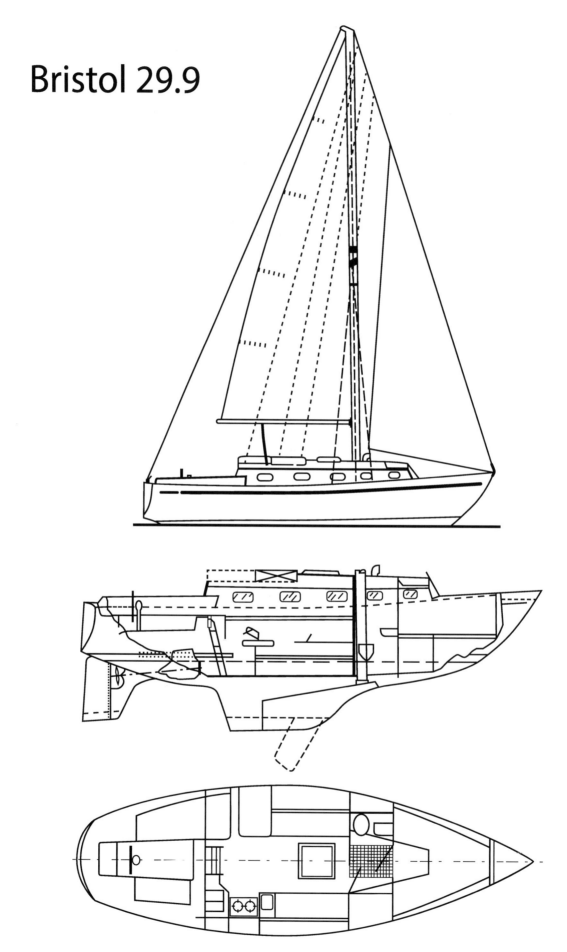

Bristol 29.9

A really big 30 footer that sails and acts more like one of her larger sisters in the Bristol line, the 29.9 was extremely successful and because of this, many of these are available at bargain prices on the used market today.

Built from 1977 to 1986, this Halsey Herreshoff design was created for the MORC (Midget Ocean Racing Club) rule and features a relatively flat run and hard turn of the bilge which translates to good form stability. Her stiff hull with high freeboard and commodious storage below makes this 70s racer/cruiser an ideal long-term cruising yacht for a couple or small family. With berths for up to six, the quarter berths on many are often just used for storage, and only when company comes along would you likely convert the portside dinette to a double. With its large volume stainless steel water tankage located below the cabin sole, the area under and outboard of the settees makes for great storage and the small but comfortable cockpit feels secure offshore.

Early models may have had Universal Atomic Four gas engines, but most you will find have either Universal or Yanmar diesels. While the fuel tanks are a bit on the small side for long-distance cruising, there is room under the cockpit to augment this.

Available as a three and a half-foot keel/centerboard version and a fixed keel of 'four and change', either option makes for a terrific Bahamas exploration vessel. Both a tall rig and a standard rig were available and either one, properly outfitted with safety gear and a self-steering windvane would be suitable for long-distance sailing.

Well-made and with over 200 built, these great little boats can be found for as little as low teens while a super nice one with all the goodies for cruising might command low thirties.

Bristol owners are typically very proud of their vessels and so finding one of these that's been well-loved is more common than running across a neglected one.

Heavenly Twins 27

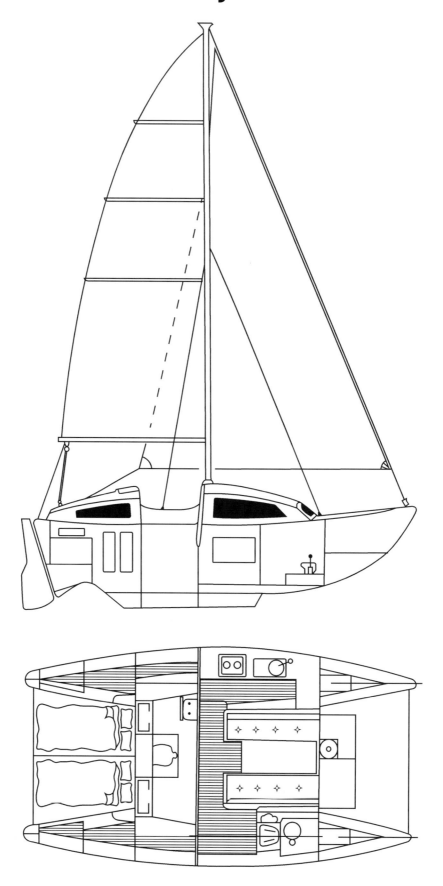

Heavenly Twins 27

Originally introduced in 1971 as a 26-foot single outboard powered auxiliary, the Heavenly Twins is for sure a minimum size cruising cat. With improvements in hull design and interior layouts, by 1976 it had been lengthened to 27 feet and the final MK 5 versions (when you can find one) were 28 feet with better headroom and twin diesel engines. The Heavenly Twin developed a cult following and to this day you will occasionally see these cute little catamarans out there cruising the world.

While I have made my opinion about catamarans well known, if you plan to cruise coastally and to spend large amounts of time in shallow areas like the Bahamas or the Florida Keys, then a Heavenly Twins with its 28"(or so, depending on loading) draft might just be the ticket. The hulls were solid laminate and the comfortable double berths in the two aft cabins offer good privacy. There is a full-standing headroom head compartment forward in the starboard hull while a good size galley is in the port hull.

While headroom in the hulls is adequate, there is only about 5' in the saloon so you'd spend most of your time sitting rather than stooping. Usable space on these boats is however quite comparable to a much larger monohull and yes, they are narrow enough that in many cases when hauling or docking, you can get by without being charged the typical 1.5 to 2 times monohull rates... as long as you find a dockmaster who isn't too greedy!

With a nearly 25-year production run and many of these available (mostly in the UK), prices for a Heavenly Twins are all over the place, but with careful shopping, a good one can likely be had for as little as mid-teens for an older version while a late model MK IV or V might command as much as the high thirties or low forties for an immaculate well-equipped 28.

Mariner 31 & 32

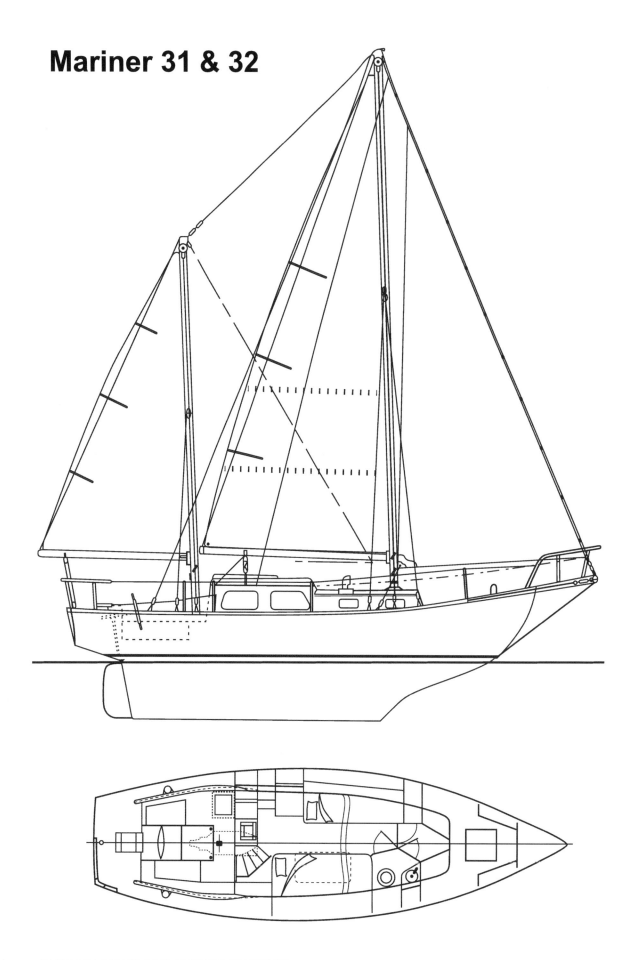

Boats 31-39 Feet and Up
Mariner 31 & 32

One of the best cruising boats of the 1960s and early 70s, the Mariner Ketch was originally built in Japan of wood and later converted to fiberglass construction. While the 31 and the 32 share the same hull and the same basic layout below decks, the 31 had a more secure and comfortable cockpit with high coamings, while the 32 featured a flush-to-the-deck aft cockpit and 'trail boards' on the bow, giving her more of a clipper ship look and extending her overall length slightly.

The glasswork of the hull was excellent and they are quite strong. With a full keel and fairly heavy displacement, they need a bit of a breeze to get going but have a superb hull form and an easy motion offshore for such a small vessel.

The boats featured Sitka spruce masts and reliable bronze worm gear steering. They had high-quality stainless steel water tanks and were typically overpowered with a Perkins 4-107 40 hp diesel.

The biggest issues you may run into with one of these are that the decks were made of luan 'mahogany' plywood which was glassed over so unless the deck hardware bedding has been zealously maintained, damage to the underlying decks is almost a certainty and so you will likely find most of these boat on the market these days will have had their decks replaced, hopefully with more rot-resistant Douglas fir and new cloth with epoxy resin. Chainplates should also be checked because, despite good quality stainless steel used during construction, the age of original installations suggests due diligence in this area.

A great boat for a couple or small family, they have voluminous storage and abundant tankage. With less than 4' draft they can access almost any anchorage and yet have enough stiffness to stand up well to a blow offshore. Many have circumnavigated.

Because of the wood decks, these can be true bargain boats and a fixer-upper can often be had for as little as $2K-5K while a very nice one will still likely only command mid-twenties. If your budget is tight and you want a smart looking, seaworthy little ship, try to find a Mariner 31 or 32.

Westsail 32

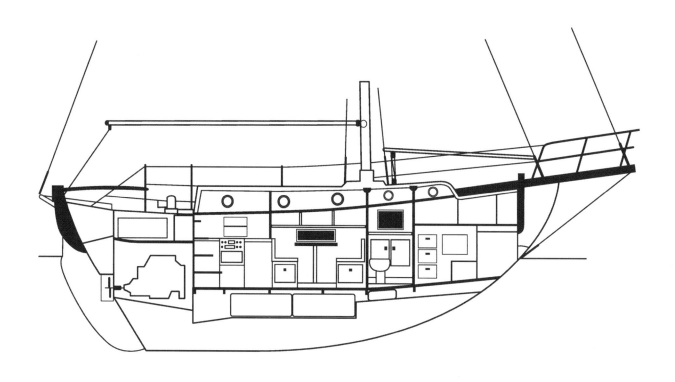

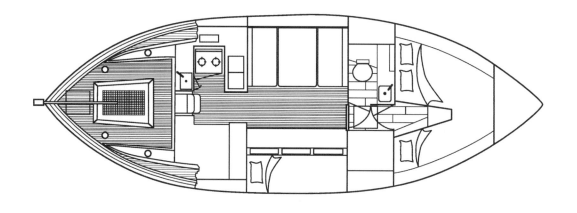

Westsail 32

Created as a fiberglass development of a 1930s wooden boat design by William Atkin of Long Island New York, an enterprising California couple acquired the molds of a defunct company that was building a boat design specifically for ocean crossings and long-distance cruising. This was a concept that had not yet caught on with the general sailing public and with a brilliant advertising campaign, the company uncovered a previously untapped market amongst the sailing populace and orders came flooding in. 852 Westsail 32 hulls were produced between 1972 and 1980.

With up to 26 layers of fiberglass in the hull layup and what is by today's standards a very heavy displacement, the Westsail 32 was the original 'bulletproof cruiser'. Stories of Westails being rammed by freighters, whales and other yachts have almost always had a happy ending with their owners making port, and countless stories of heavy groundings and hitting logs, containers, and buoys have ended the same way—with their owners getting home safely. The sailboat that was abandoned and made famous in the movie 'The Perfect Storm' was a Westsail 32 that was found washed up on a New Jersey beach weeks later, largely undamaged, having survived the storm even though her crew had abandoned her! With a reputation for sturdiness, other manufacturers and owners of flimsier designs tried to discredit this design by saying that they were slow and had poor windward performance, but most owners feel these are unjust statements. With good sails, a clean bottom, and a competent skipper, these able little vessels can make very respectable passage times and will sail as close to the wind as is necessary for the typical ocean cruiser.

So many of these vessels were built that chances are you can find one in your budget. Beware though that almost half of these boats were sold as bare hull 'kit boats', and while some of these can be spectacular masterpieces of workmanship, others can be complete disasters. Do your homework and if you end up with a good one, the far horizon will become your new best friend.

Prices for Westsail 32s are all over the map with most trading in the $30s and 40s these days while a project boat might go for as little as $10K and a super immaculate, totally outfitted one may sell for as much as $60K or more.

Southern Cross 31

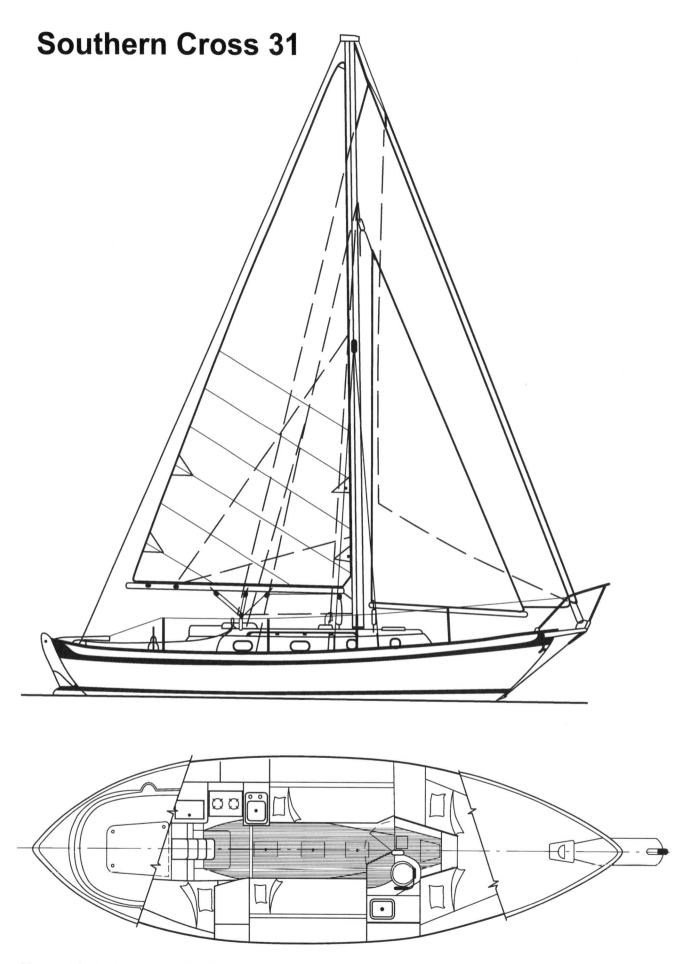

Southern Cross 31

A bigger, older sister to the Southern Cross 28, this design was a development of the first fiberglass yacht to circumnavigate; the Allied Seawind 30 by the same naval architect, Thomas Gillmer of Annapolis, Maryland, designer of the famous Pride of Baltimore I & II full-rigged schooners. The Southern Cross 31 is quite similar to the Seawind but with a slightly higher freeboard and a more robust hull featuring an Airex core, a deeper keel and an outboard rudder on a svelte canoe stern. Another terrific little seaboat and a real bargain on the used market, these are a great choice for a single-hander or younger couple and have few bad habits. The layout is simple and practical and the cockpit is small but also feels safe and comfortable.

As with so many of these true double-ender designs, the boat has tiller steering. Tiller steering offers some tremendous advantages over a wheel. For one, there is virtually nothing other than the wooden tiller itself that can break. Secondly, you can steer a tiller with your foot while navigating into a crowded harbor, allowing you to stand up on a seat to see well. A tiller allows for quick short tacking when sailing into or out of a crowded anchorage and the self-tending staysail on the well-stayed cutter rig, with the jib dropped or furled, makes it super easy to sail the boat up to anchor or to short-tack up a narrow channel. If you want real enjoyment out of sailing, a tiller is the way to go!

With its leak-resistant hull/deck joint and super stiff hull, few owners of these boats have reported serious problems. Keep in mind though that some of these were home-completed boats and so the usual due diligence must be undertaken when inspecting the one you find to ascertain its suitability for your purposes. Some owners have reported minor blistering of the first layer of laminate and so a good survey should be an important undertaking. And because the hulls are cored with Airex, checking for past repairs or improperly installed through-hulls that may have allowed water to ingress into the laminate is important. But if the hull checks out and the interior is suitable, you can't go far wrong with one of these salty little cruisers.

As with many older designs, prices can be all over the map and I know of one in sail away condition that recently sold for $9K in the BVI. An immaculate well equipped one with all the state-of-the-art gear might sell for as much as low $40s.

Pearson 365

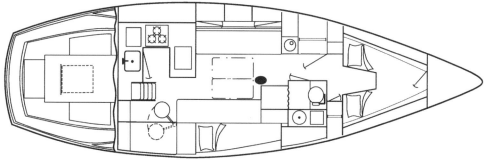

Pearson 365 (and 36C and 367)

One of the most successful medium size cruising boats of its time, the Pearson 365 was introduced in 1976 and built up until 1982 when the 36C cutter-rigged version and 367 (sloop version) was introduced. Over 400 365s were produced and these ketches are one of the better-mannered yachts of their era. With a relatively shallow draft and massive water tankage (150 gallons) this was a boat you could take for extended cruising in the Bahamas. One of the biggest selling points of this boat aside from the easily handled ketch rig was the enclosed head with a separate shower stall.

Staff designer and CEO of Pearson Yachts Bill Shaw didn't try to squeeze too many berths into this design, opting instead for copious cockpit lockers where jerry jugs, folding bikes, and water toys could all be kept out of sight and securely stowed, but still offered one good double berth forward, a convertible dinette and a settee berth plus a pilot berth, so these made great family cruisers.

I know of at least one of these boats that has circumnavigated and with proper gear and in good condition you could take off across oceans, but the 365's main attraction is that is a great shoal draft cruiser and would be a super entry-level cruiser to take to the Bahamas or farther down island into the Caribbean.

Typical problem areas on these boats are leaking stanchion bases and portlight bedding. Pearson tried (and later abandoned) using a soft rubber-like material (nitrile) gasket under the stanchions and this worked well when tensioned by drawing the nuts and bolts tight, but as decades marched by these gaskets dried up and split allowing water to intrude into the balsa wood deck cores and in some cases, especially where the boats were stored in freezing climates, delamination can occur. Another issue to watch for on these boats—especially one that's been immersed for many years in warm water—is 'oil canning' on the flat sections of the bottom of the hull aft of the keel. While this may sound catastrophic, it's pretty easy to fix and so should not be a reason to walk away should the boat you are looking at show this issue... although a hefty price reduction might be in order!

Like with most fiberglass boats, problems can be solved and with prices for a 'fixer-upper' 365 falling into the low teens and even well-maintained vessels rarely commanding more than mid-thirties, this is a great 'value cruiser' and should be on your shortlist to pursue if the size range works for you.

Downeaster 38

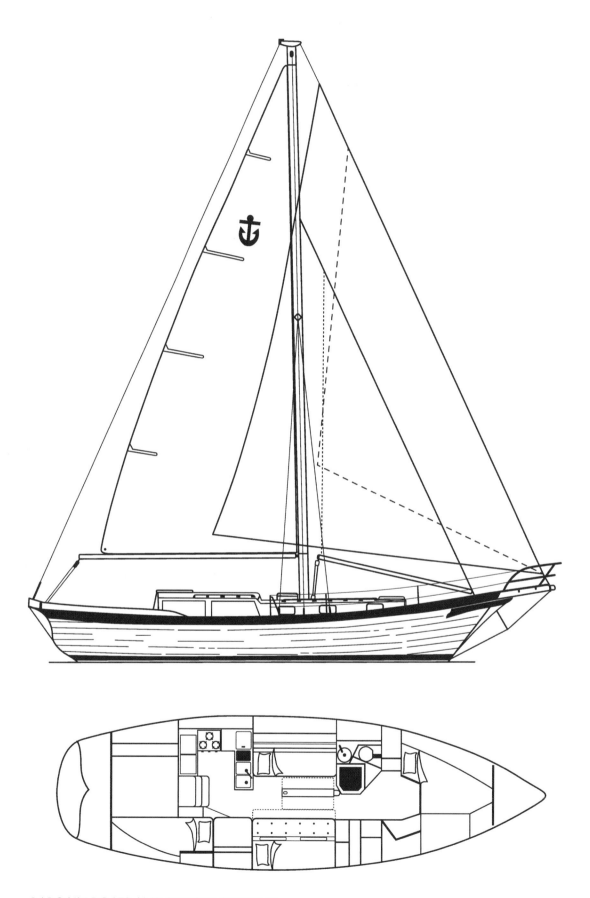

Downeaster 38 (and the Downeaster 32)

A real 'sleeper' and a terrific cruising yacht, the Downeaster 38 was one of the few American-built 'pirate ships' to be mass-produced and while most people who see them assume they are Taiwanese, the fact is the Downeasters were well made in California and while not the highest quality boats out there, they don't fall victim to so many of the common issues that similar Far Eastern vessels of similar appearance suffered from such as tank, deck, and low-quality stainless issues. The Downeasters had closed-cell, foam-cored decks and good quality stainless water and aluminum fuel tanks installed properly. And the hardware used was mostly of good quality and made in the United States.

While these yachts carried a decidedly pirate ship look, they are terrific sailing vessels, are quite fast with great carrying capacity, and are darn attractive too. Built in 32', 38', 41', and 45' renditions, the Downeaster 32s and 38s are by far the most common.

The downside of these boats is that the smaller models had a Ferryman diesel which can be quite problematic to service and yet by this time in history most of these engines will have been replaced. Another problem was that the hull/deck joints on some of these were simply screwed together with sheet metal screws and a sealant rather than through-bolted, but when you consider the good quality layup of the hulls and decks and attractive, practical interiors, replacing the screws at some point with better fasteners would not be an insurmountable hurdle to overcome.

With prices for these ranging from low teens for a fixer-upper 32 to seldom over mid-40s for a nice 38, these salty vessels fall firmly in the bargain boat category. Take a look at some of these pretty, strong cruisers. There are usually quite a few available at attractive prices!

Ingrid 38

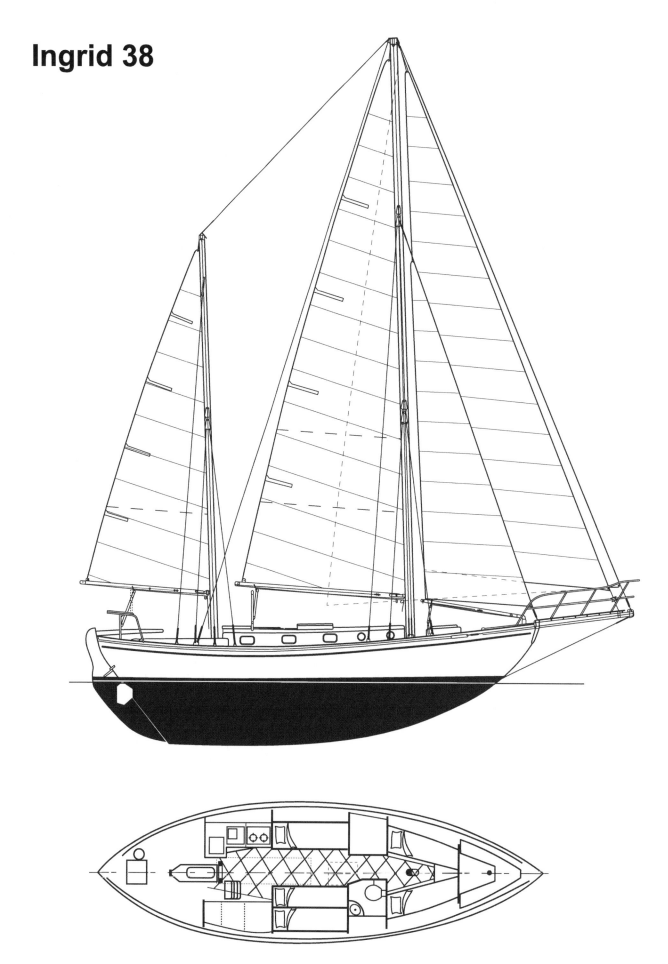

Ingrid 38

Another super well-made American production design from the 70s that was also available in semi-finished or kit form is the Bluewater Yachts Ingrid 38. This is a true fiberglass reproduction of a Colin Archer inspired 1934 William Atkin design that was a larger sistership to the enormously successful 32' Atkins Thistle/Eric, the predecessor and inspiration for the Westsail 32 and many other similar designs.

First produced in fiberglass in about 1971, and with about 143 total built, many of these were fitted out to varying degrees of expertise and because double-enders of this type have fallen largely out of style in modern times, true bargains can be found. Superb seaboats with a surprising turn of speed on a reach, these vessels have what is arguably one of the most seaworthy hull forms ever made. A scaled-down and 'trimmed' development of the Norwegian pilot boats of the late 1800s and early 1900s, they are narrow and small below by modern standards but have tremendous carrying capacity and the Bluewater Yachts models were built with all woven roving in the hull creating unequaled strength along with a superbly sea-kindly motion in all but the roughest of weather.

Don't expect to set any world speed records to windward, but a good Ingrid will ably take you wherever you are brave enough to travel and are considered by many to be a classic of unmatched beauty.

With well-outfitted models typically available from the low 30s to mid-50s these rugged cruisers represent a great value and if a good one can be found it should be high on your list of boats to check out. I owned a slightly larger custom-built sistership and cruised it many tens of thousands of miles and can report no bad habits except perhaps for a refusal to turn quickly in tight quarters!

As with any of the 'kit' boats of the 1970s, great care must be taken when looking at some of the more crudely finished homebuilt versions. While virtually any stupidness can be undone, I'd stick with one that was well done and well outfitted and hopefully only needs a little updating and modernization of systems rather than taking on a complete rebuild.

Tayana 37

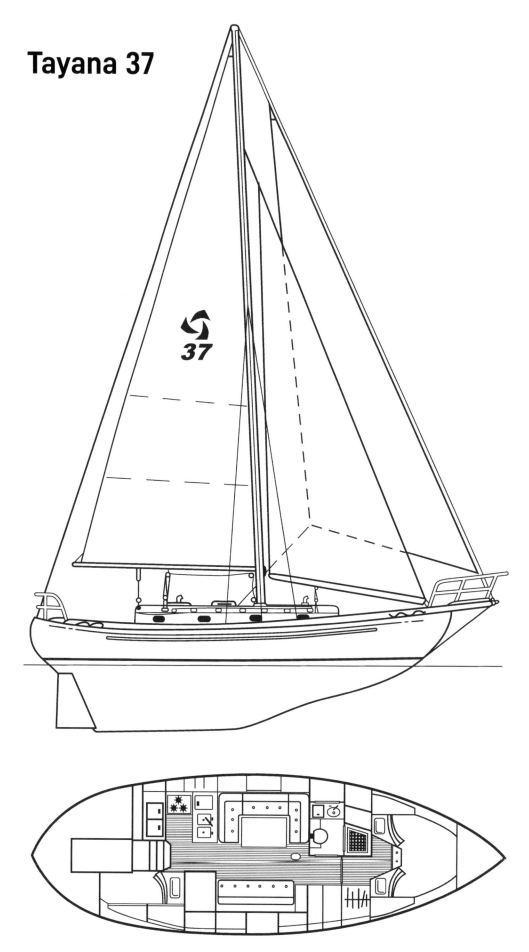

Tayana 37

At one time this was considered to be Bob Perry's most famous design and in the 1980s, it was not uncommon to see several Tayana 37s from all over the world in some far-flung anchorage.

High resale prices were common on these boats until the beginning of the new century, but now, with these boats reaching middle age, a good one can often be found at a reasonable price.

Built in Taiwan during what I like to call the golden age of fiberglass boatbuilding, the Tayana 37 does suffer from some of the issues that many of the early Taiwanese boats had. Watch out for moisture in the iron ballast encapsulation; be sure that the chainplates are recent or well maintained; and be mindful of moisture intrusion in the deck core, especially with the older teak deck versions. Earlier boats had solid wood blocks or sometimes lauan plywood squares for deck core while later boats had an end grain 'balsa' core. Fuel and water tanks can also exhibit issues but in many cases, these problems may have already been dealt with by the time you have taken over ownership.

The hulls are substantially laminated, and the gelcoat used seems to have held up very well over time. The interior woodwork is semi-custom and nicely crafted to give each Tayana 37 a unique appeal.

A deck with nice high bulwarks makes working on deck in a seaway feel more secure, but when it comes time to re-bed the stanchions, gaining access to the base of the fasteners can be a challenge. Still, the Tayana 37 makes a terrific choice for a couple or a small family and they sail well, have abundant storage, and look great too.

Price ranges for these boats may start as low as low 20s for a fixer-upper while a beautifully maintained later model may command in the high 80s. With lots of boats to choose from, surely a good one can be found that will fit your price range and skill level.

Fountaine Pajot
Athena 38

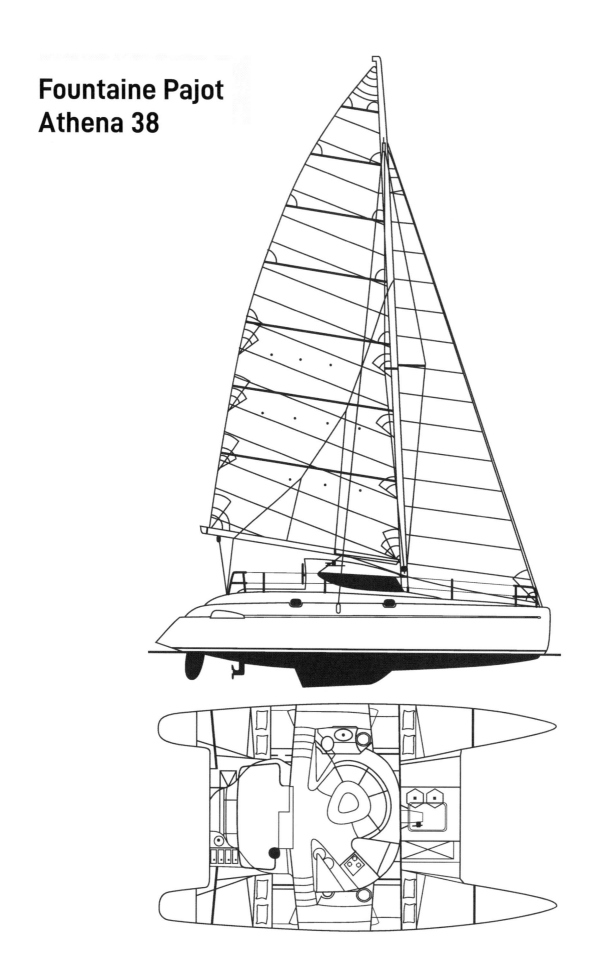

Fountaine Pajot Athena 38

Another concession to those who feel they must consider a catamaran, the Athena 38 was a tremendously successful and generally well-engineered entry-level four-cabin catamaran that was also the very first cat to be introduced into the British Virgin Islands bareboat charter fleets in 1996. Knowing this, it would be safe to say the Athena 38 launched the charter cat revolution in the Caribbean!

I'm also going to mention the Athena's immediate predecessor, the Antigua 37 as these boats are very similar. Both had twin Volvo or Yanmar diesels and four separate cabins with two heads—a very practical arrangement, particularly for a family with three kids!

These boats were initially somewhat scoffed at because they were 'non-traditional' in terms of design and construction, but then again, almost all cats these days are that way, so perhaps we can just say at this point that they were somewhat revolutionary in design concept in that they used a thin foam core and lots of compound curves to create a very stiff structure. I surveyed one of these boats that had recently circumnavigated and there were no stress cracks or signs of distortion, despite what the owners reported as some very heavy conditions in the Indian Ocean while rounding South Africa.

With some recent sales of the early nineties vintage Antigua 37s falling in the range of the high 70s to mid-80s and reported sales on some of the mid-90s Athenas selling in the 80s to mid-120s, they are stretching the parameters of being called budget cruisers, but with careful shopping, one of these at a good price might be found.

Not my first choice for world cruising but a good choice for Bahamas or Caribbean adventures, a clean well-kept older Fountaine Pajot may be worth considering.

Privilege 39

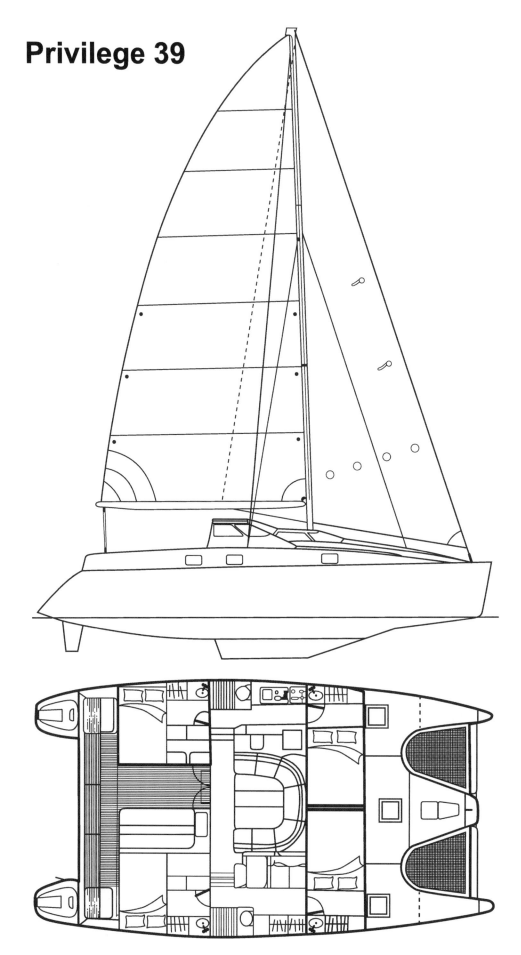

Privilege 39

When introduced in the late 1980s, the Privilege 39 was one of the highest quality and most sumptuously appointed small cruising catamarans on the world market.

Inspired by a world-class single-handed racer, two-time BOC challenge winner, and founder of the Vendee Globe single-handed round the world race, Philippe Jeantot built more cruising catamarans than any builder in Europe at the time and introduced thousands to the concept of comfortable multihull cruising.

The Privilege 39 is a heavy, stoutly built catamaran with surprisingly large sleeping cabins, a rarity on smaller cruising cats of this era and because so many of these boats were built in the early nineties, bargains can be found. With recent sale prices on some of these falling into the range of what a similar aged mid-40s size monohull might command, the enormous interior volume and good overall construction make these boats something to look for.

Problems with osmosis are sometimes found on boats that have been sailed extensively in tropical waters or left immersed for prolonged periods and the hulls should be carefully assessed before purchase by a qualified marine surveyor. These are cored hulls and so ensuring that the core has not been compromised is of the utmost importance but generally speaking, these were well-made boats and simple to repair and maintain.

The Privilege cats were unusual for their era and even by today's standards in that they had a lot of pretty teak below and in the cockpit giving them the feel more of a sumptuous yacht than the stripped-out, space capsule, all plastic feel of so many modern cats. While not intended to be gazelles on the water, respectable 7-8 knot cruising speeds are easily attained, and with a little tweaking, these boats can indeed go faster.

Expect to pay in the low to mid-70s for a fixer-upper while a nice ready to go boat shouldn't cost more than about $120K.

Having read this far in this book you know I'm not wild about catamarans for long-distance sailing, but if I were planning to just sail the Caribbean or the Bahamas for a few years and wanted to have friends or family along, I'd sure be tempted by a nice Privilege 39.

Whitby Alberg 37

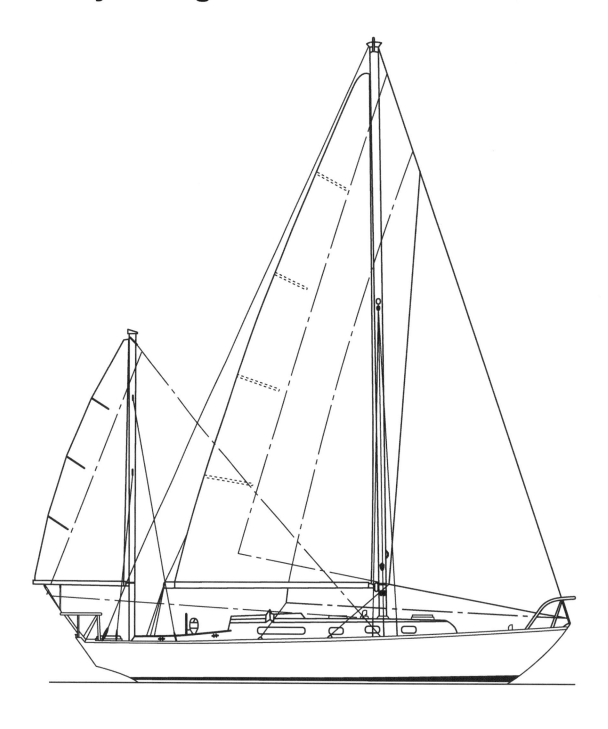

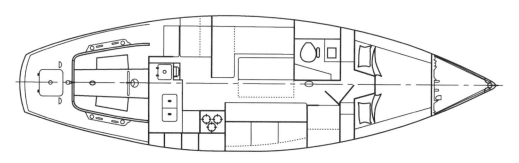

Whitby Alberg 37

The Canadian-built Alberg 37 was introduced in 1967 by Whitby Boatworks in Ontario and enjoyed a 21-year production run with two renditions. Before 1971 the original Mk1 version featured a lot of exterior wood including a wooden toe rail and a simpler, perhaps more crudely finished interior. They had wooden cockpit coamings and a solid fiberglass deck. In 1972 the MK II was introduced which incorporated a molded cockpit coaming design along with a balsa cored deck and a more 'finished' interior. Either one of these versions would be a good find for long-distance cruising and with nearly 250 of these stout cruisers built, with a little diligent searching, a good one can surely be found.

I've seen Alberg 37s in many ports around the world and with the super-strong, simple construction and the good seakeeping qualities these vessels possess, they make great budget cruisers for an adventurous single-hander, couple, or even a small family.

Featuring moderate overhangs and a longish deep keel they stand up to their sail well and are respectable upwind performers, even when loaded down for world cruising.

Internal lead ballast and a robust rudder and rig make few modifications necessary for converting one to an offshore cruiser. Add a windvane self-steering and maybe an inner forestay and you're ready for the big blue!

Some of the early boats had raw water cooled Volvo engines (Freshwater cooling was an option) and these old Volvos can be a problem. Additionally, the MK I versions featured a wooden toe rail which was prone to leaking if not properly rebedded while the MK II versions usually had a larger Perkins 4-107 freshwater-cooled engine and molded toerails. But at this point in their history, many of these yachts have been repowered. A simple quick inspection in the rain will likely reveal any substantial deck leaks.

With recent sales prices on some fixer-uppers in the low teens, even a very well equipped one rarely sells for more than about $50K, with many available in the range between.

Tartan 37

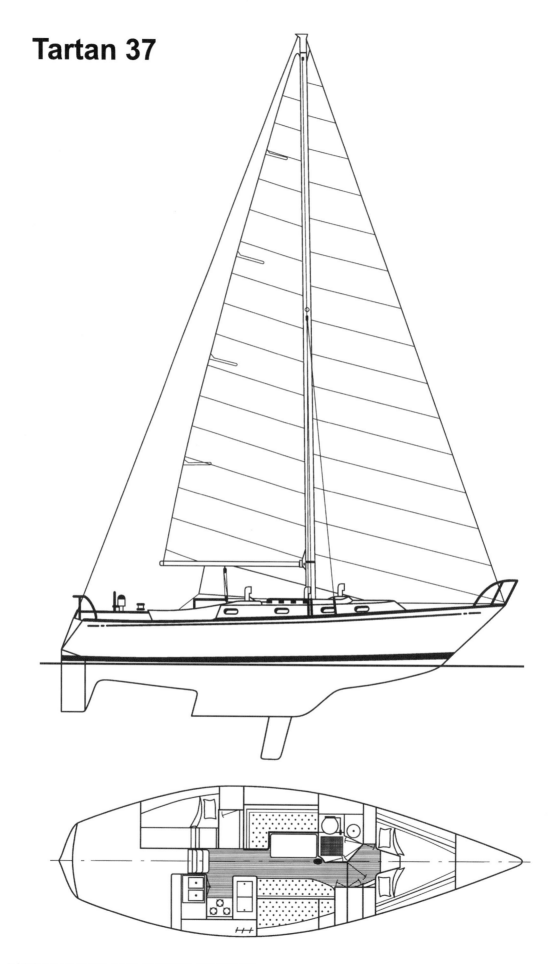

Tartan 37

The Sparkman & Stephens Tartan 37 is one of the true 'sleeper' values in the North American market.

Built to high standards in Grand River, Ohio, the Tartan 37 enjoyed a 13-year production run and was enormously successful both as a cruiser and as a club racer with close to 500 hulls built.

As one of the early 'crossover' designs, she featured the keel/centerboard design concept encouraged by the outdated CCA rule and yet incorporated some of the better fundamentals of early IOR designs which resulted in a shallow draft boat that could go upwind with the best of anything out there wrapped up in a superbly sea-kindly hull form that tracked well both upwind and off the wind, even in a seaway. A deep draft fixed keel version was also offered but was not nearly as popular.

With one of the best centerboard arrangements ever designed, this was a simple mechanism that offered tremendous flexibility for cruising shallow areas and makes it a cinch for cruising places like the ICW and the Bahamas.

A great choice for a couple or small family, there is sufficient storage for many months away from supply ports and enough space so that two or three people can still maintain a modicum of privacy when desired.

The earlier hulls had areas of plywood to stiffen the flatter sections of the topsides forward while later boats used balsa for coring in areas of the hull to create stiffness.

Beware of rudder problems and osmosis in earlier hulls but these deficiencies, should they be found, are easily remedied and because of their now largely disliked keel/centerboard design, great bargains can be found for one of these pretty vessels.

With recent reported sales prices showing lows in the teens to highs in the upper 50s to mid-60s, most seem to be trading in the mid to high 30s or slightly more. The Tartan 37 is a great value and a true 'Bargain Boat'!

Morgan 382

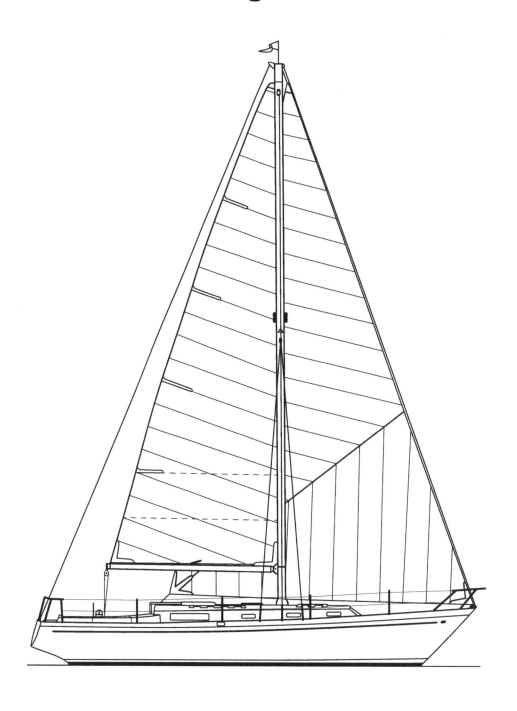

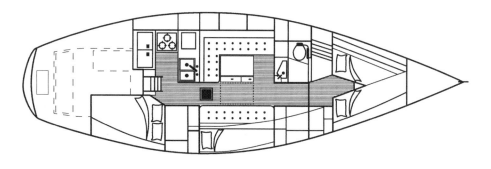

Morgan 382—384

One of my favorite budget cruisers has always been the Ted Brewer designed Morgan 382, 383, and 384.

Introduced in 1978, with some forward thinking and totally cool design features like a protected propeller inside of the beefy skeg, a cockpit scupper design which actually draws any water that might make its way into the cockpit by suction while the vessel is moving forward, plus a super stiff Airex cored hull and equally solid feeling deck, this boat has all the attributes of a beefy offshore cruiser but often sells in the same price range as much lesser built coastal cruisers.

The heavy section keel-stepped mast on the 382 model is more than adequately stayed and while the later 383 and 384 versions featured a taller rig which augmented light air performance, for ocean sailing, either version would be more than fine.

Morgan interiors are always nicely finished, but the later models of the design often featured all opening ports in lieu of the fixed doghouse types in the earlier model.

These boats point high and track well and are certainly one of the better mannered vessels in their size range.

With early 382s sometimes selling in the high teens to low twenties, even a later model beautifully maintained and fully equipped 384 model will rarely sell for more than $60K, making this super strong and able vessel a terrific candidate for long-term budget cruising.

Wauquiez Hood 38

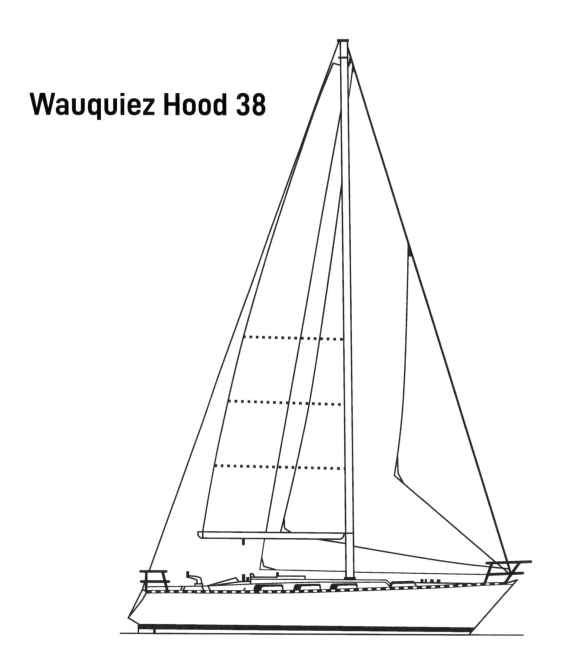

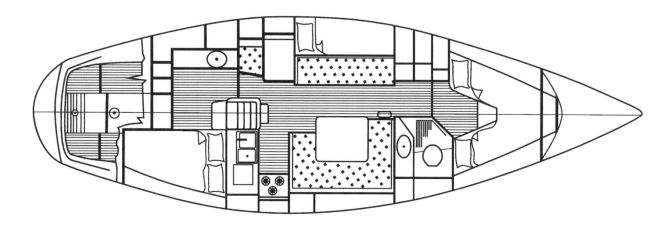

Wauquiez Hood 38 MK I and MK II

Here's another keel centerboard design! If you've been wondering why I am earmarking yet another vessel with this type of keel concept, here's why:

Keel centerboards were immensely popular from the 1950s through the 1970s because the CCA (Cruising Club of America) design rule favored this type of keel. With generally heavily ballasted hulls and an internal centerboard (retracted inside the keel when not in use) this innovation was a great way to give a boat superior upwind performance while still allowing access to shallow-draft cruising. But the real reason keel centerboards were so popular during this period was that it allowed for a better rating for racing!

Today, there is a general fear or at least a misunderstanding of centerboards and what they can do for you. Honestly folks? The biggest thing a keel/centerboard boat can give you at this point in history is TREMENDOUS VALUE! That's right. Most of the poorly informed general boating public is afraid of the 'complication' a centerboard may present. Some even confuse this type of system with 'drop keels' like on some trailerable sailboats. This stems from a lack of understanding and an oversimplification of the engineering concepts that go into creating this type of keel.

Wauquiez boats from the seventies and eighties are some of the best-built boats to ever come out of Europe and should be compared favorably with Nautor Swan and Hallberg-Rassy and are in some ways superior!

The Hood 38 was offered in two versions: The earlier MK I had a cumbersome cockpit arrangement that required going forward of the dodger to go below, but offered a terrific aft cabin while the MK II versions had a more conventional entry with a quarter cabin to one side.

Super high quality and ultra-strong, a Hood 38 MK I can be had for as little as mid-30s or less, while MK IIs might command a bit more and a super clean, well-equipped one might sell for as much as the mid-70s. But if you are looking for a fast, strong world-cruise capable boat with a shallow draft, you would be well advised to consider a Hood 38.

Mariner 39

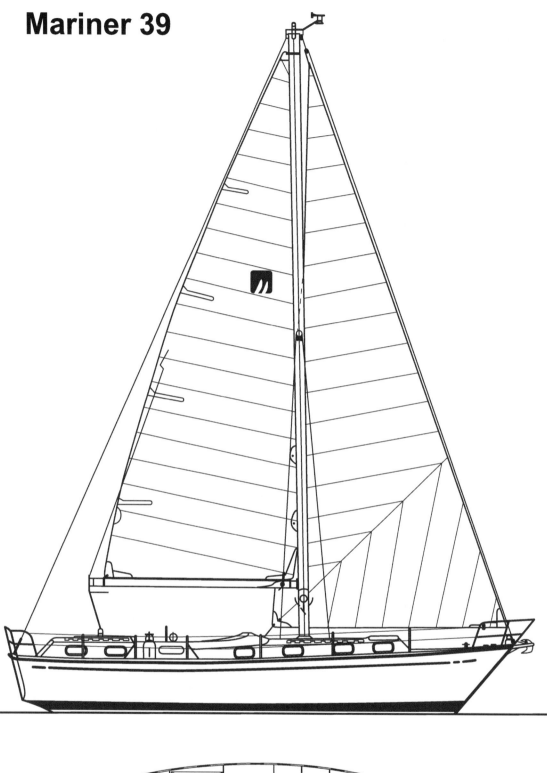

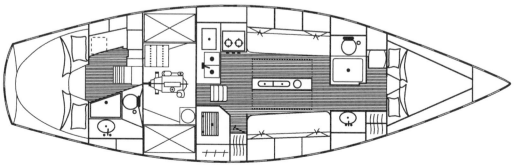

Mariner 39

Conservative yet 'cutting edge' for her era, the New England-built Mariner 39 (not to be confused with the Mariners built in the Far East) was successful in the charter fleets in the Caribbean and was widely considered to be one of the better-mannered cruising yachts of her time. Unfortunately, not as many were built as we might like to see, so finding one on the used market may take some searching. But it's worth the search!

The heavy externally bolted lead ballasted keel used Aquamet stainless bolts, arguably the best material available at the time. These boats were heavily built with a well-protected propeller inside of a substantial skeg. The Mariner 39 is a good sailing yet strong and comfortable vessel. With thick solid laminate hulls and a well-made balsa cored deck as well and a sumptuously appointed interior, these are attractive well-made boats.

While it might be said that putting a center cockpit into any boat under forty feet is 'pushing the numbers', the Mariner 39's layout works pretty well.

Offered in two layout versions, both have more than adequate ventilation with good quality Bomar opening ports and hatches.

With a narrow walk-through to the aft cabin, access is augmented by a separate companionway, and by virtue of her design, there is a good-sized, easily accessed engine room under the cockpit with plenty of space for equipment like a watermaker and extra batteries.

Because these are somewhat 'rare' boats, unfamiliarity has driven resale prices down and it is not uncommon to find a lightly equipped one of these terrific cruisers in the 20s or low 30s while a nice example with lots of gear may command as much as 70K or a bit more.

A good solid family boat and a great value on the used market, a Mariner 39 deserves a look.

Allied Mistress 39

Allied Mistress 39

Created by naval architect Arthur Edmunds and built by the well-respected Allied Boat Company of Catskills, New York, at its introduction in 1972, the Mistress 39 was one of the first true walk-through center cockpit vessels conceived solely for cruising. While also available in an aft cockpit version, the majority of the 60 or so Mistress 39s produced between 1972 and 1979 were built as center cockpits, and a raised afterdeck MK II version was finally made available which allowed for a huge-feeling aft cabin. Lots of interior volume, more than adequate storage, and a true engine room with plenty of space for a generator and mechanical systems make this design a terrific platform for a budget long distance cruiser.

The hulls on the Mistress, as with all Allied boats, were well laid up solid fiberglass and the fiberglass decks were balsa cored with plywood reinforcements in high stress areas. While not exceptionally heavily built, these boats had strong hulls which reportedly rarely suffered from serious osmosis or delamination issues and the encapsulated lead ballast was well installed so separations in the ballast encapsulation are not normally a problem.

The interiors of a stock Mistress are typically somewhat dated feeling with Formica bulkheads and simple joinery, but many owners have customized their boats, and some examples are stunningly beautiful.

With prices for these sturdy cruisers falling sometimes as far as low $20s, and even a fully equipped nicely maintained one rarely selling for more than $60K, the Mistress 39 is surely one of the best bargain cruisers of all time.

It should be noted that the Mistress's smaller sister, the 36' Allied Princess is also a vessel worth looking at.

Corbin 39

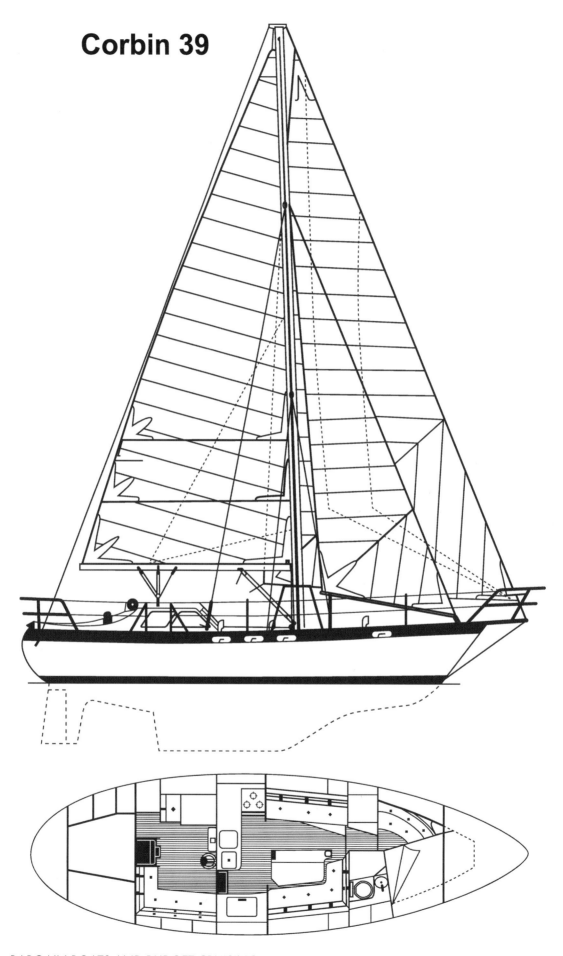

Corbin 39

Well, here's another double ender! And before people start thinking that I'm hung up on this type of hull, let me explain why so many of my 'bargain boat' examples have this type of hull. It's as simple as this: Double enders (which is an oversimplification when discussing hull shapes) were tremendously popular from the 1930s right up through the 80s and many of the real 'ocean cruiser' types that people sought out to take offshore during those decades featured this type of hull form, but through the 90s and up to today, hardly any were being produced. Because 'double-enders' have fallen out of favor aesthetically, many of these great boats built back in the day offer tremendous 'bang for the buck'.

The Corbin 39s are special boats. With virtually all of the hulls having been finished off by home builders or small yards, virtually no two Corbins are alike in either finish or build quality, and although the standard layouts offered were for the most part followed by their builders, many have quite odd interiors and some are downright terrible! But I've also seen a few claimed by their owners to be 'factory finished' that were quite nice and a few more finished by amateurs that were virtual works of art, so looking at Corbin 39s may be a wild ride for sure with some unexpected surprises, both good and bad!

The hull and decks of the boats were very well made and few Corbins have had any issues with hull delaminations or deck problems. The hulls are Airex cored, the decks were balsa cored, and the boats were offered in four different deck plans. The first versions sold were aft cockpit cutters and then later a flush deck center-cockpit design was released and then when a fire destroyed the molds for the first deck plan, an improved aft cockpit version was created and finally a center cockpit raised saloon pilothouse version was introduced.

A good sailing boat and although not tremendously fast, they track well and are surprisingly large inside considering an on-deck length of only thirty-eight and a half feet.

Prices for used Corbin 39s are all over the map with some crudely home finished versions selling for teens while super nice fully decked out world cruise equipped ones may command low one hundreds.

Bristol 40

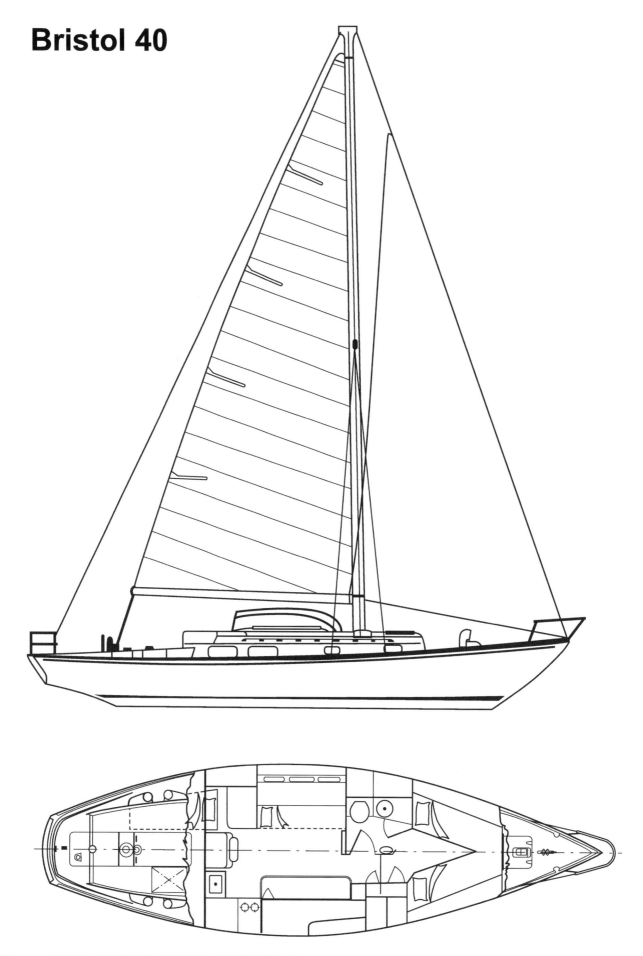

Boats 40 Feet and Over
Bristol 39/40

Here's a wonderfully built and great sailing design that truly fits the bill as a bargain cruiser. Originally built in the late 60s as a 39' CCA (Cruising Club of America) club racer, within a couple of years of introduction, the freeboard was slightly raised thereby increasing the overall length as well as interior volume and the Bristol 40 was born. With large water and adequate fuel tankage along with more than adequate storage below, converting a coastally equipped B40 into an offshore cruiser is often as easy as adding a few pieces of key equipment and updating her safety gear. Offered in both a shoal draft keel/centerboard and a deep draft versions, with their long keel and sturdy attached bronze structured rudders, they steer well with a windvane and in a large seaway, their high bow and longish overhangs provide tremendous reserve buoyancy which keeps them relatively dry, even when going to windward.

The fiberglass work on these boats was much better than average for their time and the interior joinery, usually built with mahogany (teak was an option) is finely fitted and all parts are individually tabbed into the hull thereby providing a stiff structure generally free of squeaks and movement. The quality of the marine plywood used for underlying structures, cabinetry, and bulkheads was the best available. Fittings, hardware, and equipment were chosen for quality rather than price point, especially on later, larger models and so when some of these parts wear out, substituting them with newer state of the art units can save a lot of money. For example, the pressure water pump on the larger Bristols is a $1,500 unit of antiquated design whereas a modern Shurflo or Jabsco pump costing $200 may well do the job just as well and draw less power.

Other things to watch out for are mast step issues and of course tankage and deck problems on poorly maintained vessels, but generally speaking, because Bristols were fairly pricey to begin with, pride of ownership is typical, which often results in vessels in above average condition.

Because of their somewhat 'dated' looks and also because so many were built, bargain prices can be found on these boats with lightly equipped examples selling in the mid-20s while a nice one rarely commands much more than mid-50s. If aesthetics, strength, and seaworthiness are important to you, the Bristol 40 is worth consideration.

Hallberg-Rassy 41

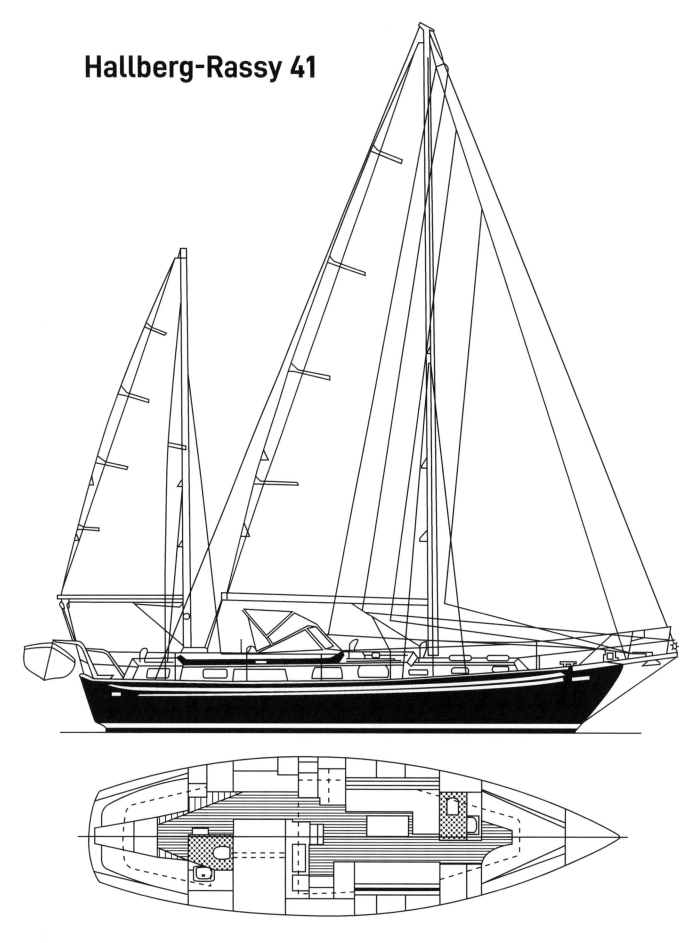

Hallberg-Rassy 41

Another super high-quality builder is the Swedish company Hallberg-Rassy and some of their older designs from the 1970s and early 80s can represent tremendous value.

The 41 is an exceptional sailboat and for her size is both strong and commodious, and quite fast too! I remember trying to catch one a few years ago in the lee of Dominica in 20-25 knots and it took me the better part of an hour to creep up on her even though I was sailing a sleek, svelte 53' Amel Super Maramu.

These HR 41s are good boats, and the engineering that goes into building them is both simple and sophisticated. With a great conservative hull form and a workable layout below, if you can locate one of these you should take a look.

I should mention here that they also made a 35' center-cockpit design called the Rasmus and with the first models of that boat built in wood, an early switch to much more mass-production fiberglass resulted in lots of these popular small cruisers being sold.

Either one of these designs, properly equipped and in good condition would be suitable for extensive world cruising.

Things to watch for are deck core issues on the teak decked boats and of course older Volvo engines which can be costly to repair. And the 75 hp versions have serious parts availability issues. But at the right price, one of these could be a great find. Re-powered with a Beta or Yanmar or even a new Volvo would give them a new lease on life.

With prices on a well-loved HR 41 typically under 100K, many that require updating can be had for much less. A used Rasmus 35 might be had for as little as the low 20s while a super nice one is rarely more than $50K.

Just knowing that you have a well-made boat under you with a reputable builder that's still in business is reassuring and there's a strong Hallberg-Rassy Owners Association that is a tremendous resource when undertaking repairs or upgrades.

Formosa 41

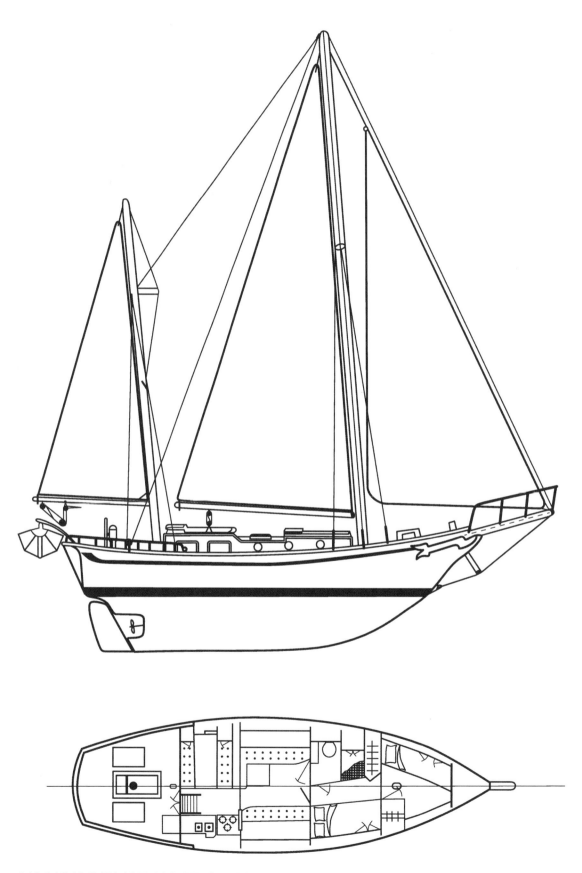

Formosa 41, CT 41, Island Trader 41, etc.

I would be remiss while presenting a cross section of bargain cruising boats if I didn't mention the proliferation of William Garden (and Garden-inspired) boats built in the Far East back in the early 1970s through the middle 1980s.

In the 1960s a couple of inspiring sailing crews took similar-looking wooden, traditional designed boats on extensive Pacific cruises, and while one wrote extensively about his family's exploits and was widely read, another made a feature-length movie which inspired hundreds, well maybe thousands of sailors to the romance of taking off for the South Seas in a salty looking Angelman ketch.

By the early seventies William Garden, who carried on with designing vessels in the Angelman tradition, was inundated by requests to create something similar to the Angelman Sea Witch but that could be built in Taiwan where a good boat could be built at the time for pennies on the dollar compared to US or Canadian shipyards. The resultant explosion of boatbuilding encompassed most of the yards in Taiwan and also some in Hong Kong and even Japan, but no designs received the notoriety of Bill Garden's 40' and 41' ketches. Note that many clones and copies were made and designer royalties were not always paid!

The Formosa shipyard turned out hundreds of these boats and legitimate (and pirated) clones and copies were built by competing yards all through the seventies. While some of the building practices used, particularly in the Formosa and CT yards, caused big maintenance headaches for owners later on with bad decks and shoddy tanks, so many of these boats were built that many are still sailing today and most have had their problems solved.

With ultra-strong low-tech hulls and conservative rigs, these boats can withstand tremendous punishment. One of my good friends survived three weeks stranded on a mid-Indian Ocean reef in one of these boats and when finally towed off, sailed the boat two thousand miles to South Africa for repairs and that boat is still sailing today.

Prices for these boats are all over the place from free to as much as a hundred thousand or more for an immaculate one, I have seen some exceptional examples and with careful shopping a decent and structurally sound one of these salty cruisers can likely be had at a very affordable price. And with one of these vessels, you can fly the Jolly Roger without looking like a dork!

Tayana Vancouver 42

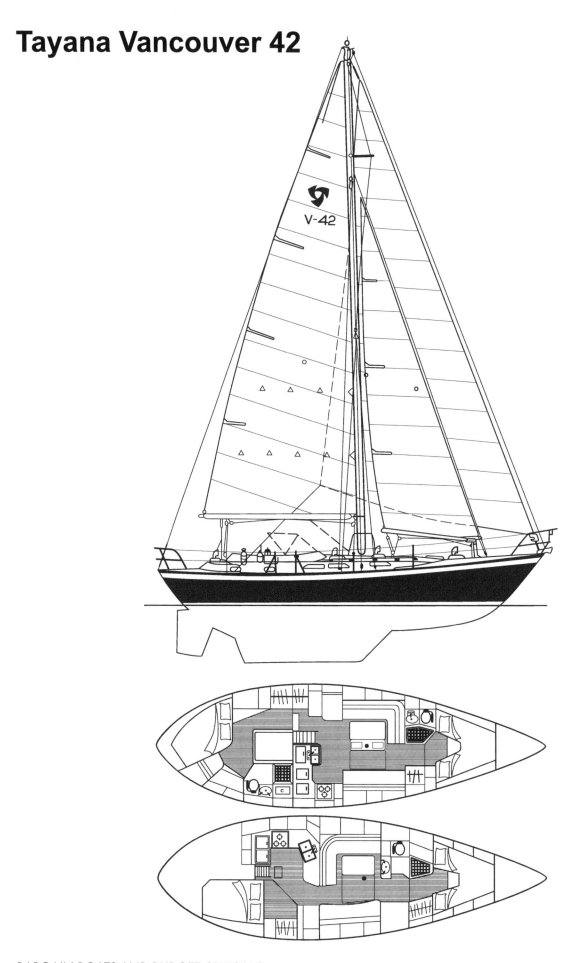

Tayana Vancouver 42

I can't say enough good things about this incredible bargain world cruising design. After the introduction of the original stepped cabin trunk 'Vancouver 42' version, the Tayana 42s were virtually all created on a semi-custom basis with the owner's ideas incorporated as the boats were being built. So after about 1979, almost no two Tayana 42s were exactly alike below deck. This can be great or not so great depending on the original owner's experience level and tastes. But the hulls and rigs were very well made to conservative specifications and these yachts are often available at bargain prices on the resale market.

Sea-kindly and spirited, the Tayana 42 does have a very rounded rocker and a fairly round bottom which means she may hobbyhorse and heel a bit more than other newer designs, but off the wind on your circumnavigation, you will be hard-pressed to have a more comfortable ride in a large seaway. Upwind they manage to 'keep their noses dry' better than most newer designs and their thick hulls, made up of hand-laid alternating layers of 24 oz woven roving and mat along with their long keels and fully skegged rudders means you can take a grounding or strike a heavy log with a reasonable chance of coming through unscathed.

Things to watch out for: bad deck cores on teak decked versions and aging stainless water tanks and black iron fuel tanks which can be challenging, although not impossible to replace, and occasionally the aluminum toe rails have needed work. Before 1986 Tayana used orthophthalic resins for their hulls, which were somewhat more prone to blistering than the later hulls which used isophthalic gelcoats for their superior resistance to osmosis. After 1992, Tayana used Vinylester resin in their hulls but the basic layups were done very well and so seldom have significant problems developed.

Available in a center cockpit or aft cockpit version, these make a terrific boat for a couple who have friends or family visiting from time to time or a small family out for a few years of adventuring, the Tayana 42 is one to look at for sure.

With prices on the used market in the low 40s to mid-80s, and into the low 100s for a near-perfect one, a Tayana 42 can be a great choice for long-term budget cruising. Over 200 hulls were built even up until today (yes, a new one could be ordered), with a little diligent searching the chances of finding a T-42 to fit your budget are pretty good.

Beneteau
Oceanis 430

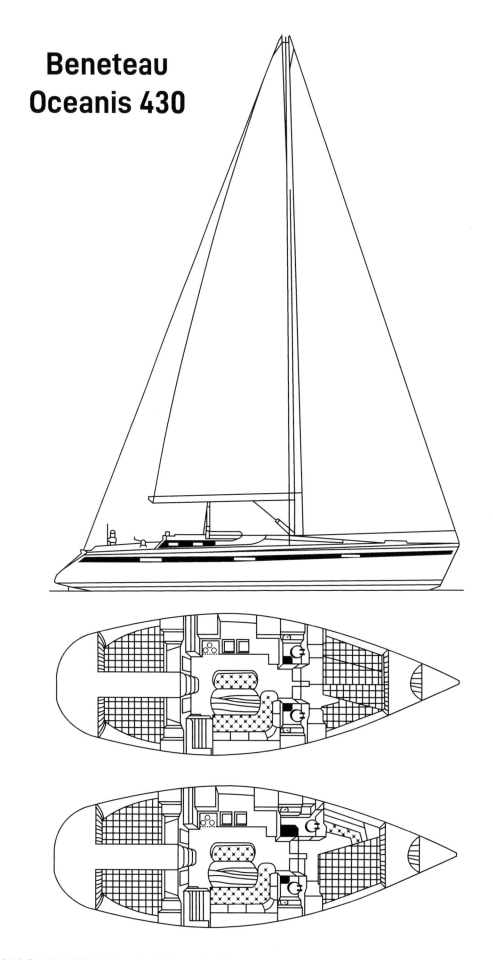

Beneteau Oceanis 430

Okay, okay, some of you might be asking, "What's a Beneteau doing in here?" But hear me out....

Beneteau is one of the oldest shipbuilders in the world and has been hugely successful in making sailing attainable for tens or possibly hundreds of thousands of people the world over. As a high-volume production builder, they have always been at the forefront of innovation with ways to create 'more for less.' One of these innovations was borrowed from American innovator and yacht builder Warren Luhrs, a development incorporating a huge time-saving production method using an Internal Grid Unit or 'IGU' as it is commonly known today.

Built in the early 1990s, the 430 is a great example of one of the first 'full-IGU' designs out there and is worth a serious look. With a strong well-rounded hull (as opposed to one with harder chines or a flatter bottom), these boats don't typically 'pound' when going to weather like newer designs and the partial skeg hung rudder is much stronger than later spade rudder models. The internal grid structure is securely fiberglassed into the hull, giving these boats a solid, stiff hull.

With a huge beam and a commodious interior, a nice 430 (or one of her contemporaries) could make a good cruising home.

Problems to watch for are aging keel bolts and leaks at the water tanks, but these are easily solved, and replacing the bolts on a Beneteau's iron keel is straightforward and simple to accomplish.

Well-mannered for a fin keel boat and reasonably fast, it might be worth considering a B430 for your future cruising home.

Prices for these fall in the range of low 30s for one that needs updating to mid to high 60s for one that's ready to sail the oceans. Lots of choices are out there in the 'between' ranges.

While perhaps not the prettiest boat out on the water to some, if form follows function, it may be difficult to get more boat for the money than with a nice Beneteau 430.

CSY 44

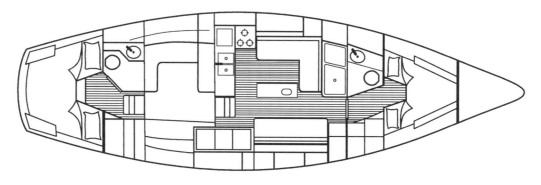

CSY 44

Created specifically for the charter industry, this Peter Ellis design was commissioned by Caribbean Sailing Yachts to be the largest boat available for potential charter yacht owners in their fleets which also offered 33' and 37' models. Both of the smaller designs proved to be great entry-level sailboats and a good number were built, but the CSY 44 was a huge success, and many hundreds were built over a six-year production run.

Available in a shoal draft or deep draft version and with a standard rig or a tall rig, these were versatile cruising yachts and had a couple of unusual features; the deep draft version was identical to the shoal draft hull except that it had an additional 18" extension on the keel that was filled with concrete and this helped hugely with assisting the boats in the stiff Caribbean trade winds. But then if an owner so desired, the bottom 18" section could be sawn off, the remaining lead-filled keel faired and painted and he or she would be left with a 5' draft boat that was perhaps more suited to cruising the west coast of Florida, the Bahamas or the Chesapeake Bay.

The second feature that has helped these vessels stand the test of time is that the decks were built of a heavy layup of fiberglass and no deck core. So the deck problems that plague so many of the older designs do not affect the CSY 44s. Built in three versions, the walk-over model that requires entering the cockpit to go aft to the master berth is by far the most numerous while the later walk-through models were for a time much sought after and still sell for a bit more. A pilothouse ketch version was also produced but this model never really caught on so may represent a good value if one can be found.

Strongly built, well-mannered under sail, and with huge tank capacities, these CSYs are regularly seen in many of the far-flung ports of the world. With a bit of personalization and a splash of ingenuity during outfitting, one of these sturdy old designs can take you far and wide.

Prices for CSY walkover over models will be mid-30s for a fixer-upper to high 70s for a well-equipped vessel. Walk-through models may be 10-20% more while the rare pilothouse version might fall somewhere in the middle.

Care should be taken though as some of the last boats built were made by Antigua Yachts and the build quality was not nearly as good as the CSYs.

Passport 40

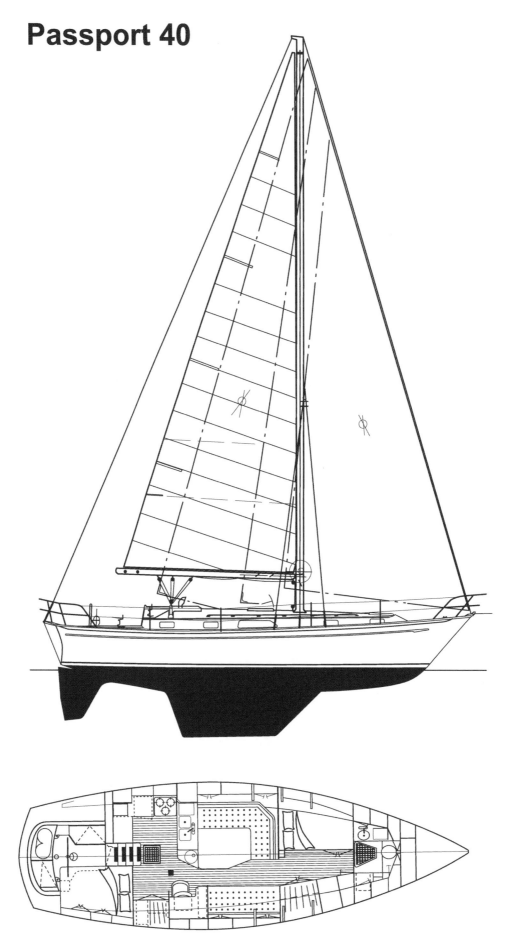

Passport 40

Before I am accused of always praising Bob Perry's designs, I have to say that this one, in particular, is one of his best.

The Passport 40 shared many of the same sailing characteristics as the renowned Valiant 40 while providing a more commodious interior complete with what was to become a trademark Perry galley with plenty of space for two to share in the cooking and a large comfortable cockpit for entertaining in port. With two basic interior versions available, this boat was able to fit many people's set of ideals and hundreds were built in the 1980s and into the 90s when the design was tweaked to become the Passport 42. An extended transom version of the earlier Passport 40 was also made and called the Passport 43.

Like many of the Taiwanese boats, they enjoyed a high quality of finish below decks, but often sported teak decks which can be a real problem as they age and begin to leak. You will find that many Passport owners have removed these decks and fiberglassed over the surfaces. The boats had fiberglass water tanks and iron fuel tanks so care must be taken when examining the fuel system. With terrific engine access and a huge 'garage' under the cockpit for storage, these boats make great long-distance cruisers and price ranges in this day and age can begin in the low 40s to as much as $100K or more for a super well maintained and outfitted one. Many are available in good condition in the middle 70s price range.

The handy cutter rig was standard although some were sold new as sloops and certainly, for coastal sailing a sloop has some advantages over the more complicated cutter-rigged versions.

When shopping for a Passport 40, take special care inspecting the chainplates and the rudder quadrant support as these are areas that have caused issues for most owners over time and so many have been replaced, or if not, will likely need to be renewed on your watch.

The moderate draft allows for good upwind performance while still allowing access to virtually all the popular anchorages and the excellent hull form keeps her on her feet well, even in stronger winds. A great all-around choice for liveaboard long-distance cruising, you can't go far wrong with a Passport 40.

Pearson 424

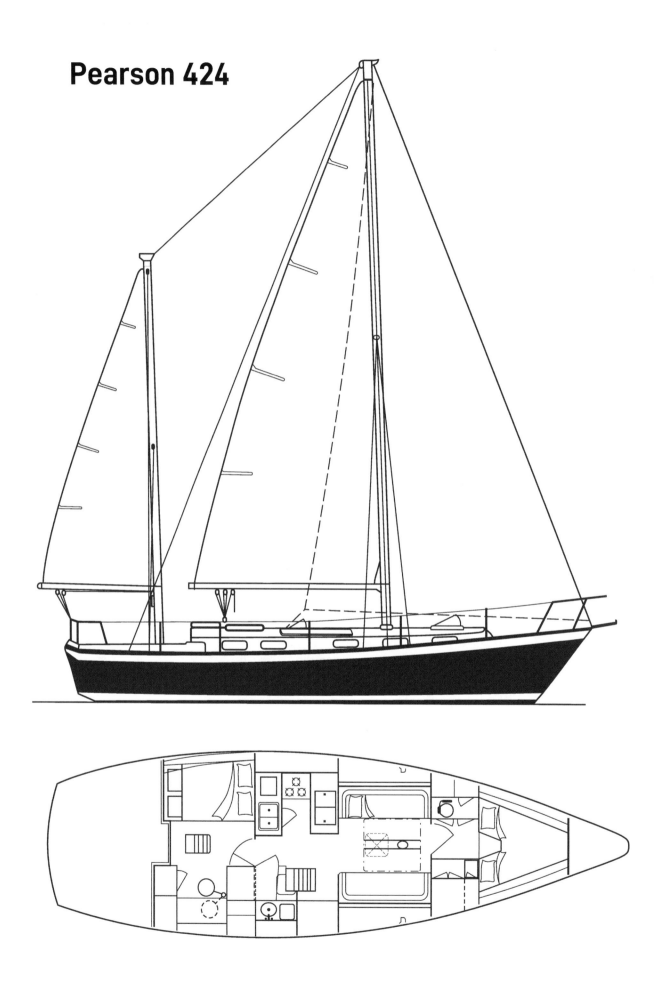

Pearson 424

Bill Shaw, then President of Pearson Yachts, was also a well-known yacht designer and penned the 424 Pearson as an aft cockpit development of his earlier Pearson 419 center cockpit ketch. By raising the freeboard a touch and with the availability of three different stock interior layouts, he created a boat that was very well received and so the Pearson 424 enjoyed a long production run. Today, you will often see at least one of these boats at anchor out there in some far-away place with budget-minded cruisers enjoying the spacious living accommodation and good overall sailing performance.

Things to watch out for are soft decks and osmosis issues. The 424 models used a Walter V-drive, which is a durable system that allowed the engine to be placed farther aft, thereby opening up the accommodations area below, but as time goes on, these eventually need to be replaced. Rebuilding them is typically not cost-effective and a new V-drive runs close to $4,000. Another potential issue to watch for is that they used a soft rubber-like nitrile gasket material on their lifeline stanchion bases and bow and stern pulpit bases and as time has gone by, these gaskets typically have dried up and split, allowing water to enter the deck cores and so on almost any older Pearson of this era, some re-coring of the deck may be necessary. But this is not that hard to accomplish, and these issues can all be solved.

Tankage was adequate with typically 150 gallons of water and 80 gallons of fuel. The aft cockpit is dry and comfortable and offers a good feeling of security. I have heard some people say that the cockpit is a bit too large and a few 424 owners have added extra scuppers to allow for quicker drainage should they be pooped by a large wave, but most owners do not feel this is necessary.

With their relatively shallow draft, these boats lend themselves well to some of the skinnier cruising areas like the Bahamas, areas of the Caribbean, and Central America, and would allow access to the lagoons in such exotic places as Aitutaki, Cook Islands, and, closer to home, the Jumentos Cays or the Bight of Crooked-Acklins in the Bahamas.

At the right price, with a well-cared-for boat, it is hard to beat a 424 as a bargain cruiser. Expect a good selection of used 424s in the mid- to high $50s, with top of the market prices coming in at around $75K, while a fixer-upper might be had for as little as $25K or less.

Westsail 42

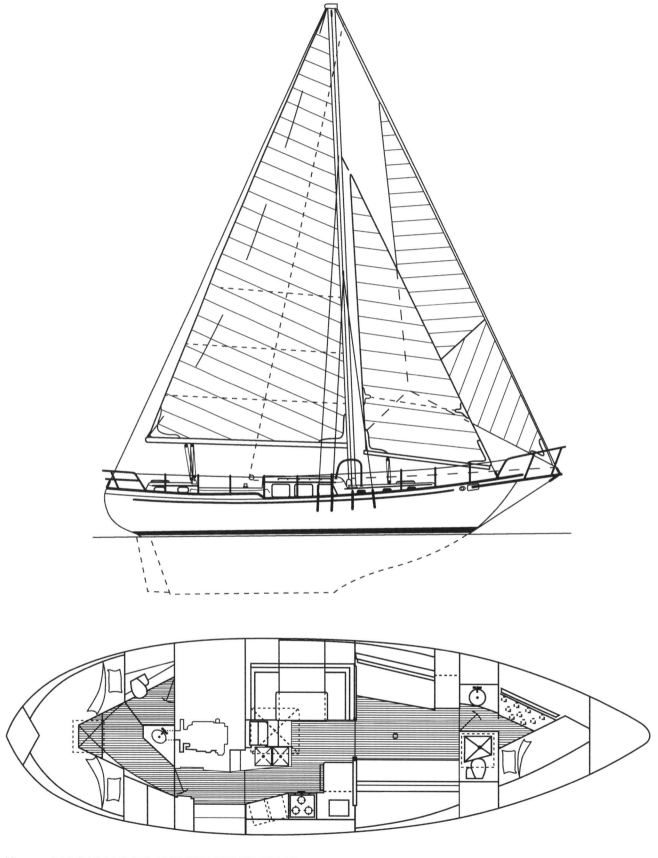

Westsail 42 and 43

Another not so well-known design from the 70s, the center cockpit Westsail 42 and the aft cockpit Westsail 43 shared the same 42'11" hull and while many were sold as kits, quite a few were ordered as completed boats. After about 1981, some were completed by one of a handful of custom yacht builders and like the Westsail 32, the quality of workmanship on these boats can vary quite a bit depending on who finished them and who owned them in the years since they were launched.

With a super sturdy solid laminate hull, internal lead ballast in the full-length keel, and a well-stayed rig with outboard chainplates, calling a Westsail 42 anything but conservative would be preposterous. That having been said, with their wide double-ended stern and fine entry and more than adequate freeboard and reserve buoyancy at their ends, these are superb seaboats. Because nearly 300 were built, they are still relatively easy to find on the used market and a good one of these can make a terrific cruising home for a small family or two sets of friends out for some real adventure.

Tankage is typically more than adequate and the well thought-out seagoing layout makes for a comfortable cruising home. It is easy to say too many good things about these boats, but because so many were built as kits, some of these home-finished vessels can be rather crude. Be sure to research your future purchase carefully! Some of the home-built boats were very well crafted, while others may require extensive rebuilding or refitting to get them truly prepared for sea.

Because of the wide variance in finish quality of these boats, prices can vary tremendously with some of the home built, lightly equipped vessels going for as little as high teens to low twenties while most of the factory finished or well-completed boats seem to trade in the $60-70K range and some extraordinarily well built and equipped Westsails might command high 100s! We even saw one recently in New Zealand that looked like it was in showroom condition and was equipped with all the latest gear. If it had been for sale, it might have commanded somewhere in the mid- to high 200s! One thing is for sure though; if you get one of these all set up properly and take her cruising, you will always feel safe and secure knowing that your boat is super strong and able to handle almost anything nature can throw at you.

Kelly Peterson 44

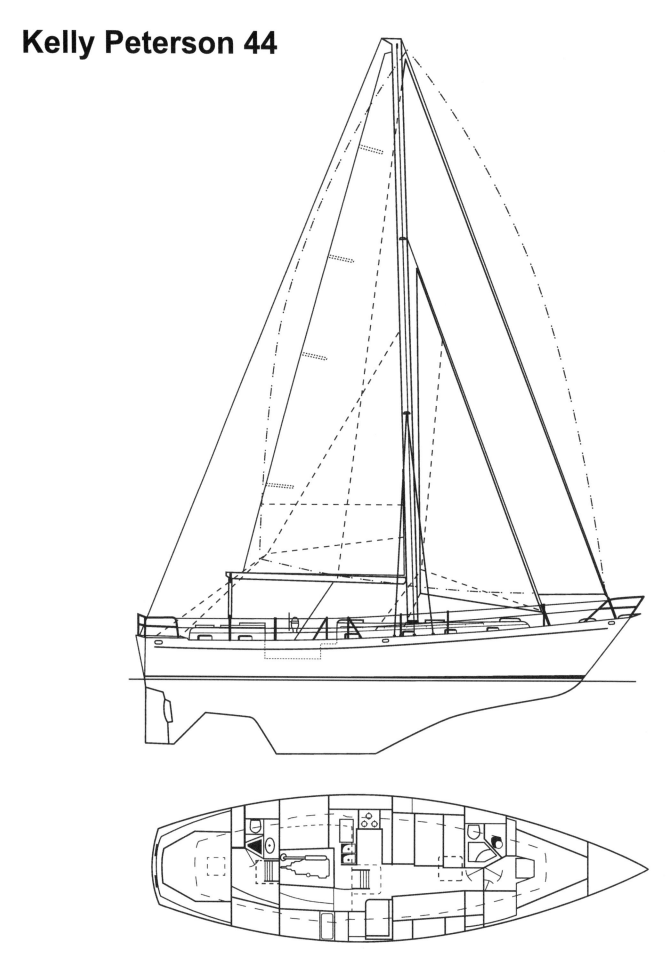

Kelly Peterson 44

Introduced in the mid 1970s, the Peterson 44 was for almost two decades considered to be the quintessential big offshore cruiser. These vessels were so revered by aspiring world cruisers that the basic hull design was copied, plagiarized, modified, and reintroduced by several different builders in Taiwan up through about 1990. While clones like the Formosa 46 were not as well made, the Liberty 458, Delta 46, and Passport 45 were basically 'bootleg' adaptations of Doug Peterson's 44 underbody and hull form, and the majority were at least reasonably well made.

The Kelly Peterson 44 featured a deep, well-rounded underbody but with less fore and aft rocker than many designs of the era and coupled with a long fin keel and a full skeg hung rudder with a protected propeller aperture, the KP 44 was a revolutionary concept at its inception in 1975 and is still one of the better-mannered cruising yachts ever built.

The boats featured thick hulls and nice high bulwarks around the deck with a small but well-sheltered cockpit which helped them to have a 'safe' feeling offshore while 10,000 pounds of internal iron ballast and tankage under the cabin sole and outboard of the engine gave them a low center of gravity so that they could stand up well to their sail. The long waterline and easy motion made it not impossible to achieve daily mileage runs in the 180s and some people have reported 200-mile days in the right conditions.

Like many older Taiwanese boats, the KP 44s have their inherent problems. Things to watch for: wet deck cores (especially on the teak deck versions); chainplate and chainplate knee issues; genoa track leaks; and leaks within the raised bulwarks can be time-consuming to resolve. With black iron fuel tanks and low-grade stainless water tanks, these must also be carefully assessed although, at this point in history, most owners will have already dealt with these issues.

The 'walk through' to the aft cabin is more of a stoop-through and the aft berth is a 'crawl in and turn around' affair, but these are minor annoyances in an otherwise fine design. Prices for fixer-upper Peterson 44s might be as low as $30K, while a nice one with all the latest gear and sails will still command over a hundred. Many are in acceptable condition and trading in the 60-70s.

Whitby 42

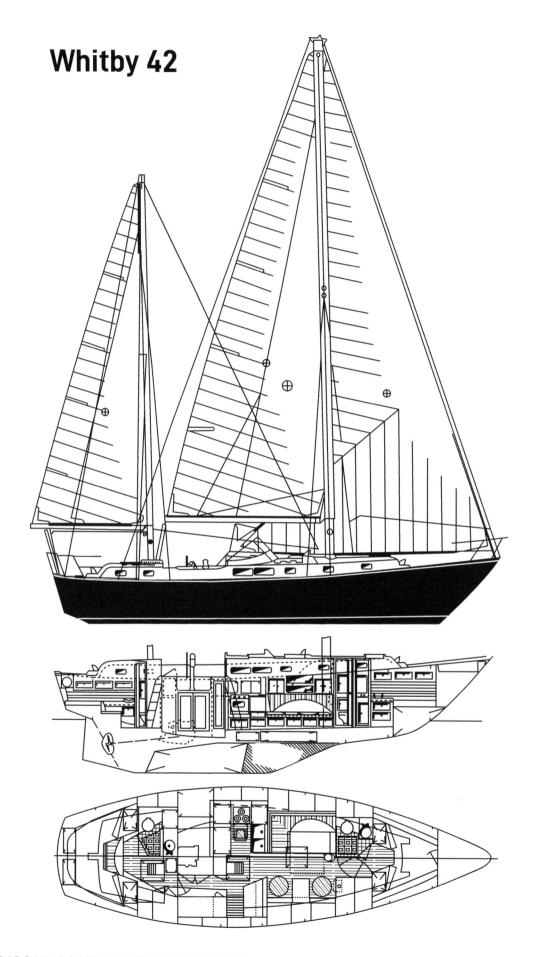

Whitby 42

Designed by Ted Brewer to meet early 70s market demand, the Whitby 42 featured enormous tankage, a high freeboard for the era, a voluminous interior, and an easily handled ketch rig in a center cockpit true walk-through design.

Tankage, like on the Kelly Peterson 44, is below the cabin sole and outboard of the engine. Storage is more than adequate and sailing performance, while not exemplary, is adequate to allow for consistent 150 mile days offshore in good conditions.

Problems on these boats are usually the result of bad ownership. With balsa cored hulls and decks, making sure that moisture has not intruded into the core of the hulls is vitally important, so if the boat you are looking at has had additional through-hulls installed for watermakers, generators, or the like, be sure to check for moisture or delamination around these fittings. Ditto for a boat that may have been damaged. The only other major issue to watch for is flexure to the aft area of the cockpit. Several Whitby 42s have lost their mizzen masts when in a heavy seaway the hulls flexed enough to allow the rigging to slacken and the mizzen masts jumped out of their deck steps. Lastly, early versions were sometimes equipped with a rudder that was a bit too small and pop-riveted hull/deck joints. Many older boats will have had these issues addressed.

If all these potential problems sound too intimidating, just know that there are hundreds of happy owners out there who have dealt with these challenges and are enjoying a commodious, safe yacht that they probably bought for a very affordable price.

As a sidenote: These boats were so popular that at one point sisterships were being built in Ft. Myers, Florida under license from Whitby and then the design was modified to have 4'6" draft with a centerboard and a separate skeg hung rudder which was called the Brewer 12.8 and finally the design was morphed into the fixed keel Brewer 44, which had a small sugar scoop stern and were built up into the early nineties.

Prices for an old Whitby 42 needing work might be as low as $25K, a tricked-out Brewer 44 might go for over $100K, while a turn-key mid-seventies Whitby 42 might be found for $50-$70K.

Morgan
Out Island 41

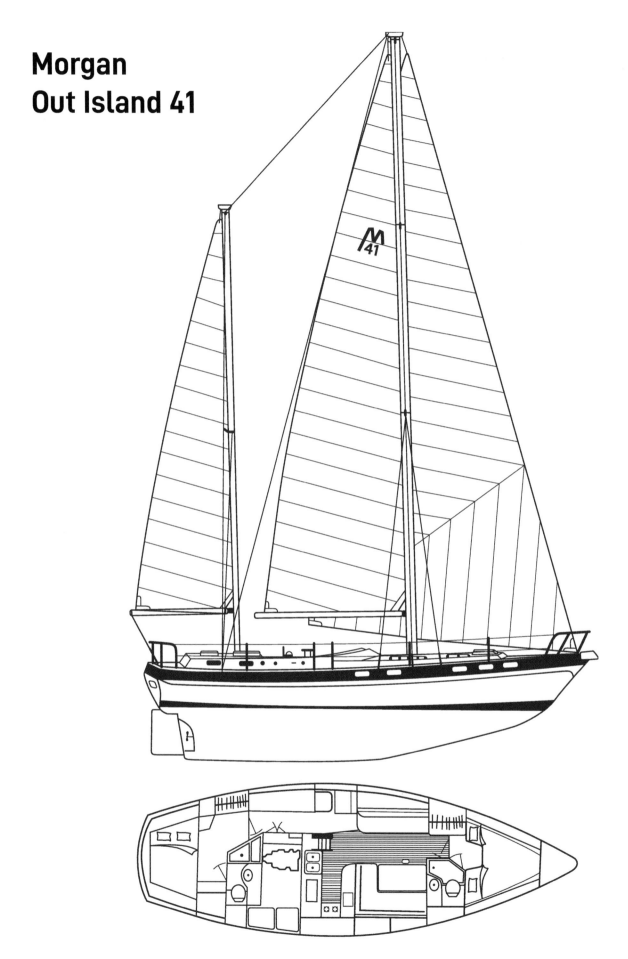

Morgan Out Island 41

In the late 1960s, Charlie Morgan was enjoying an extremely successful career as a racing boat designer which apexed when he penned and built a touchstone design dubbed 'Paper Tiger'. She was a 41' full keel/centerboard sloop that ate up the SORC (Southern Ocean Racing Conference) and launched Charlie into the forefront of yacht design. Charlie turned this design into the Morgan 41 Keel/Centerboard production model which was very well received.

By the early 1970s, with his new Morgan Yachts facility in full swing, he was approached by another Charlie—Charlie Carey—who had founded a bareboat charter company based in the BVI called 'The Moorings'. Mr. Carey wanted a design built specifically for the charter industry that would be rugged, sail well, and have good space for two or three couples for his new fleet. What Mr. Morgan appears to have done was to simply modify the lines of his 41' race boat by widening its hull and making it flush decked for more space below, eliminated the centerboard for simplicity, and the Out Island 41 was born.

Built with quality materials and with heavy layup schedules, these boats were immediately successful and popular in the private market as well and along with orders from various charter fleets, hundreds were sold over the next decade.

Sailing writer Earl Hinz, who in the early seventies had recently retired and wanted a new boat with which to explore extensively in the Pacific, ordered a new Out Island 41 and commenced two decades and approximately 250,000 miles of sailing crisscrossing the Pacific in his stock Morgan Out Island 41, proving the seaworthiness of the design. With approximately 1,000 41s built, these vessels are well represented in many ports around the world. The 41s went through several model improvements and when Morgan Yachts was sold in 1986 to Catalina, the new management introduced a very similar boat with some further modifications that they called the Classic 41.

Any of these vessels, properly equipped and in good condition, can take you far and wide and prices are all over the map. Simply engineered and well made to start with, a budget of as little as $20K will likely find you a fixer-upper 41 while a super nice one will still only be around $65-70K. The newer Classic 41 model may be a bit more. A good choice, especially if you plan to sail shallow waters, these Morgan yachts have stood the test of time.

Vagabond 47

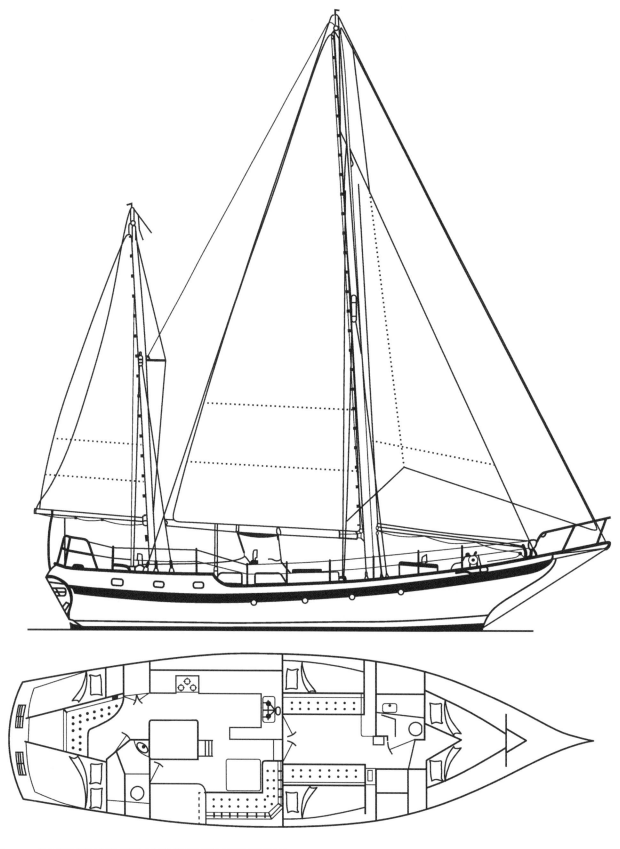

Vagabond 47

One of William Garden's most successful designs, the Vagabond 47 enjoyed one of the longest production runs of any Taiwanese yacht. Originally penned in the late 60s and built of wood, in 1971 it was first built in fiberglass and introduced as the Garden 47. Later production was undertaken in the Bluewater Yacht Builders facility and the Vagabond 47 was born. With new Vagabonds being sold right up into the mid-90s, it is quite common to see these boats turn up in almost any major port of the world.

A charter industry friend of mine reminisced that back in the early 80s he ran a Vagabond 47 in charter for two years and that "In 15 knots of wind, you carried full sail. In thirty knots, you still carried full sail!"

At just under 47' on deck and 40,000-pound displacement, these are substantial vessels! No gazelles to windward, they make up for that by being super comfortable off the wind, reaching, and have enough carrying capacity for real off the beaten track long-term cruising. Shoal draft gives them access to many areas off-limits to similar-sized more modern designs.

The build quality of the Vagabonds was far superior to the majority of the similar-looking yachts coming out of Taiwan during the 80s and so these vessels have held up well over time without many of the attendant problems experienced by lesser builders. A truly well-proportioned 'pirate ship', never mind what some reviewers who have never sailed them may say, these boats also sail quite well. Aside from the usual problems with aging teak decks, chainplate, and tankage issues, the hulls were for the most part trouble free, and with their beautifully appointed interior accommodations, they would likely be impossible to build in today's market for less than a million dollars.

Typically available on the used market from the low 40s to low 100s, the Vagabond 47 makes an excellent choice for long-distance cruising and living aboard and if you keep the extensive teak work up and the hull well-polished, when you sail into port after a long passage, you can be sure you will be admired by every sailor in the harbor, and most of the people on shore too!

Stevens 47

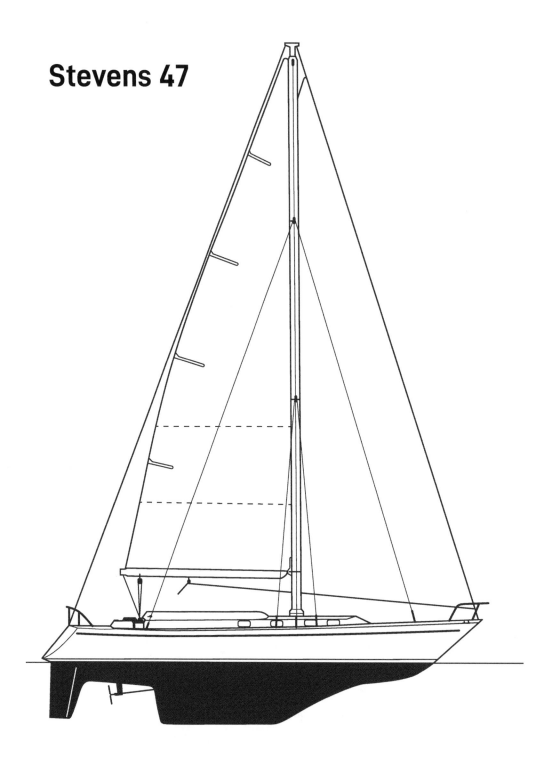

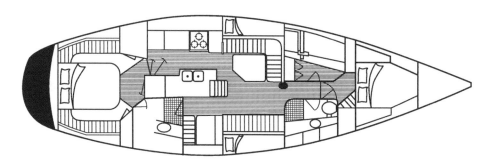

Stevens 47

Once one of the most sought-after big cruising yachts, the Stevens 47, later known as the Hylas 47, has continued to enjoy a good reputation as a fast passagemaker and strong cruising home.

Well suited for a family, the three-cabin layout offered a commodious aft cabin with either a single and double opposing berth on early models, or the more popular centerline queen, the most common layout. Storage is more than adequate, and the decks are wide and uncluttered.

These boats sail quite well and are noted for good upwind performance. 180 to 200-mile days are not out of reach and with good tankage and copious storage, they are well suited for long-term cruising.

The chainplates are accessible for inspection or repairs and the decks are cored with an Airex-type, closed-cell foam, so they seldom have problems. The hulls are solid fiberglass and the ballast is internal, so problems in these areas are rare.

Things to watch for: stress cracks along the connection of the skeg to the hull which is easily reinforced; and fuel tankage issues, which require creative repairs as they are built-in under the cabin sole.

Expect to pay a little more than your typical bargain boat for one of these vessels but with careful shopping, one can surely be had for less than $100K. I've even seen some trade in the $70K range.

With a usable third sleeping cabin, these make great family boats and a quick Google search will turn up lots of details of sailing families that have made long-term living aboard or circumnavigating a way of life.

Hardin 45

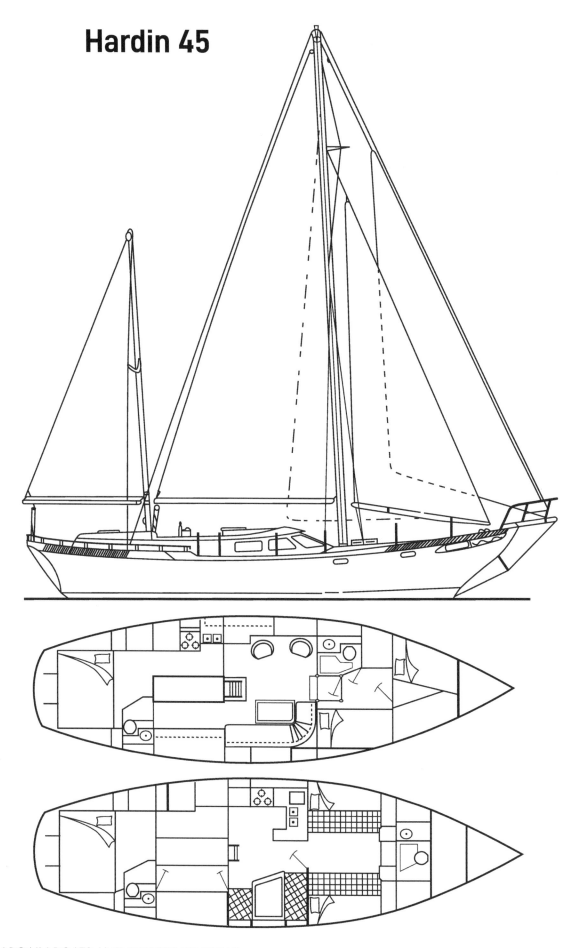

Hardin 45

While not a particularly fast sailboat, the Hardin 45s have a small but loyal following and can be seen in many anchorages around the world.

Unlike many of the Taiwanese 'Pirate ships' of their era which often had poor quality fuel and water tanks that were difficult to replace, the Hardins featured all fiberglass water and fuel tanks and so did not suffer from issues with these wearing out as they have on most similar looking designs. The vessel was offered in four different layouts, from two to four separate sleeping cabins, and featured commodious volume, copious storage, a sea-kindly motion, and an ultra-strong hull. Well-loved by their crews for their comfortable accommodations, a Hardin owner once told me, "She's our home. For a sailboat, she's not fast, but for a house she certainly is!"

Things to watch for: issues around the mizzen mast step; and leaks on the big forward-facing windows in the main salon; plus of course chainplates and bobstay fittings.

Many of these had teak decks but most will have had those removed by now. Rotten plywood deck cores under the old teak are more problematic to repair, but the broad, fairly flat surfaces make undertaking this type of upgrade relatively simple, if labor-intensive, to accomplish.

These boats were also built with a slightly different, more traditional deck plan and called the Island Trader 45. Both of these versions are readily found on the used market for between 30-50K and only the very nicest ones command much more, so if you're on a tight budget but looking for a big strong, safe and comfortable cruising home that can sail you to distant shores, consider looking at a Hardin 45.

Morgan 462

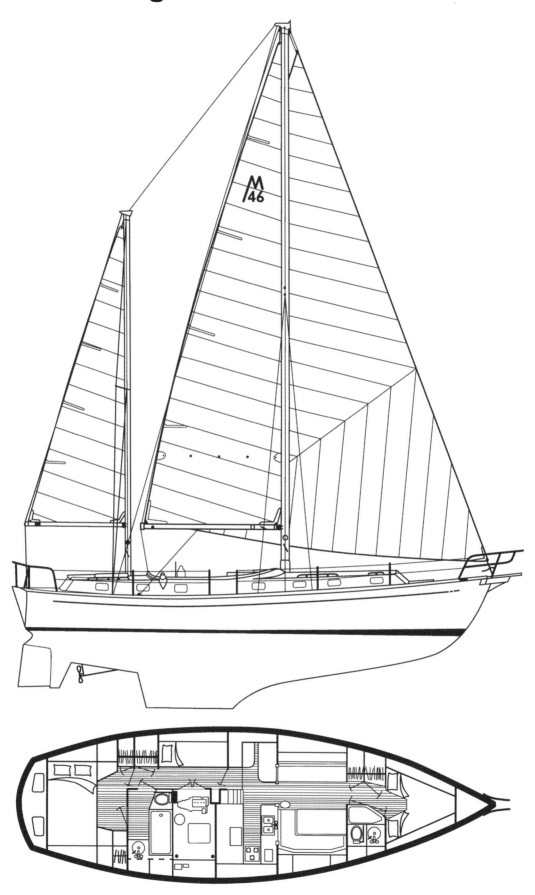

Morgan 462

By the late 70s, bareboat chartering had become such a success story that the Moorings, based in the British Virgin Islands, required a larger boat with three sleeping cabins to augment their fleet of two-cabin Morgan 41s and smaller yachts.

Charley Carey, the owner of Moorings, once again approached Morgan Yachts who suggested their new model called the Morgan 45. This boat was designed by Henry Scheel and the molds had recently been acquired from the defunct Scheel Yacht Company.

With a redesign of the deck plan and interior to allow for a better mid-cabin and by replacing the ketch rig with a sloop rig and a deeper keel to deal with the strong Caribbean winds, the Morgan 46 was born. Another extremely successful design, the majority of these sturdy vessels are still out there sailing the world's oceans. The engineering is simple and tankage and storage are more than adequate. The Morgan 46 was also available as a shoal draft ketch and either of these versions makes a terrific choice for a family or larger crew.

A lot of these boats were originally put into charter and one of these in stock configuration was sent on an around the world voyage via the five capes with a revolving crew of guests.

With external chainplates, heavy-duty hardware, substantial spars and rigging, these boats, even with no significant upgrades, rise to the challenge of world cruising. The decks are basically solid with a plywood 'stiffener' glassed at the base of the laminate so are not 'cored' in the traditional sense and subsequently rarely have deck delaminations. Things to watch for are mast step issues and osmotic blistering, but these are solvable and with good sailing performance, great engineering, and rock-solid construction, the Morgan 46 offers a lot of boat for the money.

It should be noted that after catastrophic Hurricane Irma in the Caribbean, several Morgan 46s were damaged in the storm but suffered relatively minor abuse, whereas other vessels around them were pounded to pieces.

Priced on the used market from the high 30s for a fixer upper to low 100s for a tricked-out cruiser, many of these in great condition regularly trade for $60K and $70K.

Bristol 41.1

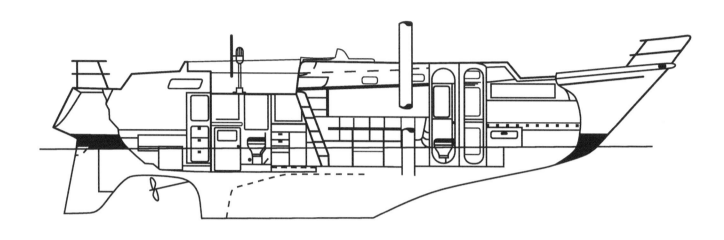

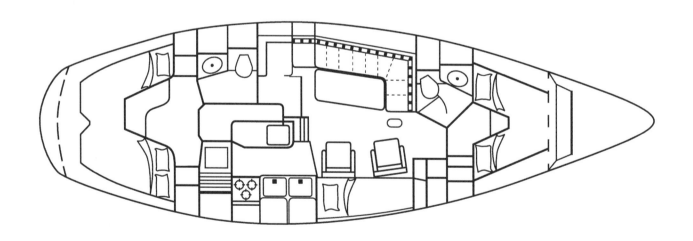

Bristol 41.1 and 45.5 (and the 35.5 and 38.8)

The Ted Hood 'decimal point boats' were the second generation of designs built by the enormously successful Bristol Yacht Company of Bristol, Rhode Island. During the late 1970s and into the early 90s, they produced a series of terrific cruising boats from 24 to 54 feet. While I consider the 41s and 45s to be their best designs for long-distance cruising and living aboard, many of the smaller models have made epic voyages, including a recent circumnavigation by a friend (a double amputee) on his 35.5 model, and another recent circumnavigation by friends of mine on a stock 38.8.

The 41.1 is a favorite of mine and is undervalued on the used market. These super-high-quality boats are often trading in the same price range as much lesser vessels and feature heavy displacement (read that as strongly built), shallow draft, and have copious storage all in very pretty hulls with easy to handle sail plans. They sail well to windward and handle heavy weather as comfortably as can be expected on any small vessel.

Although exceptionally well designed and built, problem areas can be found with the larger models which had tankage all below the cabin soles with access to these quite limited. Most owners have at some point had to cut the soles out and recreate better access but once completed, this upgrade makes for easier access later.

Many of the earlier boats had a Westerbeke diesel for which some parts availability issues have arisen, but later boats often featured Yanmars on the larger boats and the Universal diesel on the smaller models.

Starting in late 1986, Bristol used vinylester resins on the outside layers of the hulls and so consequently, osmotic blistering is often not a problem. On older models that have been in the water for extended periods you may find some blistering but generally speaking, this is not as much of a problem on these boats as with contemporaries from other builders.

Prices range all over the place, but at the lower end of the spectrum expect to find a fixer-upper 35.5 for low 20s, a reasonably well-maintained 41.1 at around $70K, while a tricked out 45.5 might command mid 100s. Lots of these boats were built, so careful shopping will likely turn up a real bargain.

Afterword

As I've said before, the vessels shown within these pages are by no means the only good choices out there and are simply a sampling of some of the terrific bargain boats available. Keep in mind that many others might also be great for your purposes. Please bear in mind the potential issues, concerns, and things to watch for that I've addressed in the preceding chapters, and try to make your decisions based upon logic and clear thinking rather than emotional desires or romantic visions.

There is a wonderful world out there, full of high adventure, and sailboats are the very freest and most flexible way to travel still available to us. Once out there sailing the world, you will meet many amazing people and see unbelievable beauty and astounding natural wonders. While it may seem sometimes that because of air travel and modern instantaneous communication that the world is shrinking more and more each day, once you are out there sailing across oceans at 6-7 miles per hour, watching every wave go by and seeing new landfalls gradually emerge from the horizon, the true size and magnitude of our wonderful planet will fill your senses with the wonder we might have first felt as children, eager to learn and excited about each new day.

It's so encouraging to me to see so many new sailors joining the ranks of the world-cruising community and I truly hope that the pages you have just read have made it easier to make wise choices when searching for your new bargain boat cruising home. Don't ever let land-based friends tell you what you can or can't do and don't fall victim to xenophobic beliefs that you are only safe in your own country. Raise your sails, up your anchor, and set your course for the distant horizon to experience the world in all its wonder and splendor.

It's been an honor to share some of what I've learned over the last forty years here on the water with you all and if you have any constructive criticism or anything to add or to augment a future edition of this book, please don't hesitate to email me at Sailadventurer@gmail.com. Alternatively, if you happen to see me at anchor somewhere in the future, please do drop by and share your experiences with me! Remember: it's not just the places we go that make world cruising so special, but the people we meet along the way that cement these memories in our hearts forever.

Todd Duff, S/V Small World IV, Tortola, BVI

Acknowledgments

To write an accurate and complete acknowledgment to all of the amazing, wonderful people who have contributed to the inspiration and creation of this manuscript is daunting and no matter how much time I spend in writing it, I will surely leave out many who deserve mention. However, here is my attempt to thank some of the most influential individuals who contributed to the inspiration and creation of this work.

Many decades back, when my dreams of sailing far were first being formulated, Lin and Larry Pardey's early books about minimalist sailing inspired me, and years later when I finally met them, they continued to encourage me and so many others to take on the amazing lifestyle of world cruising, even if on a minimal budget.

I'd also like to thank the authors of so many of the touchstone books by people like Hal Roth, Tristin Jones, Donald Street, and of course the incredible story of young Robin Lee Graham immortalized in the National Geographic series of his solo circumnavigation back in the 1960s.

Countless other inspiring authors have helped shape my own thoughts and beliefs that world cruising can be accomplished with minimal funding and to so many of these authors, I thank you for your contributions and to the knowledge you made available to those who seek it.

And then there are the terrific editors and publishers who have encouraged me in my writing endeavors over the last three decades such as Herb McCormick, Jen Brett and Mark Pillsbury of Cruising World Magazine, George Day of Blue Water Sailing Magazine, Gary Brown of All at Sea, Karen Larsen (now retired) of Good Old Boat Magazine, Sally Erdle of Caribbean Compass and many others, but none more so than Bob and Jody Lipkin of Latitudes and Attitudes Magazine who took me under their wings, so to speak and published so many of my early stories and opinion pieces.

And this acknowledgment cannot ignore my many friends and colleagues within the marine industries including notable surveyors such as Don Miller SAMS (now deceased), Bill Bailey SAMS, William Howe, Fred Hecklinger NAMS (recently deceased), and many others.

Also influential was Chet Pawlowicz of Martin Bird and Associates in Annapolis who mentored me while in my thirties to work with all seekers of cruising boats with the same diligence whether they were looking at small, cheap boats or new, ready to go vessels and who would always clear a desk for me to work upon my return from my year or more long absences while I cruised with my kids over two decades of sailing.

And I wish to personally thank my good friends Gary Felton and Deb McDonald for their input on minimalist cruising and also for the excellent cover images and for their input and ideas toward helping make a better manuscript.

Thanks too to Sailboatdata.com who provided many of the traceable images for the design section and I also thank my sailing partner of many years Gayle Suhich and my good friends Garrett Scott and Libbie Oliver who provided encouragement and acted as sounding boards over the last few years while I assembled this volume.

And lastly, I'd like to thank my many friends and colleagues in the marine industries and the cruising community who have, over the last four decades, taught me so much about boats, cruising and living simply.

Oh, and thanks especially to Joe Janson and the whole Seaworthy Publications team for making this idea into a reality.

Fair winds to all!

About the Author

Todd Duff

SAMS accredited marine surveyor and lifelong sailor Todd Duff has been involved in the marine industries for over forty years and has worked at various times as a marine contractor, yacht broker or marine surveyor in the US, Caribbean, Central America and the South Pacific.

Also a USCG licensed master, he has sailed to 37 countries; most of these with his children aboard and has been involved in the sale of over one thousand sailing vessels.

He lives aboard his sailboat and is the author of many articles for the major sailing magazines as well as 'Kidnapped from the Caribbean', a fast paced adventure novel based on actual events, available from booksellers worldwide.

You can contact Todd through his website at:

https://www.bargainboatsandbudgetcruising.com

Made in United States
Orlando, FL
10 January 2024